Praise for *Look fo*

"Blown. Away. Luke Russert's story of heartbreaking loss and hard-earned self-discovery captivates from start to finish. This is the memoir of the year, if not the decade."

—ELIN HILDERBRAND
#1 *NEW YORK TIMES* BESTSELLING AUTHOR OF *SUMMER OF '69*

"A rich and compelling account of family, grief, and coming of age. Luke Russert turns tragedy into rich lessons of life."

—TOM BROKAW
LEGENDARY JOURNALIST AND AUTHOR OF
THE GREATEST GENERATION

"In *Look for Me There*, Luke Russert traverses terrain both physical and deeply personal. On his journey to some of the world's most stunning destinations, he visits the internal places of grief, family, faith, ambition, and purpose—with intense self-reflection, honesty, and courage."

—SAVANNAH GUTHRIE
CO-ANCHOR OF *TODAY*

"A beautiful, well-written story of a young man coming into his own, finding his faith, and understanding his purpose."

—MARIA SHRIVER
ACCLAIMED JOURNALIST AND FOUNDER OF THE *SUNDAY PAPER*

"One book, two remarkable and compelling journeys. Luke Russert puts to the test—and beyond any doubt validates—his perhaps unrivaled storytelling DNA. . . . A colorful, insightful, and meticulously detailed travel diary that transports the reader to some of the world's most intriguing cities, hidden corners, and fascinating cultures. And with those travels comes a mourning son's poignant and brutally honest personal journey: to process devastating loss and grief, to wrestle with his sense of self and place, with questions of faith and family—and, ultimately, to balance the burden of expectations with the freedom of picking his own path."

—JOHN KING
CNN CHIEF NATIONAL CORRESPONDENT
AND HOST OF *INSIDE POLITICS*

"This starts as the story of one father and one son, and soon grows into something much deeper and more profound: a meditation on loss and grief, a search for home, a journey to find a missing hero that leads the author finally back to himself. It is Luke Russert's story, but in the end, the main character is you, the reader."

—WRIGHT THOMPSON
SENIOR WRITER FOR ESPN AND THE BESTSELLING AUTHOR
OF *PAPPYLAND* AND *THE COST OF THESE DREAMS*

LOOK FOR ME THERE

LOOK FOR ME THERE

GRIEVING MY FATHER, FINDING MYSELF

LUKE RUSSERT

HARPER HORIZON

ISBN 978-0-7852-9182-4 (Ebook)
ISBN 978-0-7852-9181-7 (HC)
ISBN 978-0-7852-9187-9 (SC)

Library of Congress Control Number: 2022948237

Printed in the United States of America
24 25 26 27 28 LBC 6 5 4 3 2

In memory of Dad, in honor of Mom, and for all those who welcome the stranger.

Oh dear dad

Can you see me now?

I am myself

Like you somehow

I'll ride the wave

Where it takes me

I'll hold the pain

Release me

—EDDIE VEDDER, "RELEASE"[1]

Contents

CONTENTS

Author's Note

Thank you kindly for picking up my book. It's a story about a years-long personal journey, both internal and external, that took place in numerous physical spaces, including sixty-seven different countries and a number of American cities. I don't write about every place I went to, just the ones that made the greatest impression on me. I've changed some names of people in order to protect privacy and to preserve truth. The conversations are recounted as I remember them and as I recorded them in my journals.

Prologue

Today is the first Monday in October 2016, roughly a month before the most consequential election in modern American history. A former reality TV star is running against the first female nominee of a major party. NBC News, where I've worked for eight years, is scoring record-high ratings. There has never been a better time to be a political reporter like me.

But I'm not on the campaign trail. I'm carving out my own, in the backwoods of Maine on day five of my first solo travel adventure, far from the life I've lived and everything I've known. I am terrified of what lies ahead, in part because I will always remain for certain people in Washington, DC, Luke Russert, son of America's most beloved political TV journalist, Tim Russert, host of *Meet the Press* and a man gone too soon. I've spent eight years building a broadcast TV career at NBC News like my dad, building a rapport with the audience, reporting from Congress, and even anchoring the occasional MSNBC show.

But I've just left that job and my entire media life. Lots of folks think I'm crazy. Hell, some days *I* think I am. Yet this drive—to give up my golden opportunity and everything I've known and be alone with my eight-year-old pug, Chamberlain, in the truck my dad gave me a few years before he died—is the beginning of trying to answer a question: Is it wrong to seek something else from life? The power circles of Washington, DC, and television news left me unfulfilled and unhappy. What am I missing in this world? And why haven't I felt whole?

In Maine I seek some form of liberation, a freedom from the expectations placed on me. I'm traveling for myself. Having always been on a trajectory that

1

was never my own, I finally feel, in Maine, a little bit free. Deep in the rural, remote forest, on my way to Jackman, a western village known for its moose hunters, the weight of my past, the grief of my father's death, the shackles of DC society, and the noose of inescapable technology cannot reach me. Maine is verdant heaven.

On the remote dirt road ahead of me, rays of autumn sunlight pierce the tiny gaps in the canopy of timber trees. The quiet of the surrounding woods is disrupted only by my truck, hard at work navigating the potholes, gravel, and dirt of the private logging road deep inside a working forest in the north-central part of the state. Chamberlain, riding shotgun, peers over at me with his big brown eyes. Then he wags his curly pug tail at me and stares out the window.

Vibrant reds, yellows, and oranges are on the trees. Foliage season is starting, a brush of color in a massive swirl of dark green. A real sense of wildness in these woodlands. At times, trimmed-back parts of the forest, areas that have been logged, allow for glimpses of a river that rushes alongside the road. With my truck window down, I can make out the forceful yet calming sound of the running water. Even Chamberlain is impressed. He's joined me because we were inspired by John Steinbeck's *Travels with Charley: In Search of America*. Also, I felt it appropriate he saw the home state of his namesake: Civil War hero Union general Joshua Chamberlain. Truthfully, though, I need him by my side. Even on my first solo adventure, I cannot go it totally alone.

I guess that's why I drive the old truck too. Dad and I took it on a few road trips. Old pens of his still sit in the center console. His handwriting marks "registration" on an envelope in the glove box. He took care of the truck for me when I went off to college: starting it up every day in the winter, getting it washed and gassed up before I came home. Big, tough, and dependable, his spirit is inside the cab, watching over me and probably quite concerned.

His only son has never been this unpredictable. I see his frame lodged into the front seat, his hand reaching for the center emergency brake that does not exist on this truck, as if he could stop me from hurting myself. "Take it easy on the turn, watch that pothole, brake slow." To avoid this paternal cautiousness, I'd played something for us to get lost to on the radio. And that's what I think of now. This week the field for the Major League Baseball playoffs has been set. Dad and I could listen to baseball on the radio for hours together. I fire up a baseball podcast I'd downloaded earlier. And as I listen on this October day in Maine, I'm taken back to a day in Baltimore some twenty-two years before.

"Programs, get your programs. Five dollars. Pencil included. Programs!" The vendor yells from his booth elevated just above the crowd streaming into Oriole Park at Camden Yards. The cathedral of the "retro design" parks has recently opened, and most every game has sold out. Dad has season tickets, a point of pride for a man who as a boy was lucky to attend one MLB game per year—on his birthday, making the three-hour drive to Cleveland from Buffalo. Now, in 1994, as host of *Meet the Press*, he fits as many games as possible into his busy schedule. Holding my eight-year-old hand ever tighter, Dad fights his way through the sea of people. He gets claustrophobic in crowds. Though I know this, I ask him to stop for a second.

"Dad, may I get a program, please?"

He can't hear me over the noise of the crowd.

I yank on his hand.

"What? What is it?" He stares down at me, wiping a mix of sweat and sunscreen from his eyes.

"A program. Can I get a program?"

We trek back toward the booth. He bends over so I can hear his voice more clearly. "I'll get you this program, but you have to promise to work on your reading. I want you to read it to me aloud between innings. Is that a deal?"

Excitedly, I nod my head.

He hands the vendor a five-dollar bill, then places the program in my outstretched palm. I see the smiling faces of Orioles stars Cal Ripken Jr. and Brady Anderson on the cover. I know I'll tape it to my wall when I get home. For now, I hold it like a loaf of bread. We work our way back through the crowd. A few steps behind, holding Dad's hand, I keep my eyes affixed to the back of his white polo shirt. The outline of his wallet is visible through his back pants pocket, stained into the old khakis. A hanky to wipe his brow creeps out of the other pocket. He clips his beeper tightly to his belt—it's his post-work Sunday casual uniform. As we move faster through the horde, the sweat on our palms intensifies in the humid mid-Atlantic summer day. For a second, his grip slips and we become disconnected. I fall back a few feet as people aggressively pass by.

I never lose sight of the man in the white shirt. Immediately Dad turns around, his face concerned but focused. He jogs back and grabs my hand tight, locking his big thumb and fingers around my wrist. He pulls me in. His other hand now sits across my shoulder, a protective hold. "Buddy, if we're ever separated, just look for me there," he says, pointing at a hot dog stand with a big, memorable Oriole bird logo.

He pauses and looks me up and down. "But we won't ever be separated."

PART 1

ONE

June 13, 2008

I glance down at a familiar number on my phone, one that traces back to NBC News in Washington. *Probably Dad checking in.* I slip outside the crowded Florentine bar, passing a throng of Italians cheering their squad in a European Championship soccer match. My girlfriend, Jeanie, sits at the table, beer in hand, eyes transfixed on the digital camera pictures we took today of the statue of David. As I answer the call, I can see her through the bar's window.

"Luke, is your mom there?" my dad's assistant, calling from Washington, asks.

"No, she's at the hotel nearby. Does Dad need her?"

"Well. Um. Well, we just can't get ahold of her."

"I think she's getting ready for dinner. I can find her. What's going on?"

"Um, it's that, it's um, well . . ." I can tell she is searching for words. "Your dad fainted and he's on his way to the hospital."

"Fainted?"

"Yes. Can you please get your mom to call us back here? Your dad's office line."

I know Tim Russert better than anybody, and Tim Russert does not faint. I suspect Dad is dead.

It's June 13, 2008, I'm twenty-two years old, and right now it feels like the world is slowing down and speeding up at the same time. I furiously knock on the window to get Jeanie's attention. "We've got to go now!" My voice carries beyond the glass. The look on my face is enough for her not to question why.

Jeanie and I joined my mom, Maureen Orth, on vacation following my graduation from Boston College last month. Dad was with us in Rome two days ago, our last day together as a family spent at the Vatican. He then went back to Washington to tape *Meet the Press* on Father's Day.

"What's happening?" Jeanie asks now.

I'm flushed, but I get the words out. "That was NBC in DC. Something happened to my dad. He fainted or something. We need to find my mom."

"Isn't she out to dinner with those Italian friends of hers?"

I glance at my watch. It's dinnertime, but, knowing Mom, there's a good chance she's late and just now walking out the door. I begin to run quickly up the street, Jeanie following behind. She grasps at my shirt to keep up.

I need to find my mother before anybody else does.

Inside the hotel we take the stairs. No time for the ancient elevator. In front of Mom's room, I pound the door, desperate. It opens quickly. Mom stands there, dressed fashionably, pulling out the sleeves of her blazer jacket to smooth the wrinkles.

"Luke, what is it? I'm late for dinner."

"NBC is trying to reach you," I say between exasperated breaths. "Check your phone. They just got me. Dad fainted at the bureau."

"He fainted? What does that mean?" She understands the same thing I did: Tim Russert doesn't faint. Fainting is laughable for a man who prides himself on his durability and his work ethic, who reads six newspapers a day while pumping the pedals on his stationary bike and listening to Bruce Springsteen. To prepare for weekly interviews, Dad has sheaves of news packets mailed and faxed to our home every day, sometimes twice a day. He outworks everyone. He takes work seriously. It is his duty. To faint on the job would be to disgrace it.

"I'll call NBC now," Mom says. "Stay close to me."

Jeanie leaves the room. Instinctually, she knows it'll be just mother and son facing the news of the next hour.

I sit on the couch as Mom calls the NBC desk. My eyes fixate on the ridges of the wooden coffee table. It's Friday, midday in Washington, DC, and I'd spoken to Dad just hours ago. He phoned me from my apartment. Ever the kind and doting dad, he'd gone over to set up the cable TV and Wi-Fi. A nice head start before the arduous task of moving from Boston College back to Washington. The conversation we had runs through my mind. It had all seemed so normal.

"Buddy, I'm over here at your place. This green thing. The Nintendo box?"

"You mean the Xbox?"

"Yeah. This guy here, he can hook it up to the TV audio system. He's going to leave you directions on how to get it going. I think it's best that he does it. These new systems are complex."

"Sounds good, Dad. I appreciate it."

"Of course you do." A slight tone of sarcasm comes through the phone. "You're off palling around Italy and dear old Dad is back at the fort, getting things done. Working! Working hard for the money! Enjoy your time in Europe. Just how I grew up!" He chuckles mightily at the last line. When Dad graduated from college, after paying his own way, his summer was spent working on the garbage trucks of South Buffalo, New York, trying to make enough money to go to law school. A far cry from the privileged life he's bestowed on me: a monthlong European vacation.

"Thanks, Dad. I really do appreciate it." I wasn't lying. The guy was doing me a solid, which very well could be the story of the first twenty-two years of my life—Dad guiding me, taking care of me, and, on this Friday before Father's Day, doing the thing he loved most in the world: providing.

"Okay, buddy, I'm going to get back to this. Talk later."

I wonder if that's the last conversation we'll ever have.

It is.

"Listen to me: Is he dead? Did he die?" Mom asks. "Just tell me!"

Somebody at the hospital confirms the news. A fatal heart attack, a type known as "the widow maker." Mom sinks back into her chair. She has been perked up at the desk, pen in hand, taking notes about the details. She is a celebrated journalist in her own right, a special correspondent at *Vanity Fair*, and till that moment she remarkably remains in reporter mode. But when the confirmation comes, the terrible truth sinks in. Tears stream down her face. She puts the phone down and motions for me to come over. We hug. She doesn't say a word. Mom does not wail. Not once. My throat chokes up, but I have to say it; I need to face this horrific reality, this new normal. "He's gone."

Mom nods her head. I don't feel pain. Just shock. It's the beginning of somehow trying to accept that our world has forever changed.

The news business never stops. Through tragedy, death, despair, or dysfunction—the news goes on. Even when an autocrat tries to censor it, some-how, some way, the news gets out. Those in the business know this truth, how it's not just part of the game, it *is* the game. For that reason, I do not consider it odd that no more than five minutes after finding out that Dad has died a higher-up at NBC News calls my phone.

"Luke. I'm so sorry about Tim, and I'm sorry to have to say this." His pain is real, as is his empathy. "We want to control this story. We want to report it first. The longer we wait, the more likely it is that somebody at the hospital could leak it. It could be out of our hands. Please alert your relatives as to what happened. They need to hear from you, not us. We need to get on air as soon as possible."

Mom overhears the conversation and jumps into action. She grabs the phone from my hands and yells, "This news should absolutely be held back from the public until our family has been notified! Tim's father cannot find out from a news bulletin flashing across his TV that his only son has died. If the news breaks before we can phone everyone, mark my words, I will never forgive you!"

I sit next to her as she rings my dad's sisters, Bea, Kiki, and Trish, and then her own family. Once somebody is sitting with my grandpa, Big Russ, she rings him. On each call she cuts to the point but maintains her empathetic grace. This strength inspires me. When she's done, she tells me to give the network the green light.

I call back the executive.

"Our family has been notified. Go ahead."

"It'll be Tom."

Tom Brokaw, the legendary former anchor of *NBC Nightly News*, was exceptionally close to Dad, one of his best friends. There is no better choice.

By the grace of God, my mother and I cannot see the report in real time. NBC News doesn't reach Florence, Italy, and social media apps are not yet as ubiquitous and invasive as they will be in the years ahead. This turns out to be an enormous blessing. In the hours after Dad's death, our news updates are the phone calls of friends and not an endless stream of politicians and fellow journalists offering up remembrances on Twitter or the national airwaves. Instead we find ourselves, mother and son, walking the streets of the beautiful Renaissance-era city on a perfect summer night—phones off, only each other to lean on as we peer down at the Arno River and try to catch our breath.

"Want to get a drink? Talk this out? This is probably the last time we'll have for ourselves in quite a while."

"That's a good idea, Mom."

We duck into a lobby bar of some nearby hotel. The crush of death is still raw but not quite all-consuming. At that table we pledge our loyalty, affirm our love, and make a pact of strength and togetherness as a family. Our grieving will be dignified. Our attention will go toward honoring Dad's legacy and picking up the spirits of those as sad as us. Mom mentions we are blessed. Now is the time to rely on our Catholic faith. We hold hands and say a Hail Mary.

Once back at our hotel, I beg my mother to sleep. We have an early morning flight, and chaos will greet us upon landing. I keep my phone off and get into bed. Jeanie has been a saint during this entire process and holds back her emotions so as to not upset me. It's lying next to each other in that bed, staring up at the beige ceiling and processing the events of the day, when reality hits me.

I'll never speak to Dad again. He is gone.

I burst into tears, clutch the pillow, and scream into the night. Jeanie holds me and reminds me to breathe in between my hysterical wheezing. I cry about losing my best friend. I cry for the grandchildren he'll never meet. I cry for all the lessons ahead that I know I needed to learn but will not receive from his calm and trusting voice. I cry knowing the fabric of my being is forever torn. I cry because he never got to see the Bills win a Super Bowl.

When we land in DC, the whirlwind begins. Mom and I are whisked into an airport meeting room. Copies of various newspapers lie on the table; "Russert Dead" reads a headline. NBC executives and producers gently ask us questions about funeral planning. It becomes apparent: Mom and I aren't burying just a husband and a father but a giant of a man. From the preparations already underway, it begins to sound like a state funeral. Tim Russert's death is being felt well beyond his home. There is a national outpouring, unexpected by us and, in its own way, intensely comforting.

When we get home, I walk through the kitchen door. My high school classmates from St. Albans are there waiting. I'm an only child, so they're like my brothers. My friend Auguste, tall, broad, and muscular, a terrific athlete who played football at the University of Virginia, grabs the back of my neck and pulls me close. I weep into his shoulder, enough to soak his shirt. I look around the room—so many sad eyes, but so many people seem to be looking to me for guidance. I tell myself this is the last time I'll cry hard. I want to pick people up. Plus, it's apparent from the questions posed in that conference room that there's no time to cope. Any energy that could go toward grief is going toward logistics. Where will he be buried? When will the funeral be? Where will it be? How will the viewing work? Who will speak?

Two days after Dad's death, Mom and I sit in our living room with our local priest. "Who is going to do the eulogy?" he asks.

I look at Mom and speak before she has a chance to. "That would be me, Father." I know I can do it. I can maintain composure and hopefully leave people uplifted and not saddened. Plus, writing the eulogy will be my way to honor the man who was so much more than just my father.

I retreat to my empty DC apartment and turn off my cellphone. This space is where Dad was on the day of his death, setting up my cable box and Wi-Fi. The lights on them blink, reminding me they're alive. The place is barren now but for appliances and some counter stools: the wired TV, the lasting relic of his short time inside the space; the Xbox he asked about, now plugged in. I throw a six-pack of beer in the fridge and stare at my laptop. To ground myself, I title the page, "Dad's Eulogy." A phrase beyond surreal to type.

I stand up and pace.

Where can I turn for help in writing the most important words of my life?

It dawns on me. Why not the man himself? I remember he had written about loss. I rush out to grab a copy of *Big Russ and Me*, my dad's memoir. In it he talks about death through the prism of faith:

> The importance of faith, and of accepting and even celebrating death, was something I continue to believe as a Catholic and a Christian. To accept faith, we have to resign ourselves as mortals to the fact that we are a small part of a grand design.[1]

He continues in the chapter:

> We can't withstand major crises and the huge changes they bring about alone. We are not strong enough. We really aren't. When people are confronted with a crisis, particularly the death of a loved one, the most important thing is to reach out to them. Help them, because they can't go through their loss alone. It is inexplicable in their lives at that time. You have to be there for them and help them to understand, *There is something here to accept. This is out of your control; this is a power far beyond yours.*[2]

Dad does not leave me alone in the apartment. I feel he is showing himself. Almost immediately I internalize his spirit. Perhaps he is writing through me or there is a more divine connection. The words flow out. I write at a level of focus I've never reached before. The writing is continuous. When done, I give it a look over. I don't know where it came from, but there it is. I crack two beers. I toast the man and thank him.

"Where are all those people going?" I ask. "Is there a service at the National Cathedral today?" I notice a long line snaking around the block by St. Albans School, which is located at the base of the grand church.

The funeral director riding in the front seat of the black car looks confused. The hearse carrying Dad moves along ahead of us.

"No, Luke, those people are here for the wake. They're here for your dad."

"They're here for the wake?!" Mom is stunned too.

The line must be a mile long. My eyes start to well up as I look at the people through the tinted glass. All ages, genders, races, and creeds. It's the American quilt.

The casket comes into the school through a side entrance. My closest friends escort it as I trot behind. It lies in the school's refectory behind two large bouquets of white flowers. Mom, along with me and the rest of our extended family, stands behind in prayer. When the blessing is done, an official-looking person in a suit walks over. I don't recognize him. "Luke, just wanted to let you know President Bush and the First Lady will be arriving shortly."

We have heard that somebody from the White House was going to pay their respects, but we did not know that it was going to be the president. The sirens from the motorcade are within earshot. The president and Mrs. Bush walk in, escorted by one of my old teachers. President Bush, famous for giving nicknames, has one for me. "Big Luke! Come here, brother." He brings me in for a bear hug. "So sorry, your dad was a good man."

"Thank you, sir."

Mom and I pray with them. She holds their hands. They then follow us to the school library to meet the rest of our family. President Bush stays for an hour and greets every single Orth and Russert.

"Thank you for the time, sir," I say.

"My honor," says President Bush.

The son of a garbage man, getting a US president to his wake? I can hear Dad mouthing, "What a country."

Soon after the president leaves, the funeral director approaches me. "Luke, what do you want to do? You want to say hello to anybody? You can also just rest up. It's going to be a long day tomorrow with the service."

"I should say hello. There are so many people out there. I'll do it for an hour and see how it feels."

I walk into the refectory; the crowd has started to shuffle in. One by one they walk up to me after passing the casket. People have come from everywhere—Minnesota, Tennessee, North Carolina, New Hampshire, California, Buffalo, and beyond. It's a testament to how revered Dad was; I knew he was popular, but not like this. For many it's like a member of their own family died. It's difficult to grasp in the moment. Each one shares a kind word or a special story of what Dad meant to them. Each one gives me a hug or a handshake; each one gives me a little bit of strength.

"Osman! Is that you?" Osman, an immigrant from Sierra Leone, manages the nearby Steak N Egg Diner. He has seen me at all hours and in all conditions. Slowly he puts his hands on my shoulders. He makes sure we lock eyes; his are moist and teary. "Your dad taught me American politics. Because of him, I could understand what was happening in my new country. I loved that man."

Remarkably, I'm able to stay composed. Perhaps it's that transfer of strength.

I button up one of Dad's crisp white dress shirts. It's a little big, but I need all the magic today. I'm comforted by the smell of him in the collar, a man's musk in a well-worn shirt. Before the funeral, there's to be a final goodbye. I stand off in the corner as my extended family pays their last respects to the open casket. Then I motion them to leave. It's just Mom left. I give her a moment with her husband of nearly twenty-five years. Then I respectfully ask her to go. Four years ago when Dad dropped me off at college, he asked Mom for a final moment alone with me, man-to-man. He knew I was moving on to that next chapter of independence, out of the house, navigating the world on my own. He hugged me close that day and told me, "Laugh hard, study often, and keep your honor." Now it's my final moment with him.

It's a simple casket, unpretentious, with an American flag sewn into the light blue velvet lining. A reminder of his love of country. The man who hated

15

suits is going home in his trademark look: blue blazer, charcoal-gray slacks, crisp white button-down shirt like the one I'm wearing, red striped tie, and black leather rubber-sole shoes. I place a Buffalo Bills football, Washington Nationals hat, and Bruce Springsteen CD in the casket, along with a copy of *Big Russ and Me*, signed by Grandpa, Dad, and me. "Things to bring into the next world, Dad."

I grab his hand one last time; it's cold and firm, the opposite of his soft and warm personality. There are no tears; he needs to know I'm strong. I put my fingers through his and clasp inside the thumb.

"Dad, thank you for all you've given to me, the loyalty, the lessons, the love. This beautiful life. Keep watch over me—I'll never not need you." I bend down, kiss his forehead, and whisper, "I love ya." Then I give him a final fist pound on his shoulder, like he always gave me. I don't turn back as I walk out. Finality comes with the sound of the casket being locked by the mortician.

I walk down the aisle of Holy Trinity Catholic Church in Washington, DC, steps behind Dad's casket. My focus is on Mom and nobody else. So long as she stays strong, I know I'll be fine. The priests have the rest under control. That is the beauty of the Catholic faith. If nothing else, we know how to do death, following the thousands-year-old script.

At the appropriate time, the priest summons me to the pulpit for the eulogy. I stare out into a sea of friends, family, and official Washington.

In the pews I see Barack Obama, John McCain, Nancy Pelosi. Joe Biden's face looks especially pained; he is a man all too familiar with grief. The same can be said of Ethel Kennedy, whom I lock eyes with for a brief moment. If I stand any chance of delivering a good speech, I understand I'll have to look beyond the luminaries to my friends in the back, the ones from St. Albans and Boston College, who have known me for years. To them I'm just talking about my dad. Not some legend; just Dad. They loved him for his parent role, and their faces give me the support I need. I speak to them.

My knuckles grow white as I grip the lectern. There's silence. I look down, thinking about all the faces from the wake. I'm determined to make them proud and make him proud. After a deep breath, I jump off. A powerful wave of calm washes over me. There are no nerves. This is exactly where I need to be. Fifty-eight years of Tim Russert's life concentrated into twenty minutes. The jokes hit. The emotional moments resonate. I can feel the warmth from the congregation and can hear, toward the end, Dad's voice in my ear: "You're doing great, buddy. Bring it home!"

Then I move to the closer: "Well, my dad was a force of nature. And now his own cycle in nature is complete. But his spirit lives on in everybody who loves their country, loves their family, loves their faith, and loves those Buffalo Bills. I love you, Dad, and in his words: 'Let us all go get 'em!'"

Senator Obama stands first and starts to clap. Others join him. Soon it's a full standing ovation—an anomaly at a Catholic funeral. I glance at the priest. He smiles and nods that it's okay. I take a slow walk to the pew. I don't cry. I simply whisper, "Thanks, Dad."

Later in the day there is a public memorial at the Kennedy Center, televised for the world to see. This morning I didn't know if I should speak at it, but now I feel I need to. I want to have the last word on my father in public, like I had in private. I follow remembrances from Dad's friend Maria Shriver and old boss Mario Cuomo. There are so many people in the audience; I can't recognize anybody. But I'm far more relaxed than in the morning, and crisper in my delivery. I play to the energy of the crowd, which is rooting for me at every turn. Again, I hear my dad's voice: "You're doing great, buddy. Keep at it. Hook 'em and reel 'em in. You're doing it. Yes!"

They like what they've heard. I see James Carville and Mary Matalin in tears, leading the audience in applause, and then a bear hug comes from Dad's friend Mike Barnicle. My uncle Tony Scozzaro, a gifted guitarist from Buffalo, plays Springsteen's "Born to Run" as a closing tribute. Then, unexpectedly, Bruce Springsteen himself is piped in via satellite and performs "Thunder Road," Dad's favorite song. That makes me shed my only public tear.

I take a moment backstage to think. Tim Russert died at the height of his career. He died as the nominees for the 2008 presidential election were being settled on after a historic primary season. He died as television media reached its pinnacle, in the last hours before a new digital world. He died just after his son graduated from a Jesuit college. He died days after praying in the Vatican. He died in his favorite season: summer. He died on the Friday before his favorite holiday: Father's Day. The man who wrote books about fatherhood, which caused so many people to reconnect with their dads, actually died on Father's Day weekend.

A fitting ending.

This is only reinforced as I walk outside of the Kennedy Center for a reception. Our family requested that another one of Dad's favorite songs be played as people leave the remembrance service: "Somewhere over the Rainbow." During the program a light summer rain soaks Washington, and then, miraculously, over the terrace of the iconic arts center and the Potomac River appears a magnificent rainbow. I run to it. I'm alone and stare up at the sky. This is my father saying hello and letting us know he is okay. I'm convinced of this. I find some comfort in it, even as I still feel so much pain.

A group of TV executives finds me afterward at a bar with my friends.

The speech was great, they tell me. One of the best they've heard. I'd shown such poise. They begin that day and in the weeks that follow to talk about my future.

That single eulogy, that remembrance, will change my career trajectory—and my life.

Out of my worst day will come my biggest opportunity.

TWO

Peacock

A TV executive calls and says, "You have a gift. You could be a very good presence on air. TV needs more young people." It's flattering, but I don't know if it's the right thing to do. Am I more than a name to them? What do I offer beyond remembrances of Dad? My original plan after Boston College was to go to graduate school and pursue a degree in international relations. I believe that getting anchored in something other than media should be my immediate future.

But then, a few weeks later, a random call from a number with a Los Angeles area code comes through. I think it's another executive, but instead it's Larry King, the famed nightly presence on CNN. He asks if I'd be willing to come on his show that week.

"Listen, Mr. King. Oh, I'm sorry, call you Larry, right? Listen, Larry. I really don't want to talk about Dad's death anymore. I've done it on the *Today Show* and in a few print interviews. I don't want to seem like I'm milking it."

King shifts his ask. He says he wants to talk politics, specifically youth issues—and perhaps mix a question about my dad in there.

I agree to it. To me it's a nice trial run. How will I do on TV outside of simply reminiscing about Dad? If the interview goes well, maybe taking up NBC or CNN on their offer to be a youth presence during the summer's political conventions makes sense.

Walking into the CNN studio in DC, I'm at ease. The smell of the gaffer's tape that ties down the power cords, the lights brought up to live-on-air mode—they remind me of the times I went to the studio with Dad. Sometimes he would bring me onto the *Meet the Press* set. For me it meant free candy and kind smiles from Dad's colleagues. He'd take me into the control room, where I was mesmerized by the buttons, graphics, screens, and colors. People explained their jobs to me. I soaked up the information and found the production of TV fascinating.

My favorite times on set were when Dad did remote shoots. We'd get to travel together and I'd be attached to his hip. Childcare was sitting next to Dad during production meetings, strategy sessions, and rehearsals. The rules were pretty simple: do as you're told, don't cause problems, and stay out of the way. While it was beyond cool to watch Dad interview Bill Clinton, Bob Dole, Al Gore, or George W. Bush, the highlight for me was just being with him. He'd make me feel like part of the team. Whether it was carrying his research folders or keeping track of his knapsack, I felt included. This would carry over to extremely early wake-up calls, either to be in position for an interview or to make a flight that would get me back to school on time.

Because I grew up around the TV news life, it never feels foreign to me. In fact, it feels comforting. It's a life I've always known, dominated by the man I admired most.

So, on the day of the CNN interview, Larry King sits in LA, and I'm to be interviewed over satellite in Washington. I have no nerves waiting for the interview to start. The chair almost feels familiar. I don't like how my hair looks in the monitor, but who cares? I laugh thinking about some of Dad's colleagues who spent hours on their hair.

Then I hear Larry King's voice in my earpiece and, like that, we begin a conversation. I enjoy his personalized style of asking questions and giving me a chance to talk about something beyond Dad, specifically the importance of young people getting involved and voting—something I was passionate about in college.

When the interview is over, an older cameraman in the studio comes up and unhooks my microphone and earpiece. "Kid, I've seen a lot of people interviewed in here. For one of your first times—that was really good."

"You're just being nice, but I really appreciate it."

"No, no, no. I'm serious. You're good. If you want, you can do this."

I know from time spent with Dad that a lot of the techs are a crusty, hard-nosed bunch, not keen to dole out compliments.

Maybe he *is* being sincere.

The calls from the executives at CBS, CNN, and NBC increase after the Larry King appearance. They want me to be on air, on their networks. This really is a once-in-a-lifetime opportunity available for the taking, but is it the right decision? I spend each hot and muggy July DC day grappling with this question. I'm not so naive to think I'd be free from criticism. A twenty-two-year-old kid landing a network news gig? Nepotism charges would be intense. Hell, they'd be understandable. It would be an enormous privilege afforded me, one that many reporters toiling for years in local news markets would give their right hand for. I could be seen as the poster child for white elite privilege—from private school to riding Dad's coattails. The opposite of meritocracy. It's far from my father's son-of-a-garbage-man, earned-everything-he-ever-got, working-class-hero narrative.

But Dad's life was also providing for his only son the sort of opportunities he'd had to claw his way to get. He wanted me to have it easier than he did. It gave his life purpose. Why not pursue the path that he'd cleared for me?

As I weigh the choice, I'm reminded of one of my father's favorite Bible verses, one that I had tattooed on my inner arm—Luke 12:48: "To whom much is given, much is expected" (my paraphrase). I cannot help but think there is some higher purpose in everything that's happened. I get out my legal pad and debate the offers.

I settle on NBC, a place that has long felt like family. While it's tempting to forge my own path for a different team, I can't quite turn my back on the peacock. Perhaps it's destiny. When I was a newborn, to differentiate my crib in the maternity ward from others at Lenox Hill Hospital in New York City, Dad had affixed a small NBC News hat to the railing.

God works in mysterious ways. I feel I have some natural talent in communications and, with the right tutelage, could put it to worthwhile use. Maybe I could inform my generation like my father had his. Perhaps it's my purpose. Before I phone NBC, though, I call my mother.

"What do you think, Mom?"

"Luke, we're supposed to use the talents God had given us, and for good. You have a talent. You've had it since you were a little boy." Mom always likes to tell the story of how, when I was six and a budding showman, I would emcee

21

my parents' parties, mic and portable speaker in hand: *Thanks for coming. The hors d'oeuvres are to your right, drinks to your left.*

"But Dad's legacy will follow me everywhere, won't it?" I ask Mom. "I mean, it's always going to be the first line of my obituary: 'Son of Tim Russert . . .'"

"Yes, and it doesn't make the challenge of living up to the legacy any easier. On the other hand, it's your name. You shouldn't be afraid to use it."

"That's true."

"But, Luke," she sighs, in a way she knows I find to be overly emotional but in this moment is appropriate. "Do you think you've really processed what happened? Have you grieved enough these last two months? This is a lot to handle."

"I don't want to sit around and just think about it, Mom. Doing something makes it easier."

From the silence on the line, I know she understands. Mom and I have talked about my going to grad school, getting a master's in international relations, seeing the world in the way she had as a young woman. Travel influenced her life as much as politics influenced Dad's. No path of mine is the guaranteed right one. The only thing I know, and she knows, is that I have to choose while the offers are there, and that means soon.

"Think about it. Pray on it."

I do.

A day later I open up a fortune cookie after eating some Chinese food alone in my apartment. Whether it's God or the universe, I feel like we can find our way if we're willing to be aware. I crack open the cookie and out pops a little piece of paper: "The greatest cure for misery is hard work. Chinese proverb."

I call NBC.

I'm a "Special Youth Correspondent At-Large" for NBC News. My contract runs for one year—the perfect amount of time. If it doesn't work, I'll go on my way. The one-year contract also forces NBC and me to find a role after the election is over. My office is at the DC bureau, around the corner from where Dad used to sit. Some days it scares me. Other days I purposely walk by and hope he'll pop out from behind the door. It does one thing for me: keeps our connection alive.

Many of my early assignments focus on the youth vote. I travel to the Democratic and Republican conventions in Denver and Minneapolis and interview various young people. I file stories about the convention's youngest delegate or the country's youngest mayor and what the campaigns are doing to drive youth turnout. I find one story when I take a walk outside of the convention center in Denver. A group of regal young Muslim women in hijabs are purchasing some Obama 2008 merchandise. I start talking to them about why they like Obama and what they're doing for the campaign. They mention they've been canvassing for him in Colorado, a swing state, and very much believe he could more effectively communicate with the Muslim world because he understands the faith via his Muslim father and his time spent in Indonesia. Later that day with my camera crew, I ask them questions about Obama's appeal.

"Would you see Obama as the first Muslim president?"

To my surprise they go silent, laugh nervously, and say, "No comment."

These young women, essentially my age and just as American—listening to pop music on their iPhones, dressing in stylish clothes, downing Starbucks frappuccinos—feel their support of Obama could hurt him. To hear them say they worry about hurting a presidential candidate with their support because of their faith tears at me. It demonstrates the degree of the division within our nation and the prejudice faced by so many who are nonwhite or non-Christian. It tears at a lot of people at the network too. The piece runs on MSNBC and Andrea Mitchell is kind enough to put it on during her hour. It gets positive feedback because it explores what has not received a lot of attention: young Muslim Americans finding a personal connection with the candidate Barack Obama.

As is true for anyone starting out at a new job, there are growing pains. Understanding the internal office dynamics of network and cable news is not easy. Different shows operate as self-ruling provinces. They're competitive with each other over guest bookings, correspondents, live-shot locations. What makes it especially difficult for me is that my job description is broad and vague: "Special Youth Correspondent." Producers don't know what to do with such a title. My bosses don't either. Shows by nature do not like to incorporate new people anyway because each show has a set system that works for the program, and they do not want to spend time breaking in rookies.

There is also a toxicity to media, especially to television news. It's a hyper-competitive business, where networks compete for eyeballs, talent competes for airtime, and producers compete to run shows. Internal rivalries and vendettas are the norm. When it comes to correspondents, many fight for a small sliver of airtime doled out by various producers with various agendas. While fellow correspondents are technically your colleagues, they can also be rivals just as much as your competitors from other networks. It's a harrowing world for a kid who's just lost his father, much less one with a famous last name. The name shields me from some intraoffice poison but exposes me to even more, as anyone who'd had a problem with Dad over the years can now unload on me. It doesn't take me long to realize why some people are rude to me alone.

In previous jobs, whether it was loading freight, delivering pizzas, landscaping, interning at ESPN, or taping radio shows, I was given an assignment by a superior and a time by which to complete it. I was expecting the same at NBC. Instead, I soon learn that much of the job is actually selling myself internally. This makes me uncomfortable because I never quite know if I deserve to be here. How dare I sell myself in the same vein as a colleague with dozens of years of experience? Some kind producers help me out, but the "pitch" is not my forte.

Outside of NBC, charges of nepotism rain down hard. "Luke Russert Sucks Big Time and NBC Should Fire Him Now!" one blog post headline screams shortly after I start. "Get this fat smarmy jackass off my TV!" reads a posted comment. "The apple didn't just fall far from the tree, it rolled out of the orchard!" comes in a tweet. The catcalls on social media and in gossip columns sting deep.

There is no preparation for life as a public figure, not even a childhood spent as the son of famous parents. As a public figure you are not a person.

You are a name that can be ridiculed. And you will be. I'd expected some heat. I'm a white heterosexual male whose privilege has given him a cherished opportunity. I understand what my life and name have afforded me. But I can't renounce my name any more than I can renege on my one-year contract, both of which seem to be what many of my online critics want. I can only prove my worth by doing the work.

The high point of that first year comes on election night. President-elect Obama scores an upset win in the conservative state of Indiana. I'm stationed at the state's flagship university in Bloomington. Behind me is a human wall of college students, many elated that their candidate has won the presidency. For a few minutes I get on the network election night telecast and not only recount the turnout of the youth vote but also take a moment to explain the significance of the election for young people—those who came of age after 9/11 and have borne the brunt of the recent economic collapse. These young people are making themselves heard. This gets a cheer from the students behind me and, eventually, an Emmy for being part of the NBC News team that evening.

After that, though, the job becomes a slog. Once the inauguration passes, I don't get on air much. The youth vote beat isn't really a beat once the business of governing begins. I decide I'll leave media once my contract is up in the summer and go back to school. Yet as that date nears, it bothers me that I'm not going out on my own terms. I feel like I still have something left to give. The energy that compelled me to take the job the previous summer is still there.

After some informal conversations with colleagues, I realize NBC is short staffed on Capitol Hill. There aren't enough bodies to cover all the news. I'm under contract for another three months, so I persuade my boss to give me a chance as an off-air producer/reporter on the Hill. I won't be on camera but will be working in the Capitol building, where many of its inhabitants loved my dad. I can use my name for good, to help get calls returned, and I can gain some needed experience. Plus, working at the Capitol feels more substantial. If I'm going to work in TV, I should be doing work that matters.

I walk into the Capitol building and feel like I've been given my chance to play a part in the history of our great nation. I realize this sounds grandiose, but when you work on the Hill, it's true. Everyone from the night-shift janitor to the Speaker of the House gets to see history play out in real time and maybe even become part of it.

Though I grew up in Washington and feel like I know the pace of the city, it's a different experience working inside the Capitol every day. The campus is its own little town, complete with a chapel, restaurants and cafés, parks, a transit system, barbershops, gift stores, and post offices. There is an energy in the place, especially when both chambers are in session and thousands of aides, reporters, lobbyists, advocates, foreign dignitaries, and police scurry around the hundreds of lawmakers, all trying to look important and make their mark. Sometimes when I work late, being around the statues in the rotunda feels like being in *Night at the Museum*. I make eye contact with George Washington, Thomas Jefferson, and Martin Luther King Jr. I stand quietly alone at the center spot where Lincoln and Kennedy had lain in state as moonlight splatters through the ceiling windows. I try to hold my breath for complete silence. I think back to what the emotions in the room must have been like at those times.

I know within a week at the Capitol that it's my home. It's the best gig in Washington.

The work comes naturally: hearings, roll call votes, parliamentary procedure. It all makes sense to me. If it doesn't, I ask my NBC colleague Mike Viqueira, who is kind enough to help. Maybe because I've heard so much about it at home, or I'm generally interested, but working the Hill does not even feel like work. It feels like I'm getting a PhD in American government. And I love being a civics nerd! I make myself available at all hours, which means I begin to appear on-air again, when no one else can appear for a predawn stand-up at the Capitol on a snowy Sunday or voice a late-night radio script after a roll call vote. I do well enough in these appearances that my three-month audition as an off-air reporter becomes another yearlong contract. One more year to audition!

I want this gig. I grind; I pound the marble floors. I chase congressmen into elevators for quotes. I load up NBC's internal "hot file" used to determine coverage, with briefing notes at all hours of the day. I try to break down complex legislative procedure into discernible English. I will not be outhustled or outworked. I want to—no, I *have* to—stay on the Hill. Persistence pays off; ultimately, I'm rewarded with a multiyear contract as an on-air congressional correspondent.

"This is wild!" I say to my friend Jake Sherman of *Politico* almost every day. He's my age and we run to the Speaker's Lobby each afternoon to cover votes. Soon, I'm on a first-name basis with the Speaker of the House. Senators call my cellphone. I'd be lying if I said I did not enjoy the fame. It's intoxicating for a twentysomething. The airtime comes in spurts. I back up the chief congressional correspondent, the reliable and talented Kelly O'Donnell.

When the Hill is busy, I'm busy. When Congress is in recess, I'm not needed so much. That's fine. It gives me a chance to develop sources and work the hallways. Unlike at the NBC Bureau or 30 Rock, where my youth stands out, on the Hill I'm surrounded by fellow millennials. My producers, the indomitable Shawna Thomas, the hard-charging Frank Thorp, and the attentive and amiable Alex Moe, are all in my demographic. My personality and sense of humor are liberated. Many press aides are no more than a few years older than me and are kind enough to take me along to their favorite Hill haunts, like the Tune Inn and Johnny's Half Shell. Even some of the revered older, crusty, veteran Hill reporters, like Carl Hulse of the *New York Times* and Paul Kane of the *Washington Post*, take a liking to me. I find some mentors.

Nepotism charges never go away. At times, I'm asked around the Hill how I came into the job. It's usually a passive-aggressive question, issued with a smirk. Someone wants to knock me down a peg. The irony of my career is that by seeking more substantial work, I've walked right into the looming shadow of my father. The comparisons to him continue, and the online vitriol intensifies the more I'm on. I no longer care as much, though. I come to realize I cannot change the critics' perception of me. I'm Roosevelt's Man in the Arena now, and I can only prove myself in that arena. Proving my worth is my motivation. It's a powerful fuel.

Time goes on. News never sleeps. I work late nights. I work on weekends.

Budget fights, government shutdowns, committee hearings. I cover deeply meaningful stories like the health care that 9/11 first responders are not receiving, an issue that was dear not only to comedian Jon Stewart but to NYC-based MSNBC. For *Dateline* I spend three years off and on reporting about a murder case in New York that I'm convinced was a wrongful conviction. *Dateline* gives the story the show's full hour. It gets nominated for an Emmy. I also have a foray into weather stories—blizzards, hurricanes, tornadoes, and earthquakes.

Mostly, though, I stay close to the Capitol. I'm there even when I'm not. My cellphone rings a lot. Too much when I watch Nationals games with buddies or take a date to a restaurant: "The News Desk here. There's a campaign event in Arkansas, or maybe it's Wisconsin—can you leave in two hours?" The answer is always *yes* because the question is never a question. This is the gig. I have to be on and at the ready.

The job carries a lot of stress: fear of failure, of the competition beating me to a story, of flubbing a live shot or asking an inane question at a press conference. So I prepare more. Work longer. The news packets Dad once received become the news sites I scroll endlessly.

The work pays off. In addition to my congressional beat, I begin to guest host programs on MSNBC and appear on *Weekend Today*. At the age of twenty-six, I'm handed an hour of airtime on a national cable news network. I stand in for notables like Lester Holt, Andrea Mitchell, Willie Geist, and Steve Kornacki. I even appear as a panelist on *Meet the Press*. I'm not just in Dad's shadow now. There is a chance for me to follow his life. *MTP* is hosted by Chuck Todd, and I truly do not want his job, though some within NBC and many critics online doubt that. I love the congressional beat. I'm beginning to understand where my work can lead me: down a wide and well-lit path and toward a prestigious future, with a little luck and good timing—if not at *MTP* and its ghosts then perhaps at the *Today Show* or hosting something full time on MSNBC. I could also just be content as a long-tenured correspondent. Or there are always opportunities at other networks, too, come contract time. Dream big dreams, right?

The brass ring feels within my grasp.

"Hey, Loudmouth!" John Boehner yells at me. "We need to have a talk!"

It's the spring of 2015, and we're in the bowels of the Capitol building. Boehner is the Speaker of the House.

"Come by my office in an hour. Are you available then?"

We're friendly, but I cover him and his often unruly House Republican Conference aggressively. Maybe I've offended him. "Sir, I suspect that of our two schedules yours is a tad bit busier. I'll be there."

He smirks but doesn't laugh.

The bulky shoulder of a member of his security detail makes no effort to avoid my own as Boehner and his men pass through the narrow hallway. Why does Boehner want a personal audience with me on this day in late April? Perhaps my coverage has pissed him off? Maybe it's an off-the-record scoop? I comb my mind but nothing jumps out.

Loudmouth isn't a clue either. He's called me that for months, a nickname given to me for my propensity to shout questions at press conferences—in a booming baritone I've inherited from Dad—in such a way that no other reporter stands a chance of being heard first. Boehner has enacted the "Russert Rule": no voiced questions at all, just every reporter silently raising a hand while Boehner calls on them with a point of the finger. If anything, Loudmouth is the more affectionate name he has for me. If Boehner wants to make a point, he'll call me Shithead.

When I arrive at his office, an aide tells me Boehner is not there. He'll see me in the ceremonial Speaker's office just off the House floor.

That is strange. The ceremonial office is normally for visiting dignitaries like the pope or the Dalai Lama when they come for photo ops or when the Speaker needs to round up votes from his political caucus on a controversial bill. The room affords privacy.

An aide escorts me down the hall and then through the door to the ceremonial office. It's stately: a marble fireplace, orange carpet over a marble floor, and flags at the ready for flashing cameras.

John Boehner, in a perfectly ironed white shirt and well-shined black shoes, sits in a high-back leather chair, alone, smoking a Camel and reading a golf magazine.

He takes another puff and looks up.

"What are you doing here?" he asks.

"Sir? You called *me* to *your* office."

He cracks a smile. "No, Shithead. Not *here* here."

He puts the golf magazine down and motions for me to sit opposite him. I do.

"What are you doing on Capitol Hill? You've been here awhile now, huh?"

I know Boehner was educated by the Jesuits, and this almost seems like a Jesuit mind game: *Who are we and why are we here?*

Still, I play along. "Yes, I've been here about six years now."

"How old are you?"

"I'm going to turn thirty come summer." Thirty is an age that's stalked me. It scares me to acknowledge it.

"Junior, it's time for you to go do something. Build something. You don't want to be a lifer here. Trust me. I've been here over twenty years."

What is he talking about? Boehner is the most powerful person in the building, second in line to the presidency. Everything in DC goes through him. The twenty years sure as hell seem worth it.

"That's kind of ironic, no?" I say. "You're telling me to leave after six when you've been here for twenty?"

"But I'm the goddamn Speaker!"

I can't help but laugh just as Boehner does: from the belly. But I don't have his smoker's cough. When we settle again, he continues.

"Look, you're a young guy. At one point you up and realize you've spent your entire life here and never once got out into anything else." He pauses, then continues, "I get it. It feels like the center of the world here, but there is more out there. It gets too easy here."

I've never felt like the work of the Hill is too easy. The days are long, the subject matters convoluted. No matter what I do, somebody is always angry at me: a boss, a colleague, a Democrat, a Republican, a viewer. Sometimes all five!

Some days last ten hours. Some last one hundred.

"Too easy, sir?" I ask.

"Yeah, too easy. With all the turnover and parties and the circuit. You can always find new women to date, guys to drink with. You're never settled."

I learn that Boehner worries about my long-term well-being. Worries that I've given my life to an institution where time is a flat circle. Where it's entirely too possible to wake up fifteen years down the line and not know what happened to yourself or the outside world. If you knew people only through politics, then you didn't really know people.

"There's always some big story," Boehner says, "some next bill, blah blah blah. You don't want to become a creature."

Is he warning me about his own life? I'd done a piece on him. He was one of twelve kids and grew up on a rural hillside outside Cincinnati. His family ran a local bar. They never went hungry but never lived easy. Boehner worked as a janitor to get through college. Yet when he got to DC, he became a consummate Washington insider, albeit one with emotion; he often cried during speeches. He lived in the apartment of a lobbyist, was once chided for handing out donation checks from the tobacco industry on the House floor, and was a regular at the steak houses within a half mile of the Capitol. Even now he rarely turned down fundraising appearances, many of them corporate-backed at swanky DC hotels or resorts in the nation's most desirable locales.

"Are you a creature?" I ask, half-serious.

"Shut up, asshole."

He swallows his smile, his upper lip hugging his top teeth. But I can tell the question, even in jest, stings just a bit.

"Look," he says, trying to refocus the conversation. "This is always going to be here: Congress, politics, Democrats, Republicans, et cetera. You'll want to see more than just here."

He pauses.

"Now get out. I got some diplomat coming for something."

"Oh, so that's why we're in this office?"

"You thought it was for you, Shithead?" he cackles. "Oh, maybe it was!" He smiles wide.

"Thank you, sir."

I stand to leave and look at him a final time: fingering his cigarette, a man who has it all. Yet he has one message for me—get the hell out of here.

As I walk out, I'm not angry at him. There is no rush of *Don't tell me what to do, old man.* Instead—and it takes me a while to realize this—in his own unintentional way, Boehner channels the spirit of my father. He pushes me to think. A man who reaches the summit of Washington from humble means, just like Dad, is astutely aware of all the mountains he will never see.

His advice haunts me. I ignore the work emails piling up on my smartphone. I duck into a modest café on the Capitol's first floor, buy some frozen yogurt, and take it outside to a bench in full view of the rotunda. I need time to think.

The truth is, Boehner has awakened a spirit within me that I've been trying to ignore. A spirit formulated in questions that are hard to answer and even harder to ask. Questions that have been entrenched deep inside ever since I joined NBC. What *am* I doing here? Am I trying to live up to my father's legacy? Am I trying to show Dad, beyond the grave, that his boy could be like him? Do I even like this job? Am I addicted to its fame and notoriety? What's my plan for life after thirty? Forty? Fifty? Dad died at fifty-eight; how much time do I have?

I've never quite sat back and contemplated if I was happy or fulfilled. As a believer in fate, I feel Boehner's words came from a higher place than just his heart.

The conversation in his office sets off a period of deep self-reflection. I face uncomfortable truths. I become skeptical of things I'm supposed to enjoy: the spotlight of TV, the power of Congress, the high-society gatherings of Washington, the adulation of fans. It's absurd beyond measure, so much of it—an endless supply of food, booze, and transactional relationships. My parents kept me away from it for so long; my youth had been so grounded: school, sports practice, and uninterrupted time with friends. Now I was squarely in the middle of the swamp. Yet what did any of this matter if I was left thinking, *Is this really it?*

A hollowness inside me widens, and I can't ignore it. I have been using journalism as an altruistic shield, but it is not enough to protect me from thinking I'm letting my life slip away.

I think about my future, about marrying somebody deemed "worthy" by DC society, seeing my kids go to the same high school as I had, then attending the same galas I'm attending now, getting older, never leaving, ending up in the same cemetery as my dad. It suddenly feels terrifying.

Yes, I've stayed up late with too many attractive lobbyists, and I've eaten dinners seated between a senator and the director of the CIA. I've found myself on a first-name basis with the highest-ranking people in government. The president knows my name and face. I'm living the dream of so many people. Yet despite this I feel shattered and inadequate. What do I know aside from the world curated for me? The awesome power of nature, the pulse of vibrant cities, the pull of curiosity—I've never seen them. I know pain, but it's internal, ever-present grief. Am I using that grief as a crutch? As an excuse to stay too comfortable and confined?

Months pass and the weight of the questions grows heavier. One night I take out a notepad and list the reasons for staying at NBC and in Washington. After an hour, the *nays* beat out the *yeas*.

I spend the next few days reflecting. I have the job of a lifetime, but it does not feel fulfilling. Some of that is the stress of the position, the internal pressures of network/cable TV. You're always disposable, depending on the regime. Constant jockeying behind the scenes to improve your position, to get on the air, or to snag a coveted assignment. The job is hard enough—the internal politics are suffocating—but throw on top of it the seemingly constant criticism from Twitter, and those who reach the summit of TV success have to wonder about its cost. I'm certain it took a toll on Dad, but boy, has it taken a toll on me.

I know I've suffered from anxiety since my father died. A therapist even confirmed it. Any routine pain or shortness of breath makes me think I'm going to have a heart attack. That I'm going to keel over and flatline just like he did. The feelings intensify during work hours. Breathing techniques help. Beers at night do, too—the irony, of course, being that any hangover only strengthens the anxiety tenfold the next day. I still tremble when I have to go into an audio tracking booth and record a script for a piece. Dad died in a tracking booth. Each time I enter one, it feels like walking into his coffin. I imagine his final moments, how he fell backward, what must have been going through his mind when he felt that chest pain. I count the seconds till I can leave, lest it happen to me too.

Pulsations, sweats, and shakes can creep up on me at any moment. As can a gnawing emptiness in the pit of my stomach that is debilitating. One particularly stressful day, I fall over in the basement of the US Capitol. By luck, I'm able to catch myself on an exposed water pipe. A passerby asks if I'm okay.

"New shoes. Guess I slipped!" I reply. The shoes are so worn they have holes in the soles.

I'm having a total panic attack. I'm late to a live shot, worried I've made a mistake in my reporting, and I'm just feeling terribly anxious. My tie is too tight, choking my neck. The uniform, the job—it all feels like it's literally suffocating me. I compose myself as best I can and go on live TV. Nobody seems to notice a thing.

I never tell a soul how intense the panic can get. Not even Mom. I internalize everything, suppress it and go on. If anything, I throw up a shield of jocularity, confidence, and bravado—nobody will ever see me sweat. My parents were the ones to teach me as much.

While I never truly sour on it, the last few contentious years of rancor and divisiveness in Congress has had an effect on me. I've grown cynical—something my father never was. Devoting my life to covering lunacy, including those who loathe government and yearn for turmoil, begins to lose its appeal. I also instinctively know that things will get worse in Congress before they get better. The presidential primaries begin to prove that point.

Donald Trump sucks up all the oxygen for political coverage on TV. Stories and assignments shift from actual legislation to members of Congress reacting to the latest thing Trump said. This is exasperating for reporters and politicians alike. All programming seems to have become "Trump TV." The story that does me in is in late May 2016. Harambe, a famous gorilla at the Cincinnati Zoo, has been killed by keepers after a child fell into his enclosure and he dragged the boy in a menacing manner. Whether or not Harambe deserved to be shot becomes a topic of debate on TV. As I prepare to go live with a substantive report from Capitol Hill, I'm bumped for Donald Trump's reaction to Harambe the gorilla.

I understand that the news as I knew it will never be the same. Trump is a sound-bite machine. He'll influence almost all political coverage. It will be a slog to cover him for four years if he somehow wins. Celebrity had won over substance. Not the most attractive thing to somebody who likes the nerdy side of government.

During lulls at work I begin searching Google Maps. I cyberwalk the streets of Tokyo, Buenos Aires, Dakar, and Jakarta. At Boston College I'd majored in history with a focus on foreign policy. I was the son of a woman who in her own youth had been a Peace Corps volunteer in Colombia and who still said to me, "Travel while you're young." I had wanted to see the world at twenty-two, but now, at thirty, I wonder if I can truly break away from being a DC creature.

What pains me isn't just a latent wanderlust. The last eight years have been such a whirlwind that I've never fully processed my grief for Dad. It's apparent that I've spent so much time honoring his legacy that I've never truly accepted his death. Worse, by honoring that legacy, I have failed to forge my own life. I'm thirty years old and have no idea who I am, independent from my parents. As I cyberstroll these international streets, I dream of walking away from my gold-plated destiny and figuring out what *I* want from life, away from television, away from my hometown and its nurturing yet confining streets. The power and money that so many seek, at NBC and in any profession, seem pointless if those things don't give your life purpose. I have no idea what my purpose is.

Do I have the courage to find out?

THREE

I'm Really Doing It

Chamberlain grunts as the truck dips into a large divot; some dead pine and dirt kick up on the windshield. I slow down and reorient myself inside the forest. I've never traveled solo for longer than a day. Even then it was usually for a work trip. There was always a parent, a girlfriend, or a group. A purpose, a distraction, or a tether to "real" life. But here I am, in October 2016, and I'm doing the craziest thing I've ever done: leaving my life behind—NBC, journalism, my career, and even DC itself—to find myself in travel, first in Maine, then perhaps abroad, for six to nine months, the exploration under-written by an insurance policy from Dad's death combined with money I've been saving. I'd give all the money back if I could have one more day with Dad. But because I can't, well, I'm doing this.

It scares me. This travel trip, this career postponement, this career suicide, even—it's the craziest thing I've ever done. I have enough doubts about it without Twitter and the gossip sites piling on, which they do. So I decide to turn them off.

And instead, I turn on to Route 1, the drag that hugs the Maine coastline, and see the barreling waves in Ogunquit. This is an expedition but also a personal audition. Can I handle the travel life I so desired? Sure, I'm in my truck, with my dog, so there is familiarity, but I'm really stripping myself down to the core. Nights in motels, hours alone on the road, frequent unplanned stops. I do not know what I'm looking for and do not know how it will appear, but I'm convinced it will show itself through travel. It has to.

Why Maine? Well, I'd just discussed that with my friend Reilly. A dear friend from Boston College, Reilly invited me to spend the night at his South Boston home before I departed for Maine.

Reilly thinks my career postponement was a little odd. "Wait—just driving around Maine with your dog? No real plans? Just drifting along?" he asks.

"Yeah, man, Maine. Going to see what it's got. I figure it's a nice time of year, see some foliage, shoulder season so the motel rates aren't too bad. I've never been, and it's the one place on the Eastern Seaboard that still has that wilderness feel on the coast. Think it's a good place to get lost for a week or so and explore."

"Wow. Unreal."

"Hopefully it's real."

We share a laugh. Reilly is due to become a dad within weeks, the first of my close friends to achieve the milestone. He and his wife, Becky, are well inside the proverbial "red zone" as to when a baby could come.

"How are you feeling, Reilly? This all must be so surreal."

"It is. Check it out."

We walk upstairs to a newly constructed nursery. I start to make a wiseass crack about golf posters being replaced by teddy bear wallpaper, but the enormity of the moment stops me. Becky is lying on her back in their bedroom across the hall, visible through a crack in the door, half-asleep and cradling her stomach.

"Wow. What a room, buddy. This kid is already so loved."

Reilly smiles and nods. He is proud of himself—he's thirty-one, the same age as me, but married, promoted, with a home mortgage, and now preparing for life's most important job. The epitome of secure and stable.

"Good night, Luke. I got work early in the morning."

I have trouble sleeping. I can't help but juxtapose the life I've just chosen against Reilly's. To the world I knew, Reilly is doing it right. He is a good man. The consummate provider. The American ideal we cherish so much in a dad. In my own way, I was on that path before I left NBC. And what am I now? Some privileged kid in a quarter-life crisis? Who would my dad want me to be? The wannabe beatnik on the road in Maine or a model of humble stability like Reilly? I don't know.

Maine will start the process of finding answers.

Nowhere else offers such a chance to escape by the sea—away from the sterile and strangling high-rises and ultradense communities that make up so much of the American Atlantic coast. The spectacular rocky shoreline augmented by the rustic rolling farmland, lakes, and forests of the interior, northward to Canada and west to New Hampshire. Everything appears like a painting. Perhaps that's why Edward Hopper and Andrew Wyeth spent so much time in Maine.

I'm introduced to this beauty when I come across the Nubble Lighthouse out on Cape Neddick Point in the town of York.

I do not have a plan to visit the Nubble Lighthouse. I simply follow the signs on Route 1 that make it seem important. In a state of lighthouses, Nubble may be best—it is so stunningly beautiful. I learn that a picture of it was placed by NASA inside the *Voyager 2* space probe so that if aliens were to ever make contact with the satellite, they can see it as an image representative of life on Earth. Nubble rests atop a small island maybe twenty or thirty yards from the shore. Farther down, perched on the side of the hill, is a small red barn. It is one of the most photographed places in the state. I can't help but think of all the souls who used Nubble to get home and all of those who saw her but didn't end up making it back.

I drive all of Route 1 on the coast, to the end of the line. Eastport is appropriately named, the easternmost city in the United States, nearly touching New Brunswick, Canada. A gray, hazy fog engulfs the place when I drive in soon after sunset. The spookiness fits. A drunk man on the street asks to buy the pug for fifty dollars. I laugh it off but ask where he got his buzz.

"The Happy Crab," he says.

What a bar! A wooden box with a good jukebox where dollar bills from folks passing through are taped to the wall. The barkeep lets the pug inside. I sidle up to a man in his late fifties who is wearing a flannel shirt and has peppery gray hair. He asks me what my business in town is, and I tell him about my romantic traveling dreams. He is more interested in my past as a political reporter. Feeling comfortable in our conversation, perhaps aided by the potent Maine IPA beer, I ask him for his current take on America. He tells me he feels that his community is being destroyed by opioids. He's lost a family member to the epidemic. Nobody cares and nobody is doing a thing about it. A lifelong Democrat, he says he'll vote for Trump because "Democrats are talking about bathrooms in North Carolina while kids are dying from these damn opioids." I try to explain the complexities of the North Carolina gender-assigned bathroom story and how it can be considered offensive to marginalized people but soon realize it's not worth it. He won't be moved. I can see the pain in his eyes as he talks. His world has changed too much.

Route 1 delivers me and the pug 170 miles to the north. Way up into Aroostook County, the super-rural agricultural wonderland of Maine known to locals as "the County." It's the largest county by land area on the East Coast and one of the largest east of the Rockies. We drive by lakes and forests and then out into potato country, finally resting in Caribou—a former hub for fur trappers and timber cutters. The next day I decide to take a different way out to Jackman, Maine, in the western moose-hunting country, via Fort Kent in the north near Canada. I want to challenge myself more, do something radical.

Why not take an old logging road, get off the grid?

Perhaps this was illogical, but for a city kid, a three-hour drive through old logging roads deep in the heart of a forest in northern Maine might as well have been scaling Everest. After passing a sign put up by Katahdin Forest Management LLC saying to enjoy their forest but give way to the timber trucks, the dog and I enter the woods. I save the route on my Google Maps and take a screenshot. We'll lose reception, but the phone will charge through the car and we'll stay on the route via Google so long as we follow it correctly.

Once inside the forest, we see no civilization, aside from passing trucks or fellow thrill seekers, for two hours. This drive is one of the most adventurous things I've ever done. It's pretty sad that, in my thirty-one years, a drive through a working forest on old logging roads qualifies as adventure. But I know at that moment, as I go deeper into the forest, that an important part of my travels will be pushing myself to take risks, however small or pathetic. Cradled by my dad's truck and my pug, ever eager and peering out the window as we drive into the woods, I'm sure it's the right decision.

Lost in the beauty of the dense trees, snaking my way alongside a creek, I do not pay much attention to an approaching dust cloud. There is too much to notice and to feel. I'm so far from my past, so disconnected from my former reality, one that I now realize I did not feel totally comfortable inside of. I have longed for this moment, this freedom. This ability to be on my own and unknown.

A loud honk of a bullhorn wakes me from my romantic dreams. The dust cloud in the distance reveals itself in front of me. It's a gargantuan timber truck that does not hug the side of the road, as it *is* the road. There is no ability to pass. My only option, aside from a deadly head-on collision, is to veer right and pull off the path.

I don't know if there is still any road on the side. If not, we'll go off an embankment. I do not see my life flash before my eyes, but my heart sinks into my stomach. *This may be it*, I think. I may leave this world driving off the road in a random forest in western Maine. The first time I ever go off on my own, and I can't even survive a week. I feel a bit pathetic underneath the gripping fear.

I turn the wheel and dodge the timber truck. I can feel the weight of the truck and its angry hiss as it darts past, coming within inches of turning the pug and me into roadkill. I stomp on the brakes, and the tires squeal as they lock on to dead leaves and, beneath that, gravel.

Momentum carries us a few yards. The seconds are harrowing. When we stop, we are just three feet from the edge.

I've survived!

Dazed but relieved, my prayers have been answered.

"Jesus, take the wheel!" I belt out, followed by a nervous laugh.

"And *he* did!" I joke to the pug.

I get out and touch the ground. I take a deep breath and mutter, "*Wow.*" It was a gut-wrenching experience, but soon after, I realize it has injected me with new life.

We're running through an enchanted forest, not a soul around, the sky covered by the trees, clearing only above the creek and part of the road. This road has no name, and that fits the feeling. For the first time in my life, I really feel off the grid. Sure, I have the luxuries of a truck, a charged phone (but no reception), and my pug, but at this moment, deep in a working forest in Maine,

41

I cannot be found. This feeling is both surreal and liberating. Most important, it is a reawakening, a powerful reminder that I like what I'm doing.

And I want to find this feeling again, in as many places as I can. Having been on call for my eight years as a journalist and never too far out of my parents' sight before that, here I am—man, truck, dog—absolutely free.

In that forest I find peace. It's fleeting, as I know I have to eventually leave the woods, but I also know I can find a real peaceful freedom through travel, through pushing myself to do the very thing that scared me.

This is my zen moment.

The power of aloneness—those hours, those miles, alone in my truck, with only my dog, my music, and my thoughts—has helped open my mind to self-discovery. I'm free to understand myself. To think about all that has happened—Dad's death, my career, my future. I know I've not done enough to think beyond what is expected of me. What do I expect from myself?

At a bend that offers a stunning view of the creek and of the clear water rhythmically running over the smooth rocks, I pull over. I carry the pug down to the water, splashing it on his coat and then on my own face. This is our baptism. We are reborn into the church of living free.

I make a promise to myself. For too long I have been too small-minded, too risk-averse, too defined by a legacy.

I want to find my own way.

That new way, my way, cannot be confined to Maine either. I'll need to measure myself against the world. I need to know what's out there, to chase that feeling of freedom and self-discovery. And it can only happen alone. Solo travel is the vehicle. It'll force me to think, to challenge, to ponder, to be. I decide by the creek that I'll go to Latin America. My mother was a Peace Corps volunteer in Colombia. It was where she first adventured and found her calling in life.

Maybe I'll also find mine there.

PART 2

FOUR

Patagonia

Behind me I wheel a new compact carry-on bag, and a fresh beard covers my face. I trudge up the jet bridge, backpack hanging off my shoulder. I may aspire toward some wannabe Hemingway with a splash of Bourdain, but this is my first solo trip abroad, and I'm giddy but nervous.

The flight is eight hours overnight from Miami, and my excitement overrides any fatigue. I'm here a few hours before connecting to Calafate, a lake town in Southern Patagonia that hugs glaciers, near the end of the continent and literally the end of the earth.

When I confided in my mother that I was leaving my career to find myself in solo travel, she not only welcomed the idea but made me promise to see Patagonia. She'd visited in her past, and it had left a spellbinding impression on her. It was, in her mind, a gateway to a mystical dreamworld. She was so intent on Patagonia that I decided to go there first. Mom would guide me over text and recount her past experiences. I would send her pictures in real time. Google helped plan the rest. I'm trusting online reviews and pictures for guidance. Hitting landmarks of importance and keeping my fingers crossed. Solo travel for beginners, with a badass mom—in other words, a safety blanket still draped over a son's shoulders.

I find an ATM for local currency. Attempts at withdrawals of $200 or $100 worth of pesos go nowhere. I look around, confused. A kind British man taps my shoulder.

"The most they let you take out is seventy-five dollars," he says. "They charge a ten-percent transaction fee. They want you to take out seventy-five dollars multiple times so the fee adds up."

"Oh, is that the issue?" I do my best to not be the big, dumb American tourist. I notice a few slick-looking guys approaching. They do an exchange out of a bag with a lower rate. The Brit waves them off.

"It's better that you take a hit with these machines. You can trust the money is real. Remember, lad: in Argentina, count everything three times and make sure you have what you want in hand before giving anyone money."

I nod, grateful.

With a wad of cash protruding from my pocket like a tennis ball, I walk to the security line. I'm the only gringo, but thanks to my mom and her insistence on cultural immersion, I've spoken Spanish since I was age three.

"Señor, párese aquí." A woman about my age tells me to stand to the side. She looks like she's auditioning for the role of Lara Croft: a tight-fitting blue polo shirt tucked into darker blue cargo pants that drape over shined black boots with a tall heel. She's pulled her dark hair back to expose piercing dark eyes.

"Why are you making me stand here?" I ask her in Spanish.

I get no response.

For a half hour, nothing changes. I'm just standing to the side while every other passenger passes through.

The TV show *Locked Up Abroad* pops into my mind. I begin to search for the number of the US Embassy on my phone. I write it on my palm. At last, a short man approaches.

"Espera para el perro."

Wait for the dog? I ask myself. *Oh my God. They think I have drugs!*

Sweat beads form on my nose. I remove my sweatshirt to cool off. I tell the person in charge that I've boarded from Miami that morning, that they screen very thoroughly for drugs there, and why would I bring drugs into Argentina? Wouldn't it be the other way around?

The short man tells me that Americans routinely bring drugs to Argentina and to sit down and shut up. I retreat submissively to the bench and realize my bags have not been in my possession for close to an hour.

Will they plant something in my bags?

Lara Croft motions for me to stand. A beagle emerges from a back room. Takes a few sniffs. My heart races.

Maybe they *are* framing me!

Or is this some sort of elongated attempt at eliciting a bribe? Why, during my first day pursuing this dream, is this happening?

The beagle has no reaction to my bags.

I smile at him and grab my backpack, assuming I'm free to go.

"No te vayas."

I retake my seat.

My Ziploc bag of vitamins and probiotic pills that I take for my stomach makes Lara Croft suspicious. In Miami, I took them out of their boxes and combined them into one bag to save space, but I now realize how other people—people working in airport customs—could confuse them for narcotics. Though the beagle smelled nothing, Lara Croft insists my vitamins be tested with some sort of chemistry kit. It has now been over ninety minutes. "I might miss my layover," I say, incredulous.

No response.

Nervousness turns to anger. I decide to push back, convinced these folks are targeting me for being American and are happy to make a probiotic become crystal meth. I've also by this point seen dozens of other passengers with pill bottles in bins move through with no issue.

I forcefully yell in Spanish, "Vitamins! All vitamins! Test them all. Waste your time and do it. Why would I bring illegal drugs in a Ziploc bag? You think I'm that dumb?"

Blank expressions.

They do think I'm that dumb.

I sit back down.

From where the beagle emerged walks out a smiling lady in a lab coat. She takes the bag of vitamins and disappears. Forty more minutes go by. I see the embarrassing headline in my head: "Luke Russert Arrested for Suspicion of Drug Smuggling in Argentina." The lab lady returns, smile still frozen. She informs the security personnel that everything in the plastic bag is in fact legal. She tells me next time to keep the vitamins in their bottles. I thank her for her kindness and turn my back on Lara Croft. She has flexed on me, a fellow millennial. Perhaps it made her day to inflict so much fear—good for her. I'm flustered from the ATM rip-off and vitamins-turned-drugs-turned-vitamins fiasco and go to lie down on the filthy carpet in the terminal. I want to sleep.

Just as I doze off, a loud wail jolts me upright.

The screams, mostly from women, multiply and are soon joined by the shouts and whistles from men. They sound celebratory, so I unclench my fists. The Argentinian national soccer team walks through the terminal en route to their charter flight for a World Cup qualifying match against Colombia. In the middle of the group is Lionel Messi, arguably the best player in the world and one of the top five of all time. He comes within a few feet of me. Following Messi is a burly-looking fellow in a black tracksuit. His muscle. After kowtowing to the Argentine ATMs and bag checkers, I figure this is my time for a comeback win.

I'll touch Messi.

I position myself close to the barrier, stick my hand out, grab his arm, and pat him on the back, saying, "Vámanos, Messi!" The legend smiles back and the burly man promptly shoves me backward.

I laugh and kind of cry as I catch my balance. A brush with greatness. I've been in Argentina less than four hours, and I've touched their national hero and almost been detained for drug smuggling.

Welcome to solo travel! My new world.

CALAFATE

The desert soil looks like cut-up moon rock. In the distance I make out snow-capped mountains. The reflection of the sky-blue Lago Argentino makes the skies extra blue. The man I'm riding with drives respectfully through the hills rather carefully, as if to make the point that the terrain isn't his. He is a custodian. In slowly mouthed Spanish, he asks if this is my first time.

"Sí!"

He nods knowingly. I wonder what tipped him off and realize it's everything.

In this mountain valley, with a large freshwater source in Lago Argentino, Calafate is the perfect spot to live in an otherwise inhospitable desert. When the Argentine government created the nearby Los Glaciares National Park in 1937, the town became a hub for visiting Southern Patagonia. In recent years, largely due to social media, the town has risen into a tourist-fueled powerhouse thanks to some of the world's most gorgeous glaciers.

I take a walk down Calafate's main drag, Avenue Libertador. Green space divides the avenue, while on both sides of the street rise boutiques, cafés, restaurants, travel agencies, bars, grocery stores, and hotels. I see the "Ruta 40" logo everywhere, the infamous highway that runs the length of the country from the South Atlantic all the way up to Bolivia. I see, too, many motorcyclists attempting to traverse the entire route, and even some bicyclists. I long to have their courage. Am I a poseur for not doing something more badass in Patagonia? Should I have rented an RV? Hell, maybe even learned to ride a motorcycle? I'm honest enough to know I'm not capable, at least not on this first leg of the trip.

I sign up for a 4x4 tour of a surrounding mountain. Soon a white Land Rover with massive tires and a hood-stack exhaust drives up. A short, heavyset man rolls down from the driver's seat, hurriedly shakes my hand, and lifts me into the passenger side for no other purpose than to appear like he's operating at a fast pace. Behind me is a Japanese man and a Spanish couple. The driver's name is Jorge. He begins to speak in a Spanish broken by coughs and cackling laughter. With bravado, Jorge explains that we will drive to the top of Huyliche Hill. There, roughly 3,500 feet up, we'll have a view of Lago Argentino, Calafate, and the entirety of the valley and the mountains in the distance.

The 4x4 winds through the terrain. Jorge gets out to show fossilized rock by the side of the trail. In the prehistoric era this was either under or near the water's edge. Some of these fossils trace back to a cousin of the shark species. There's a beauty in the barrenness and in the remnants of life.

On a turn around the hill, we encounter a group of what looks like wild horses. Their speckled coats stand out in the dried desert grass. Not ridden or harnessed, they roam the land at will.

They're used to visitors, and when one approaches, Jorge encourages me to pet it.

The horse obliges, but when it sees I have nothing in my hand to feed him, it reacts angrily.

I jump back in terror.

This elicits a squealing cackle from Jorge, the Spaniards, and the Japanese man. Jorge has conveniently forgotten to hand me the bag of carrots he keeps in his glove compartment. After retrieving them, I offer my apologies and the carrots to the horse.

Jorge yells, "Good job, Gaucho!"

It's a humbling feeling, being the butt of a joke that cuts across three languages.

We arrive at a plateau that extends out from the steep face of the hill. In America this hill would be a mountain, but because the Andes tower nearby, in Argentina it is simply a hill. I walk toward the edge. Jorge cautions that the winds often pick up without warning—don't get too close, he says. I veer slightly off course, climb some ensconced boulders, and find my own little summit away from the group. The baby-blue color of Lago Argentino matches the sky. It's made even more radiant by the brown desert, which acts like a natural frame. Gratitude sweeps over me.

Just as I'm about to offer my thanks in prayer, I notice a bird high above. It's the Andean condor, so large it can have a ten-foot wingspan. From my outpost, I see more condors. Some dip and descend toward the lake, taking on the appearance of landing aircraft. Others climb in altitude and, to the naked eye, look like planes disappearing into the horizon. I'll later learn that the condor occupies a special place in Andean culture. Ancient peoples saw it as a deity, ruler of an upper world. For me, the condor symbolizes freedom—literally above it all, descending into society only for the basics: sex, food, water, and sleep.

Jorge sees how infatuated I am with the birds. Reaching for his phone, he scrolls through dozens of pictures he's taken of the condors over the years. He jokes he has more pictures of condors than of his wife.

"They are their own special spirit, Lucas."

They are now my true love as well.

I text Mom a picture of myself standing on the edge, just below where the condors hang out.

"You've made it, kid," she texts back.

PERITO MORENO GLACIER

Mom missed the glacier on her own trip to Patagonia. I feel a sense of duty to see it. Especially since the existence of glaciers feels finite due to climate change.

The Perito Moreno Glacier is visible in the distance. There's an eeriness that adds to the glacier's astounding size: the violent sound of breaking ice, which causes a serene ripple of the water. It's loud enough to be heard over the boat engine. The sun reflects the blue of the lake off the glacier, so the bright white ice appears as if someone has outlined it with blue marker. It's cold, but I decide to stand outside on the back deck for the duration of the voyage. I don't want to be inside a boat for any of this. It needs to be felt.

I laugh; far away, the glacier looks like the wall of a snow fort that kids in a Buffalo neighborhood would make after a blizzard, complete with the jagged tips to appear like a castle. Now a mere fifty yards from the glacier wall, I properly appreciate the reality of its size. The ice sheet stretches back as far as I can see. It stretches beyond that, too, covering ninety-seven square miles. The Perito Moreno is one of the world's healthier glaciers.

In the middle distance I see what look like little gnats. A crewman notices my bewilderment.

"Those are trekkers in the middle of the glacier field on a hike."

"Wait—those are people?!"

"Yes, sir."

The boat maneuvers around chunks of ice that have broken off the glacier face, some legitimately the size of tractor trailers. I've never seen anything so beautifully domineering.

I know for the rest of my life I'll be a fervent environmentalist. These cannot disappear. I try describing the sights and what they inspire to my mother over the phone. I say the dreaded, "You've just got to see it." In the case of the Perito Moreno Glacier, though, the best I can say is "You feel like a mere mortal, in front of something that is beyond comprehension."

I send some pictures, and she's so impressed that she prints one and hangs it in her kitchen. Getting on Mom's kitchen bulletin board may as well be getting shown in the Louvre.

I wish she could have seen the glacier with me. Dad and I had countless ball games together. Mom and I did not have as many bonding moments. The glacier feels like one we missed. But I guess, in some way, she did show it to me.

I'm excited to see her in Buenos Aires.

FIVE

Buenos Aires

Months earlier, when I was trip planning in DC, Mom asked if she could accompany me on part of my journey in Latin America.

"I haven't been to Buenos Aires in years," she said. "Plus, you'll be down there for Thanksgiving. We should be together."

Of course we should.

Mom's travel expertise is legendary. It makes sense to see her work first-hand. It makes sense to travel together now because, somehow, we never have. Not just the two of us. In my thirty years, and in the eight since Dad died, we'd never gone somewhere together. I hope a trip to Buenos Aires is a new chapter in our relationship.

It's inspiring to continue the legacy of what Mom did with her mother. In 1965, after a year of service in Colombia for the Peace Corps, Mom got a three-and-a-half-week break prior to her second year of work. She used that time to go on a breakneck tour of South America with my late grandmother Helen Pierotti Orth, affectionately known as "Mama-Mia" for her 100-percent Italian heritage. It was the first extended time out of the country for my grandmother, a second-generation Italian immigrant who had rarely left California. On their trip they visited Ecuador, Peru, Argentina, Uruguay, Chile, and Brazil. Mom was twenty-one, Mama-Mia forty-six, and with her youthful Italian skin and Sophia Loren curves, Mama-Mia was often mistaken for Mom's older sister. They traveled "Peace Corps–style," which meant on a budget of five dollars a day. Mama-Mia could have afforded more but believed in the spirit of the trip and never complained. She and Mom spent nights in various family-run boardinghouses, ate from markets, and used their money to sightsee and bond over wine or martinis. Coincidently, they seemed to be on the same travel schedule as the infamous Boca Juniors soccer team from Buenos Aires, then touring the continent. The players made various passes in numerous countries at both my mother and grandmother.

All overtures were allegedly unsuccessful.

From the back seat cab window, Buenos Aires has the feel of a city that used to be something. Every guidebook says it's the "Paris of Latin America," the apotheosis of old-world charm and sophistication, the most visited city in South America. On a drive through the Palermo neighborhood, I see couples enjoying wine in front of street art. An old woman who could pass for Coco Chanel is walking a Pomeranian. Well-designed buildings along cobblestone streets are, yes, fading, but fading beautifully. Seeing the boulevards, parks, buildings, and street life, I understand how there was a moment in history when its regal splendor and immigrant energy made Buenos Aires the best city in the Americas, one that many leaving Europe chose over the United States. That spirit is present, a hovering ghost, full of old victories and glories within the aging edifices and proud Porteños—citizens of Buenos Aires who have remained despite Argentina's recent, and consistent, political upheavals. Like New York City, Buenos Aires is, for those living here, the center of the entire universe. Everything else is substandard or unimportant. As the old saying about the city goes, "It's made up of Italians who think they're French and speak Spanish."

Mom made it down to Buenos Aires while I was in Patagonia, and I find her at the lobby bar of the Alvear Palace Hotel. This, too, is a relic of another era—a time when quality guest service was akin to breathing. My mother knew the place from when she wrote a 1989 profile piece for *Vanity Fair* on then Argentine president Carlos Menem. She spent hours in the Alvear Palace's bar, trying to glimpse Menem walking in with one of his mistresses. Mom glances now at an older waiter in black tie meandering around the marble floor near the bar tables.

"He was the one who served me in 1989," she says.

I can't help but laugh. Mom's memory: always its own reporter's notebook.

"Where did you sleep with your mom in your first visit here?" I ask.

"On the cold floor of a family guest room while your grandmother got the bed. You're welcome, Luke."

Mom reaches to grab her purse off the ground. "Let's go for a walk and explore. That's how you experience a city."

I follow her out the hotel doors and into the street. After a few blocks we come across a beautiful park with distinct purple trees. "Those are called jacarandas, prevalent here," she says. "Aren't they beautiful?"

They are. And their beauty is magnified by the life below them. Lovers lounge on large blankets, sipping wine and eating from baskets. Artists paint behind fountains. Students write furiously in their journals. Some men kick a soccer ball. There is plenty of well-kept grass to sit on here, but Mom wants to keep going.

"Let's see Eva Perón's grave."

To enter the cemetery is to walk into a maze. Large mausoleums look like mini cathedrals with Gothic architecture, stone saints, and gargoyles. All of them cram together along paved walkways. We circle round looking for Evita, the famed one-time First Lady of Argentina, for a good twenty minutes. It's nice letting Mom take the lead. It's almost like we're in New York City again and I'm a young kid, being led around Central Park with all my trust that Mom will always keep me safe. Mom knows best.

But not even Mom can find Evita's grave. Evita's complicated legacy is present even in the mundane act of asking for directions. One British man tells us, "That awful woman is two rows down the right." An Argentine lady says, "Saint Evita is around the corner." Some think the former First Lady is responsible for the most important social changes in Argentina, like welfare programs and women's suffrage. Others think she's a dim-witted actress who parlayed her marriage and movie star good looks into a political career, helping fascist autocratic tendencies to gain power. As with most mythical legends, the truth is somewhere in the middle.

"Don't cry for me, Argentina!" I say when we at last find the tombstone.

"Oh, she's much more than a Madonna movie, Luke," Mom says. "Look at all the people coming here today. She's somebody who will never leave the national conscience. Those who die young tend to live forever, obviously," she says.

I buy a pamphlet about the woman from a nearby stand and read back a quote of Evita to Mom: "One cannot accomplish anything without fanaticism."

Mom laughs. "I think that's right."

I can see her mind examining the quote, ruminating on it.

"To be a woman in those times. Even these times. To get anything done, you need to be a little fanatical."

Thanksgiving, that most American of holidays, will this year be spent away from my homeland. Mom's presence assures some comfort—I'm grateful for it. Mom herself used to be a traditionalist when it came to holidays, but after Dad died, she's become more open to experiences. She seeks out moments that are different from times spent in Buffalo with family. The less traditional the setting, the less that holiday stirs up memories of losing her husband. I know all this and try to find a place that'll be to Mom's liking.

I find my friend Paige. Paige is, coincidentally, also from Washington, DC. She studied abroad in Buenos Aires her junior year, fell in love with the city, and moved down shortly after graduation. She found herself a handsome Porteño and got married. It's her home now. After telling her I'll be in town, Paige graciously invites Mom and me over for Thanksgiving.

"Mom," I tell her one day when we're out sightseeing, "it'll be American expats and their local friends. I'm pretty sure you'll be the only person there over forty."

"Perfect."

I'm a little nervous at how Mom will react when she's the most overdressed person at the party, all elegant slacks and well-knit sweater and array of offbeat jewelry.

Most everyone else is in jeans and summer shirts. But Mom hits it off with Paige quickly. Mom also appreciates the vibe, which is very American: the

Dallas versus Washington football game on the TV, country music playing, the smell of turkey floating out from the kitchen.

Paige's place fills up quickly with seven Americans, two Irishmen, a Colombian, a Peruvian, a Uruguayan, a Spaniard, a Pole, a Mexican, and a few Argentines. Mom ingratiates herself into the crew, quicker than I do, frankly. She marches around the living room, asking questions, no longer just the reporter but the curious person she's always been, asking people about the things they most want to discuss—themselves—while skipping over her own background. It works well. She becomes the focal point of the party. The expat guests have all sorts of interesting jobs—business analysts, journalists, artists, energy speculators, social workers, commodities traders—and Mom and I learn they love the freedom of Buenos Aires even more than their careers. The city offers an out for whatever predestined lives they were supposed to live in their home countries. I feel a bond with these fellow millennials. "Same," I almost say.

I think Mom sees part of herself in them as well. I watch her effortlessly work the room, like a politician at a fundraiser. She even finds the shy kids and asks about their lives until she's established a connection. I've always been good socially but nothing like Mom, nothing like today. With her, in this room, there's never an awkward pause. Out of her glows a warmth that soon bathes the rest of the apartment.

Prior to sitting down at the table, Paige asks everyone to say what they're thankful for. While in the US this is often an excuse for a wisecrack—"I'm thankful for beer and football"—everyone standing behind their chair takes it seriously. I hear stories about friends, spouses, family, the troubled political times in America, the distressed and overheated climate everywhere. Somehow everyone in this room remains grateful. Mom goes last. She takes a long look around the table, her face still glowing.

"I just want you all to know how thankful I am to be amongst such talented young people. It really makes me think that the world will be okay despite the extreme political difficulties going on in my home country and here in Argentina and most of Latin America. I worked in Colombia, but for many years, due to the violence, I could not go back. Yet things got better, and I was able to return and start an educational empowerment foundation. Now, kids in remote rural schools and poor barrios learn about robotics. It took a long time, but things got better."

It's a perfect ending to the exercise.

Argentinian red wines flow. The table is all laughter and smiles, and one by one, the millennials start to ask Mom about her own career. All she's done. Why she's here. She's reluctant at first, but even though Mom is circumspect, she's also happy to stand in the spotlight when it shines fully on her. She regales everyone about her eight cover stories as a music writer for *Newsweek* in the 1970s about such luminaries as Bob Dylan, Stevie Wonder, and Bruce Springsteen. The various articles she wrote for *Vanity Fair* about topics from the opium trade in Afghanistan to actress Katie Holmes escaping Scientology. I've seen this movie before; I still enjoy it. I also know it makes her happy, something important to me on this holiday. By providing this space, I've helped her block out pain from the past.

Our new friends laugh at how Mom compartmentalizes so much of what she's seen. She finds it boring, all those stories from the '70s about hanging out at the same clubs with Keith Richards, Bob Marley, and John Lennon during her *Newsweek* days. The table sits before her in awe, both at her tales and her nonchalance.

"Did you ever party with Mick Jagger?!"

"Yes. In fact, I went to his thirtieth birthday party. It was all right, not that cool."

Mom's preference is for the deeper stuff, such as the massive income inequality that still plagues so much of Latin America.

One of the Irish kids leans over to me and says, "Mate, your mom is so fucking cool."

When the night is over, Mom and I walk off the feast, heading back to our hotel.

"That was so much fun, Luke. I loved the energy of that room."

"How do you do that? Where does *your* energy come from?"

"When I was a little girl, people told me that I talked too much. I guess I use it to my advantage now. Also, asking questions is the only way to learn something."

I can't tell if she learned the skills as a journalist or if it just comes naturally. Whatever the case, I'm in awe of her tonight.

We get back to the hotel. I walk to the bar for a nightcap. Mom heads to the elevator. She gives me a long hug. Call it a son's intuition, but I know she's thinking about Dad and Thanksgivings of the past as she holds the embrace. I also know she does not want to talk about it. The night has been too good.

"I'm thankful for you, Luke."

"Likewise, Mom."

SIX

Uruguay

The ferry that brings Mom and me from Buenos Aires across the Río de la Plata to Montevideo and Uruguay is named after Pope Francis.

I snicker.

He is, of course, the Argentine pontiff who's rejected the trappings of wealth and who projects an image of austerity to the world. This, the *Francisco*, is not austere. It has accepted the trappings of wealth, a large catamaran that's one of the fastest commercial passenger ships in the world. It cruises above fifty knots and has dining rooms in first class. As Mom and I move aboard the ship to get a better view of the ferry's bars and cafés and its massive duty-free shop, a woman in a uniform hands us shoe covers.

"Please put these on your feet."

"What?"

Mom and I are both confused.

The shoe covers will keep patrons from scuffing up the ship's floor, we're told. It's unbelievable.

The *Francisco* is less a ferry than a yacht. Light floods everything; the boat's ceiling is made of translucent plexiglass. We sit in seats made of buttery-soft tan leather. Men in black topcoats and bow ties push drink carts around. At the top of the staircase, where business class and first class meet, there is a framed photo of a smiling Pope Francis. Mom giggles loudly.

"I guess they missed the part where Pope Francis spoke of Jesus saying it's easier for a camel to pass through the eye of a needle than for a rich man to go to heaven."

I never missed that part. For all her humor, vivaciousness, glamour, and intelligence, there has always been another side of Mom: the disciplinarian. Particularly the *Catholic* disciplinarian. Mom drilled good behavior into me as a kid. Because Dad worked on Sunday mornings, it was usually Mom and me at Mass before Sunday school. She had a strong moral code and keen sense of right and wrong. She brought the Church into my life and kept it present.

One Christmas, when I was a young kid, she chastised my father for giving me too many presents. "Just because you did not get much as a kid, Tim, does not mean you have to give him everything."

Dad brushed it off, tousled my hair, and said, "He's a good kid, a really good kid."

She stared at me sternly and said, "I hope you know how blessed you are. So many kids do not get any of this. What have you done to deserve it?"

I thought that was harsh, the aggressive impartation of Catholic guilt. I may not have put it in those words when I was eight, but what I did understand back then was that Mom could work the guilt hard.

"You know, a big day for me when I was your age," she went on, "was taking the ferry across San Francisco Bay with my parents and them buying me a chocolate bar. You get more than that every week."

I was, in essence, being criticized for something outside of my control. I mean, my parents were the ones who, through their own success and hard work, had bestowed on me the privilege that, as Mom often reminded me, she had not had.

The dynamic caused tension growing up. It would manifest itself in a desire to be considered worthy. In sixth grade I made my school's basketball team. No easy feat, with thirty kids trying out for twelve spots. Dad was ecstatic; I had gone to basketball camp over the summer to improve my game. To him I had worked hard to achieve a goal. To celebrate he got me a pair of Air Jordans.

"You earned these, buddy. Look good out there!"

To Mom, the sneakers were excessive, especially for a kid who would not start and would be lucky to get rotational minutes. "Tim, he went to camp all summer for basketball—something he was lucky enough to do. Least he could do is make the team."

Moments like these fueled not only the occasional resentment but an intense internal desire to prove my ability. To show Mom I was deserving. When I turned fourteen and became of legal working age, my parents told me I'd be working every summer going forward, just as they had. Dad always romanticized hard work.

"Your grandpa was a garbage man," he said. "You need to learn what a paycheck is, how your body and mind feel after a hard day."

But my desire to work hard in these manual jobs was never to uphold my dad's vision. It was always to prove to Mom that I was tough, motivated, and not lazy. Not that she would necessarily acknowledge it. Mom rarely complimented me for my work ethic. Her expectation *was* such a work ethic.

Mom grew up in a different era, the 1950s, in a *Father Knows Best* household. When she had me in her early forties, she opted for a similar domineering style of parenting. A child was to submit to the will of their parents. They were to be a "gofer." Go for this, go for that. Snark and insubordination were dealt with sharply and swiftly: "Go to your room and don't come out." Disagreements, even requests to better understand Mom's point, would often end with "Because I'm your mother and that's the way it is." She channeled her own father.

Karl Orth, a devout Catholic and football star at Saint Mary's College in Moraga, California, could best be described as "taking no shit." Coincidentally, like Dad, he died of a heart attack at age fifty-eight. I never got to meet him. A giant of a man, he squeezed the hands of any boy who dared to ask Mom out on a date until those hands turned blue. As an accomplished athlete, he demanded excellence. Mom would bring him an A- on a paper and Karl would ask why it was not an A. I felt that same sense of judgment at times from Mom growing up. If you did something well, you didn't deserve a trophy for performing up to your abilities.

This style contrasted mightily with Dad. He believed in affirmation. He was much more sensitive and empathetic. The example I'd give to friends was to compare my parents to football coaches. Mom was the disciplinarian, the coach that challenged you at all times. You do those extra lifts, you run those sprints, not because you want to, but because you cannot be seen as backing down or, worse, coasting. Dad was the coach who knew how to manage players, who knew when to push and when to pull back, the one who took you aside when you did a great job or when you needed a reminder to be better. He'd say something like, "Whatever happens, I know you've given it your all. Have fun out there." Or "You're better than what you've shown. Focus. Pick it up."

I grew closer to Dad. I felt he gave me more of a fair shake. Even when I did well by Mom, her praise felt empty. I assumed she thought I should have done better. When I made the mistakes of any teenager—sneaking out, talking back, drinking underage—she made me feel as if she questioned my morality and intelligence. Dad, by contrast, did not question my integrity. He simply demonstrated how I fell short and needed to do better. I began to tune out Mom and focus my energies on Dad. To be honest, there was regrettably some inherent sexism, too, in my teen years. I was a wannabe macho man, prone to fits of anger, high on raging testosterone, not wanting to be controlled. My mantra was "With Mom, no matter what I do, nothing will suffice. She's beyond intense. Out to get me. Completely unreasonable."

It would be grossly unfair to say Mom was not kind. She had to deal with two bonded males. She was affectionate, quick to hug, and always put out a healthy breakfast. She took great interest in my schooling and my well-being. When I was a youngster, she guided me in my nightly prayers and made sure my room was safe to sleep in. She read to me for hours. Jules Verne books were our favorites. When Dad was gone, she'd toss a baseball or shoot hoops with me. She even allowed me to practice WWE wrestling moves on her, till I nearly tore her elbow. Some days she was very warm and engaging and tried to create special moments for us—some activity or experience or just a long conversation. I was often skeptical, however, and never could entirely go along with her way of doing things. Going along felt like giving in. That was something I could not do. I could not subscribe to her methods. Though I respected her and loved her, I framed her as a rival. I did not want to lose. I held those feelings for too many years.

They can creep up even now.

MONTEVIDEO

"It reminds me of South Beach in 1997, when I reported on the Versace murder. The art deco structures, water views close by, little gritty but pleasant." This is Mom's declaration after fifteen minutes of walking one of the rehabilitated streets of Old City Montevideo.

Mom is leading the charge, walking briskly and darting between foot traffic. It's cumbersome to keep an eye on her. At times it feels like walking with a toddler at an amusement park. We're on Peatonal Sarandí, the main pedestrian walkway, both sides lined with midsize colonial buildings, vendors, galleries, shops, cafés, bars, restaurants, and colorful artistic graffiti. Benches and palm trees dot the center.

Next, we visit the Plaza Matriz, abutting the city's eighteenth-century neoclassical cathedral. Mom notices a major juxtaposition: a gorgeous house of worship across from a tacky McDonald's. Both are dwarfed by more modern bland office buildings across the plaza center.

"It's a shame. But it's understandable. Growth is considered progress more than preservation. Especially in emerging countries."

I nod in agreement. It's best to let her lead.

"I want to go to the mall," she says.

"The mall? We're in Uruguay and you want to go to the mall?"

"I'll explain in the car."

"I'll call an Uber."

"Oh, but that takes so long. Let's grab a cab."

"Mom, it's safer to Uber. We don't have to exchange cash, and we know our driver by their profile. Trust me on this."

"So we just wait here?"

Mom has always been impatient. I try not to let it get to me.

"It'll be here in five minutes. Relax, it's all good."

After the Uber arrives, we whiz past tall white condo and apartment buildings overlooking the ocean. The Punta Carretas area of Montevideo further supports Mom's South Beach analogy.

"Why are we going to a mall?"

"Whenever I go to a prominent Latin American city, I like to check out the mall in the well-to-do part of town. You can learn a lot about a place by its malls. The styles and trends that sell. The food they serve. It's a window into the economic situation of the elite. You see how the wealthy see themselves and then compare it to the realities of the street."

I appreciate these nuggets from Mom. Even though sometimes her tone leads me to believe she thinks I'm not bright enough to grasp her thoughts and observations.

Mall Punta Carretas looks like the Arc de Triomphe in Paris. On the plaza outside sit large modern art projects in the form of colorful stiletto shoes. Inside rest Christmas decorations, a nativity scene, even a Ferris wheel with fake snow surrounding it. The shops are high-end. Brands like Lacoste, Swarovski, and Nike have their own stores. There's even a Uruguayan version of Whole Foods.

"Lots of American brands here, Mom. Also, that entrance is something else. You see all those families lining up to take a picture in front of it?"

She nods.

"It may seem inconsequential," she says, "but a lot of outside investment in a city can come from the first impression visitors have or of the aesthetics of a place. An archway into a mall with some pleasant art can go a long way."

"Your 'mall-onomics' is pretty brilliant."

I put my hand on her shoulder to show I'm not only being a wiseass.

"You're welcome," she says. "Just don't buy anything. You can get most of this anywhere. Use your luggage space for the crafts that come from authentic markets!"

BUMPY RIDE TO GARZÓN

The next day, Mom and I are to leave for Garzón, a scenic wine region Mom wants to visit. The drive takes us along the coast; Mom also wants to stop in some seaside towns.

I pace in the hotel lobby and hear Dad's voice: "Be an on-time machine."

I hate being tardy. I see it as the ultimate sign of disrespect. This makes me unbearable for some people, including Mom. She operates at a different speed. In the days before flight schedules were posted on the internet, Dad would tell her that takeoff was forty-five minutes earlier than it was in reality, accommodating her tardiness with a schedule of white lies. I just think it's rude to be late. Mom and I were supposed to leave twenty minutes ago for Garzón. I'm her driver, willingly, and I'm anxious knowing I'm tasked with hours behind the wheel in a foreign country.

I wait. Our rental car pulls up. It's a modern sedan but with a manual transmission. I can't drive stick. Ninety percent of the cars down here are manual. Mom was in charge of the rental because her Spanish is better. I told her ten times to request automatic; apparently it got lost in translation.

I wait.

Mom gets out of the elevator, unrushed.

"You're a half hour late, and the car you rented is manual. What are we doing here?!"

"I said automatic to them!"

"Going forward, I'm booking everything for us."

"Be my guest," she says flatly, coolly.

I don't back off. I know I'm being petty, but I'm triggered. "This is absurd. You didn't double-check, did you? We'll be delayed two hours. That's if they can even find an automatic."

"It's amazing that a grown man like you can't drive stick."

She knows where to thrust the knife. Mom was always quick, is still quick, to criticize any perceived softness. It fuels a sense of inadequacy in me. A part of me wants to run out of the lobby and find someone to teach me to drive a stick shift—to prove to her I'm capable. I can't help but feel small. Getting good grades my entire life or climbing my way up the NBC ladder is not good enough. In her eyes I'm still some ungrateful teen not up to the task.

I don't lash out. Lashing out is futile. Provoking Mom when she's upset only makes matters worse. So we wait—for our anger to pass. When the automatic shows up, we ride in silence for an hour to cool down.

The warm temperatures arrive. The sea air comes through the car windows. Idle chitchat about the small beach towns helps to loosen the mood. We talk about my pug and wonder what he's up to at the moment. What *is* he up to? Where's he staying? Mom loves him like a grandson.

In the distance the skyline of Punta del Este takes form. This oceanfront vista on the way to Garzón has long been a haven for Latin American elite.

"You know I partied in Punta Del Este with Mama-Mia," Mom says.

"Holy shit!"

"You don't think we actually partied?"

"No. Look up!"

A large billboard by the side of the road shows the grinning face of the then president-elect of the United States with the words in English: "Trump Tower Punta del Este—Ultra Exclusive Becomes Real."

Mom shakes her head in disbelief. "This is now America's image to the world."

I slow down to take a picture of the leader of the free world hawking condominiums in a developing country. We share a pained laugh. It softens the mood.

"Let's stop off in José Ignacio. It's supposed to be a hidden gem."

It isn't so much a suggestion as a directive. We're roughly an hour from Garzón and it's lunchtime.

One of Mom's Colombian friends regaled her with stories of José Ignacio, heaped endless praise on the place. The fewer questions I ask, the greater the decline in tension. I am once more the dutiful son, driving Mom to her preferred destination and taking care of her wants and needs. It's a role I've played whenever I want to move past an unpleasant moment.

"We'll do lunch for sure," she says.

In a way this is Mom offering me a peace treaty.

José Ignacio is a fishing village slowly turning into a hot spot of wealth. Modern art galleries and swanky restaurants have replaced tackle shops. Some old fishermen remain, but most have resigned themselves to the influx of those second-home buyers.

"La Huella restaurant—I read about it!" Mom says with excitement. "Supposed to be the best restaurant in the entire world!"

If it's not the best in the world, it's close. La Huella is on a beach. There's a thatched roof held up by wooden cylinders that appear the same as those used for boardwalks, an open kitchen with that patented Uruguayan woodfire grill. After a sushi starter, I order a fish the size of my arm. Mom gets grilled octopus. We enjoy some sips of Albariño, a local Uruguayan grape. It has a nice peach taste. If there is such a thing as a perfect lunch, this is it.

Mom is calm and joyful. She's unusually quiet, soaking in the meal and the day. This is her way to apologize; she'll never flat out say *I'm sorry*. Disagreements from earlier in the day seem petty with a full stomach, but the underlying tension never goes away fully. The reality of ramming heads for decades.

The strong sun burns the edge off. Nobody dares to bring up the morning.

GARZÓN

Through the windows we see blurs of pine groves and stretches of flat farm-land with grazing cattle, the scenery framing modest white brick homes. This is the rest of Uruguay. Rural, green, and empty. These scenes lead us from the sea to the fields that are the nation's wine country. We arrive in Garzón as the sun sets. It is small, like the set of an old Western movie. In the middle of this unpretentious place is an old brick house that used to be the town's general store. It's been struck by a bolt of opulent prosperous lightning and is now a high-end hotel and restaurant birthed from the brain of Argentine celebrity chef Francis Mallmann. Mom chose the place. She read the wine was some of the best in the world. Friends of hers concurred.

The town's quaintness is a welcome relief after stops in major cities.

I have some time to kill before dinner, so I venture outside the hotel. I hear a loud shrieking noise. It's an animal. I follow the sound, and to my amaze-ment, two young baby foxes are chained to a stake in the front yard of a house. Two kids kick a soccer ball in the back. I walk up and ask how they got the foxes. It turns out the mother fox had been hit by a car and the family took the babies in. The family fed the foxes what they fed their dog and gave them milk.

The kids offer one up for me to hold. I tamp down any fear of rabies: if these kids can hold the foxes, so can I. They feel like young puppies. I hand the kids a few pesos and say it's for the care of the animals. I get back to the hotel and tell Mom the story.

"I want to see the foxes!"

"Why?"

She's already gone. She has this impulsive unpredictability inherited from her own mother, a free-spirited renegade. It gives me anxiety. She's always moving. To her credit, it enables her to get things done. Obstacles are arbitrary. At times it's scary. I never can predict what she'll do. I try not to anguish over it, but I almost always do.

While waiting for Mom to come down to dinner, I scroll through Instagram. Mom has already posted a picture of the foxes.

She's beaming when she gets back to the hotel room.

"Why did you run away for that picture?" I ask.

"Because I wanted the exclusive."

She smiles, not a smile of kindness. Of victory.

"Are we competing on our Instagram posts? Are you a tween girl?"

"You always get more likes, and I just wanted to get a good one." She is only half joking. Her competitiveness extends to social media. I'm a rival.

"Is this how you were such a good journalist?"

"As a journalist, you always want to be first." She's serious but lets out a half laugh to try to not fully admit it.

I'll never match her intensity, rushing out for something as trivial as a picture of a fox.

SEVEN

Paraguay

I've met very few people who've set foot in Paraguay. It's considered a wild place with a lawless ethos, a complicated history, and a nearly nonexistent tourism sector. Many foreign governments refer to it as a "smuggler's paradise." It has its own vast outback region. For restless wanderers like Mom and me, this made Paraguay more attractive, a country where we could write our own story.

I suggested it during trip-planning, and Mom leapt at the opportunity. We were both first timers; the appeal was learning together.

That was before the fight in Uruguay. Tensions have calmed as we drive into Asunción, Paraguay's capital, but ours is still a fragile peace. Getting Mom to and from airports gives me anxiety. She's prone to forgetting something important or switching plans at the last minute. I focus my energy on staying calm and getting her to the hotel without incident.

"Have you been reading up on the history of Paraguay?"

It's a rhetorical question from Mom—I know she's been reading the country's history—but she'll defer to the history major here. I don't mind the affirmation.

"It's incredible that the country is still standing!" I say.

I launch into what I've read.

"Okay, so there was this overzealous leader who thought it a good idea for Paraguay to assert itself in the region and fight Argentina, Brazil, and Uruguay simultaneously. Three on one! The War of the Triple Alliance from 1864 to 1870. It led a country of just north of five hundred thousand to lose nearly two-thirds of their population due to death, violence, famine, and disease. At the end of the war, the country had about thirty thousand men left. Think about that! For a long time, there was a massive gender imbalance. That meant *women* sustained Paraguayan culture, traditions, institutions. Women ran the country at a time when women throughout the world ran nothing!"

I know Mom loves a good feminist story.

"I found an article about Pope Francis's visit to Paraguay," Mom says, nodding. "He called Paraguayan women the most glorious of the Americas for rebuilding the country practically on their own."

Asunción has the feel of Houston. It is humid and hot, with an old town center. Years of limited zoning laws have scattered the city into an assortment of office buildings, strip malls, and apartment buildings, all in odd configurations. Around the city are vast pockets of impoverished shantytowns. Small structures with tin roofs and piles of garbage have been tossed into the local Paraguay River. Seemingly on purpose, the road from the airport to Villa Morra, the upscale residential and commercial area of Asunción where Mom and I are staying, does its best to avoid the realities of poverty. What's promoted are new developments and the ease of doing business. A country where it's simple to become a citizen and enjoy practically tax-free living. It's an appeal to the deep-pocketed Brazilians and Argentinians who travel through and may one day make Paraguay the Florida of Latin America. The road moves past the South American Football Confederation's modern headquarters, an organization that has put Asunción on the map, where the governing body makes the rules for all soccer on the continent. Our driver, sent by the hotel, does not acknowledge any of the hardship. He focuses on the headquarters.

Outside the hotel Mom and I walk down a street named after American politician Huey Long, a thank-you from Paraguay to the long-dead Louisiana populist for supporting their side in an old twentieth-century conflict.

"I didn't think we'd see Huey Long in Asunción," Mom says.

It's a harbinger for the randomness of Asunción. Nothing seems settled. The street carries us to a wide thoroughfare with dozens of high-end strip malls. There is a sports car dealership with a large customized Land Rover

Defender pickup for sale on a corner. Most of the shops lack any customers but showcase the finest in luxury apparel, electronics, and home goods. Men in white button-downs and khaki pants sit under umbrellas with large buckets of iced beer. At some tables each man has a bucket of beers for himself. Much of the sidewalk is uneven, the opposite of pedestrian friendly. It's apparent that the wealthy in this area never walk. They are chauffeured.

We get curious stares but also smiles and a few honks. We hang a right onto a more residential neighborhood, hopping puddles along the way. There is close to no drainage. If this is the wealthy part of town, I can only imagine the working-class areas. Many houses sit back from the street behind large stone walls or electric fences. Security cameras are the norm. Some homes even have private guards. The only person we see is a woman in jogging clothes with two large German shepherds beside her. She gives us a puzzled look, like it's weird we're out alone in the street.

Mom pays her no attention. She stands tall, walking at a fast clip. She's plugged into the adrenaline she gets when experiencing something new. It's infectious. I follow, the proverbial sidekick. After a few more blocks we see a gated shopping enclave: fine diamonds, gold, and other jewels as well as very high-end clothing. It's clearly a place out of reach for the average Paraguayan. It has all the makings of a gilded fortress. A guard pats us down prior to entry.

"Dior diamonds right off a pothole-filled highway in Asunción, and steps from decrepit poverty," I say.

"Yeah, shows you where the priorities are," Mom says.

Mom has lived well in her older years but retains the fiery passion of a Jesuit priest when it comes to income inequality. I can sense her old Peace Corps ethos bubbling to the surface. She's tired of this part of Asunción. Too sanitized.

"Let's go find a real *mercado*, Luke."

When Mom was twenty and a young midterm college graduate in 1964, she joined the newly created Peace Corps. She wanted to live the organization's slogan: "The toughest job you'll ever love." Inspired by JFK's challenge to act, Mom found herself in the mountains outside of Medellín, Colombia, living with a local family in an impoverished barrio, thousands of miles away and economic strata beneath the life she'd known in the Bay Area as a kid. She helped build a rural school the community named for her and provided educational opportunities for local children who had neither. While service guided Mom's decision, other factors influenced her choice. Women who graduated in the early 1960s were very much confined to a patriarchal social structure. Many of Mom's friends got married and had children right out of college. Opportunities beyond the usual "feminine jobs" weren't available. For Mom, the Peace Corps offered her not only a sense of adventure but independence. She was equal to her male counterparts there. Free to organize and execute. She developed a reputation for being relentless. With Mom, things were not allowed to linger; they got done. To build a school in a rural area high atop a mountain, she organized a human chain of volunteers on a Sunday to clear rocks and get them down a hill. Through negotiations, she even got Colombia's wealthy coffee growers to fund the building effort—not bad for a girl in her early twenties who had just learned the language!

Mom was a strikingly beautiful young woman, and many of Medellín's eligible bachelors, especially those from aristocratic families, had their eye on her. She dated some. She fell in love with one. Something she never forgot was the disregard many of the wealthy had for the poor. They never stopped to consider the plight of those worse off. They behaved as if money was God's will and then rationalized their behavior by having high-ranking priests over for dinner. As if God validated their lives. This never sat well with Mom, and she used it to define her own faith, one that placed selflessness at its center.

Her years in Colombia, in fact, defined so much of her. They planted the seed for a life that refused to be held back and always moved forward, full of faith without fear.

Mom fearlessly hails a cab and tells the driver in Spanish to take us to the city's municipal market.

Sprawling, sticky, crowded to the point of claustrophobia, the municipal market sells everything. Walking within it is like being in a washing machine:

constantly tossed into the chaos of a crush of people selling, haggling, and looking for a deal. The passageways are so tight that my body is crushed against the Paraguayans passing on the opposite side. I can feel sweat, smell breath. It's like a crowded subway car during rush hour in August.

None of this fazes Mom. She grabs a man by the door and asks where the ceramics are. He points into an indistinguishable sea of humanity. Without recourse, Mom plunges in. I do not know if I would have moved so swiftly if I were not following her. I know Dad wouldn't have. He would have been way beyond his comfort zone.

Mom paces quickly through rows of vendors selling everything from underwear to vacuum cleaners to TVs to live chickens. Much of the clothing is knockoff brands from China. Tables outside are covered by vinyl tarps. Inside, the market building offers little to no ventilation. It's the opposite of a comfortable shopping experience or the well-lit and air-conditioned strip malls of America. I realize we're the only gringos here. For Mom, this all feels natural.

"These markets—they're how the vast majority of people live in large South American cities," Mom says. "It's the lifeblood."

Her pace quickens as she spots ceramics vendors. Christmas is just a few weeks away. The focus is on nativity scenes and Baby Jesuses. Yet alongside Jesus are Minnie Mouse, Buzz Lightyear, and the yellow Minions from *Despicable Me.* There are also all sorts of fine locally inspired crafts of parrots, lizards, and some indigenous pottery.

She sees an assortment of unique green ceramic bowls with indigenous zigzag patterns. They'd fit in a trendy Los Angeles restaurant. Her excitement bubbles to the surface: a find! She bargains quickly and aggressively in fluent Spanish. She wants to pay a fair price and not the tourist rip-off.

Mom beams when she gets the local rate.

She rarely buys anything from brand-name stores in the United States. Her house brims with items from her travels, some of which date back to the 1960s.

"Don't be basic," she's often told me. "Surround yourself with things that have a story attached to them."

We walk outside the market into an area of calm. I wipe the sweat from my brow and take my first settled breath in more than an hour. Mom scours some of the outdoor stands, looking for one last find. Taken aback from watching her at work, I size her up. For someone in her seventies, she has not lost a step. Her energy is greater than mine. For the first time in memory, I want to be like her. I want to have this spirit to jump right in. It's something my father never had. He was measured and cautious—nothing was left to chance. Mom is exciting, a true badass. She trusts in her abilities and is curious to get the full story, no matter how raw.

I see her with new eyes.

YAGUARÓN

The next morning, a little past eight, as I head toward the coffee stand in the hotel lobby, a large, portly fellow with a warm smile greets me. He has curly black hair and wears a plaid button-down with blue jeans and white sneakers. He looks older than fifty-five.

"Lucas!" he says. "I'm Victor, your driver."

Driver?

Turns out, Mom got drinks with the daughter of a former Paraguayan diplomat last night. I'd been invited but was too tired to attend. Mom is wearing me out. That friend arranged for Victor, a government driver during the week, to earn extra cash driving us around on his off day, Saturday, to see the countryside outside Asunción.

Victor has an opinion on everything. He reminds us within a minute of getting into his 1990s Mitsubishi SUV that he always knows the real story because he knows the real people. More importantly, he knows the roads in and around Asunción from memory, navigating the all-too-common ditches, potholes, speed bumps, and bottleneck traffic jams.

"Show us something you think we need to remember about Paraguay." Mom is persistent, almost like she knows there is more out there.

Unfazed, Victor suggests the small rural town of Yaguarón. Usually a man of many words, now he becomes subdued. In Spanish, he simply says that the church of the town, the Templo San Buenaventura de Yaguarón, is the most beautiful thing he has ever seen.

When we arrive, the Templo San Buenaventura de Yaguarón appears plain and mundane. I wonder if Victor is playing a joke on us. The long red tile roof reminds me of an open hardcover book placed upside down on a desk. White pillars run the length of the church on both sides. There's a bell tower that appears like a watchtower from a World War II movie—two platforms on four legs joined together by a ladder in the middle. Victor tells us the outside is meaningless. We have come for the interior.

Unfortunately, the front door seems to be locked. Victor calmly walks to a side entrance and opens the door.

Mom goes in first. "Oh my God!" she yells out.

Templo San Buenaventura de Yaguarón, in its own way, just might upstage the Sistine Chapel. It's that beautiful. The full room is intricate wood carvings: the altar, confessionals, pulpits, and even the ceiling. Up, down, and side to side, carved faces and artistic designs emerge from the wood. They are everywhere, on the support beams and windowsills. Brilliant gold angels are suspended next to the altar, with blue pillars in wraparound gold trim. Victor tells us that the indigenous people, forced to construct the interior in the 1580s at the behest of the conquering Spanish, were working with limited tools and made their dyes from plants.

Mom walks around the altar, at a loss for words. She spots an older man off to the side, in the corner of the church. He walks slowly, as if he is always mindful of being before God. He calmly tells us that he is the caretaker and that the church appears better with the lights on. The parish has only enough money for them to be on during services. For a small donation, he'll turn on the power so we can appreciate the true beauty. Mom quickly hands him fifty dollars—much more than required but what her Catholic conscience dictates. Light floods the church. The intricate gold markings appear even more radiant. It's the equivalent of the building coming to life. Our chins move upward in unison to the heavens.

Mom laughs. "I think this is divine intervention."

"Who would have thought Paraguay had the most beautiful church we've ever seen?"

"Don't ever dismiss a place outright," she says, still looking up. "It also helps to trust a local."

She walks over and hugs Victor.

"Thank you!"

Back on the road we notice large swaths of people walking alongside the shoulder. Victor says these folks are pilgrims walking to the town of Caacupé to celebrate the upcoming Feast of the Immaculate Conception on December 8. Caacupé is home to the Cathedral Basilica of Our Lady of Miracles, a large Catholic shrine to the Virgin Mary. Mom asks Victor to take us.

Mary has been very much on Mom's mind. In December 2015, *National Geographic Magazine* published Mom's cover story about the Virgin Mary: "The most powerful woman in the world." Her reporting took her to Bosnia, Egypt, France, Mexico, Portugal, and Rwanda. The focus on the piece was the importance of Mary in contemporary society and the millions who believe in Mary's visitations to ordinary citizens. It also led to Mom establishing a deep spiritual connection with the Blessed Mother, one that had been burgeoning for years.

With Victor, Mom is instantly engrossed and unloads a barrage of questions.

Victor says pilgrims walk to Caacupé every year as a show of their devotion to the Virgin Mary. Paraguayan Catholics believe that the pilgrimage to Caacupé renews their spirit. They pray in front of a carved image of Mary that dates to the early sixteenth century, during the height of Paraguay's indigenous people, the Guaraní. Their customs inform today's faithful. The feast day celebrates acceptance and unity.

As we get closer to Caacupé, the number of pilgrims grows. It's people of all ages. Every few miles we see water stations with rows of plastic chairs to sit and grills serving up local delicacies for little or no cost.

Caacupé itself is packed with people. Victor finds parking in some guy's backyard for five bucks. The three of us make our way through the crowd and into the basilica.

A more modern church with a glass-covered atrium at its entrance, the space is awash in natural light. Eyes in the pews are either fixated on Mary or the ground below in prayer. Per local tradition, pilgrims fall to their knees and crawl with their heads down from the front of the door to the altar. This final devotion after walking dozens, if not hundreds, of miles is a powerful act of subservience. To an outsider it may appear odd and cultish. As a Catholic caught up in the moment, I see it as total commitment to the Virgin Mary. Mom walks to a kneeler and enters a state of deep meditative prayer. I sit behind her. I think about all she has seen and encountered. As a young woman seeking adventure and responsibility in Colombia, she found the value of service in a male-dominated world. She learned how to not back down and how to progress. No wonder Mary, a pious, powerful woman with such respect, carries such an appeal. Mom was influenced by this deep faith later on in her journalism career. The moralistic sense of what was right and wrong led her to writing massive exposés on the heinous crimes of the famous and powerful, even helping to defrock Catholic pedophile priests. As she prays, I begin to understand all she's accomplished and all she still seeks to do. Mom had a dream of being more than what society offered to her. She broke barriers by becoming one of the first female writers at *Newsweek*. She has always charged ahead. The strictness with which she raised me I now see as her attempt to teach me religious discipline so I might be as free as she is.

Mom says little on the way out of the church. She is still deep in thought. She smiles at the pilgrims walking in; they return her smiles. When we get to the car, she stares at the basilica in a contemplative state.

"Was that not humbling, Luke?"

There's only one thing I can say, given all I've seen and learned.

"It was."

That night Mom and I huddle over drinks in the airy hotel courtyard. She is uncharacteristically quiet, soaking in the moment. I know I'll hold this memory forever. I never once thought about holding memories of my father in real time because I expected to have him around much longer. I will not make the same mistake with Mom.

"You see something like today, Luke, you take measure of it. That's what travel does. It makes you an experience junkie."

"I'm beginning to see that. It feels like the world opens up and I appreciate so much more."

We walk back to her room, and I help her pack her ceramics. The next day we will split up; she's going to Colombia to visit her educational foundation and I'm continuing on to Bolivia, a country where it's unclear if my visa will work or if I can get in. I never received the requisite letter of invitation from the Bolivian government.

Mom tells me not to worry. To be creative and trust my abilities.

"Like you?" I say.

She smiles.

"It's kind of funny, Mom. Most parents would be terrified of their kid trying to sneak into Bolivia. But you're all for it."

"You won't get anywhere in life just sitting on the sidelines." Her eyes meet mine. "You can do it."

I've never seen her put this much faith in me.

I fight back tears.

EIGHT

Bolivia

I land in Santa Cruz, and my palms begin to sweat. I see a few Bolivian soldiers and security personnel meandering around the tarmac. Are they staring at me? Will they deny my visa? Bolivia purposely does not make it easy for Americans to enter, a policy enacted by leftist president Evo Morales in 2007 as payback for years of perceived American interference in the country. In Asunción, Paraguay, I was warned by the gate agent, "They could send you back. You sure you want to go?"

"Yes."

I was not confident in that *yes*, but I had something to prove. To Mom and to myself. Hell, even to Dad. He was incapable of putting himself in this type of situation—not in control.

Also, I've already paid for this trip; there's no gift from Mom like in Argentina. I'm on a budget now and need to get a return for my investment. I've saved a lot over the years, the chief benefit of the apartment Dad left me. I also came into some money from Dad's estate when I turned thirty. It didn't influence my choice to leave media—I left money on the table with that decision—but it gives me a nest egg. Mom would never let me starve, but it's a good layer of security.

It's kind of ironic, no? I'm using money from a death to try to explore life. I'd give it all back for one more day with Dad. Hell, I'd become a hermit for that.

This will be a test. That much I'm sure of. Maine and Patagonia had their minor challenges, and Mom held my hand in Uruguay and Paraguay. Bolivia is squarely on me.

The visa isn't the only complication in this impoverished nation of eleven million people. La Paz, Bolivia's capital, sits at approximately twelve thousand feet. Since my teen years, I have struggled mightily with altitude sickness. I'm so afflicted that I rarely go to places above five thousand feet. It's paralyzing for me. I also suffer from hypoxia, a lack of oxygen in the blood, and in my twenties I was diagnosed with sleep apnea, a condition where I stop breathing in my sleep. I'm fortunate to be on Obamacare. With such a difficult preexisting condition, I likely would have lost health insurance when I left NBC, had it not been for the law, and probably would not have been able to travel. I need a noisy machine called a CPAP to dream peacefully. Altitude makes sleep apnea violently worse. Mind-altering, horrific, three-day insomnia tends to hit me at high altitude.

Why am I doing this?

I'm so out of my comfort zone as I move through customs. I'm doing something Dad would be catatonic about. I'm reminded of a conversation I had with Dad right after my high school graduation.

"You want to go where?"

"Colombia. To see Mom's school."

Dad looked puzzled and concerned. "I don't know. It's not really safe."

Colombia had just emerged from a very violent period in the 1990s marked by kidnappings and ransoms. While tourism existed, there was still a State Department warning against traveling to the country. This warning did not concern Mom. She went frequently to visit the beneficiaries of her education programs. She knew the community and felt well looked after.

"Dad, how is it any different if I go?"

"They know your mother. She takes risks for her magazine stories. Hell, she went to the Afghanistan border right after 9/11. She knows what she's doing. I worry about you."

"Oh, come on! She'll be there part of the time."

"Let me make some calls."

"What are you going to do? Call the CIA?" My tone was that of an incredulous teenager. *Dad is being hypocritical*, I thought. *Safe enough for his wife but not his son?* He peered back at me, annoyed with my question. He didn't need to say anything. His eyes told me to leave his home office.

The next morning he came into my room and asked me to turn down the Guns N' Roses CD.

"It's not worth it. There are too many opportunities for disaster. You got a good summer job lined up. You're going to school in the fall. Just not going to happen."

"Well, I'm eighteen. I can go if I want."

"Once you pay your own way around here entirely, feel free. But you're on my payroll, and the boss says no."

Dad left my room. In the end I accepted his authority. The man was rarely wrong. But that seemed small-minded to me. He really did not like traveling outside of the US unless it was to a place he knew. Why did he limit himself so much? I mean, the guy had the number one public-affairs TV show in the US but never interviewed foreign leaders abroad. Seemed timid. Distrust—the downside of his parochial upbringing. I turned the CD player back up.

Now, years later, here in Bolivia, I walk to the front of the line, past an intimidating stone-faced soldier.

I have to see Bolivia because in my past life, I would not have been able to.

To gain entry into the country, I was to produce the following at the Bolivian Embassy in Washington, DC: money order for $160, proof of yellow fever vaccine signed by a doctor, two four-centimeter-by-four-centimeter color passport photos, letter of invitation from a Bolivian local written in Spanish, copy of plane ticket receipt to and from Bolivia, current bank statement, and two color copies of my passport. I obtained all of this prior to my departure to South America but did not have time for the Bolivian Embassy to process my forms.

I see three customs officials on duty for the international line and I select the youngest one. He has dark black hair in a bowl cut and looks like a Bolivian George Harrison.

My nose sweats. Bolivian jail would suck.

I hand over my passport.

George immediately asks for my visa.

In Spanish I tell him, "Oh, I don't have it yet. I thought I could get it at the port of entry."

He glares back at me and shakes his head. Stares down at my passport and then peers into my eyes.

I take a manila envelope out and lay its contents on the table. I've met all of the stated requirements except the formal letter of invitation in Spanish.

George carefully inspects everything. "Where's your letter of invitation? Do you have a friend in Bolivia?"

His face is expressionless.

"You're my best friend in Bolivia."

"Ahhhhh," he responds. A small smile cracks his lips.

George stands up from his chair, takes all my documents, and disappears into a side room. It feels like thirty minutes pass.

When George finally emerges again, he walks over to a woman processing visas with a laminator and whispers in her ear.

Slowly, he walks back to me. He hands over a visa form to fill out and under his breath mentions that the visa cost is $160—yet for him to be my friend, I have to give him a gift, as that's what friends do. George then pulls me closer and says, "She is a friend too," and points to the laminator lady.

I know the average monthly salary in Bolivia is a few hundred bucks. I calculate that sixty dollars for him and sixty for the woman should get me into country. I fold the cash into my completed visa form.

George smiles. He takes the sixty dollars and then pushes the other sixty dollars toward the lady. She smiles and nods at me. I hand over my passport, and within five minutes I have a ten-year Bolivian visa.

George stamps my passport and waves me through.

The face stares me down, resolute and powerful. At 21,122 feet, Illimani is the protector of La Paz. Like a man guarding a door, the mountain sizes me up as it comes into view while my flight descends into the El Alto International Airport. Survival here has never been easy. The luxuries from the modern world have made it tolerable, but it is still hard to fathom how 2.5 million people live in and above the canyons in the shadow of the peak. I take one last breath of pressurized airplane air as the side door opens, unsure of how my body will react at 13,325 feet.

I walk on the outdoor tarmac ahead of a tall indigenous Bolivian man with a long black braid and black derby hat. If I fall over, he is big enough to catch me. Within one minute I feel a sharp headache. My eyes water. Then I can't keep them open. My steps slow. My backpack feels like an anvil. As I wait for my checked bag on the tarmac, I lean sideways against a wall. I'm afraid if I sit, I won't be able to stand again. Out of the corner of my eye I notice a sign at a store in the terminal: "Oxygen." For an astronomical thirty American dollars, I buy a canister of oxygen that's like an inhaler. It could have cost one hundred dollars and I still would've bought it. I take two of the cans and immediately suck in the oxygen. My eyes open and the headache dies down.

It's a temporary reprieve. There's only so much air in the can.

The cab driver hugs the bumpy dirt and gravel roads, past tin-roof shacks. I inhale hit after sweet hit of oxygen. Driving from the airport to downtown La Paz is a drop of 1,300 feet. Every inch of the descent lessens the pressure in my head and chest.

The driver sizes me up in the rearview mirror and asks if I'm okay. "Parece verde, señor."

I *do* look green. I took prescription acetazolamide altitude medication the day before. Combined with the effects of altitude, it makes my hands and feet tingly, a pins-and-needles feeling to the extreme.

In the hotel lobby sits a vat of coca tea, derived from the plant that makes cocaine. It alleviates altitude sickness in its tea form. I gulp copious amounts during check-in. The receptionist asks if I'd like some bottles of oxygen brought to my room.

"*Yes!*"

A sympathetic porter wheels the bottles of oxygen to my room, and I feel like a man in a nursing home. I can barely breathe, and my eyes are slitted like a cat's. I settle into my room and try to focus on the sweeping views of the city, but it's scary not being able to breathe, like drowning above water. Every movement takes effort: sending a text, walking to the bathroom, unscrewing a bottle. For hours my head pounds. My inner monologue loops the same thoughts: *Why are you here? Why are you doing this? This is so stupid. You should leave.* I'm afraid to go to sleep because I do not feel guaranteed of waking up.

I text Mom a picture of me hooked up to the oxygen.

"You'll be okay. Just acclimate," she says. "You can do it. You're strong!"

I don't feel strong. In fact, I've never felt more concerned for my well-being. I think again of bailing.

But there's an odd competitive edge to me now, one I've never felt at this level of intensity before. *Better to die on this mountain than to face myself as a quitter.* An overdramatic response, sure, but I also know La Paz is a once-in-a-lifetime trip. I won't come back here again. I have to find a way to enjoy it, cherish it even.

I carry an oxygen canister and two huge water jugs outside the hotel, much to the amusement of the Bolivians. If there's a stereotype of an overcompensating gringo, I am it. I climb into the front seat of my guide's car. My guide, Alberto, is a small and dignified man, a Jehovah's Witness who, at sixty-two, has jet-black hair, wears a maroon sweater vest, and drives a minivan. In slow and deliberate Spanish, he says he'll show me everything I want to see.

We drive to a vista with panoramic views of La Paz: Mirador Killi Killi. Two things stand out about the view. The first is the degree to which the small red clay homes look like they're sliding down the hill; how exactly they're stabilized on that steep face is a feat of engineering. The second is that the wealthiest neighborhood, the Zona Sur, sits at the bottom of the canyon with the worst views. Alberto explains that the wealthy live lower because the climate is warmer, the level streets easier to navigate. The impoverished live higher up in the cold, many in the town of El Alto on top of the canyon. I can see this contrast from Killi Killi. Sleek modern homes become late twentieth-century apartment buildings become clay houses with tin roofs. El Alto is roughly 1,200 feet higher than La Paz. The poor have richer views.

"Alberto, is that a gondola?"

I see a gigantic ski lift with individual cars continuously looping up the hill to the top of the canyon.

"The *teleferico*, señor. The best thing to ever happen to La Paz."

It is the highest and longest urban aerial cable car transit system: eight lines, twenty-five stations, providing equality and opportunity for a nominal fee. I take a video and text it to Mom. She loves gondolas and credits them for delivering Medellín's recent renaissance.

"Those are so cool!" she texts back. "Just like Colombia. Ask what they do for the people there!"

I find out that La Paz's public transit system used to be a series of exhaust-emitting buses, some government run, some private, that attempted to move a metro area of 2.5 million people through windy, pothole-filled roads. For the poorest residents highest in the hills, reaching a place of employment in the town center took hours. Alberto says that before the gondola his son had to wake at 5 a.m. to make it to a 9 a.m. shift. Post-gondola, he now wakes up at 7:30 a.m., walks his children to school, has tea with his wife, and makes it to work early. The gondola gave people their lives back.

With Alberto I take the A-line from Sopocachi, the hipster neighborhood of well-off chic, and ride two stops to Mirador Qhana Pata. For fourteen minutes I'm the condor I so idolized in Patagonia. The yellow car sweeps upward, flying quietly over the thousands of homes and souls of La Paz. Below I see children playing, women cleaning pots on porches, cars turning corners, men pushing carts, police making an arrest.

On the gondola ride back down, I strike up a conversation with a young father who grasps his newborn baby boy tightly to his chest. He's bringing the baby to his mother-in-law who lives down the mountain before his afternoon work shift. His wife is still in school. Without the *teleferico*, he tells me, the journey would have been extremely difficult with a baby and vastly more dangerous. "I'm happy he gets to grow up with this."

Back at the hotel I text my findings to Mom.

She responds: "See? If Bolivia can accomplish something like that, why can't the US?"

Fair question. Getting out of my comfort zone helps me see my own limitations and those of my country. I think that's why Mom was so desperate for me to travel. What can you compare yourself against if all you know is your small little world?

I fall into the couch and hook up to the oxygen. The altitude still hurts, but I'm beginning to feel a bit better. Tomorrow I'll leave La Paz and head to the Bolivian Salt Flats, my reward for persevering.

UYUNI

If God created a place for Instagram, it's the Bolivian Salt Flats near Uyuni. Otherworldly landscapes set the scene for pictures that lack depth perception because there is no horizon. The sky bleeds into the salt.

The salt flats are dried-out prehistoric lakes from tens of thousands of years ago. At 4,086 square miles and 12,000 feet above the sea, the flats equal the size of the Big Island in Hawaii. I've been transported to a planet from *Star Wars*.

The Hotel de Sal Luna Salada is built of salt blocks. Salt floors, salt bedside table. After a shower at night, salt sticks to the bottom of my wet feet. I wake up to see the sun rising and hovering over the salt. With the absence of horizon, the juxtaposition of two worlds, one light and one dark, has never been so profound.

"Get in, Lucas!"

Juan is a kind guide who's my age. He does well for himself. Whereas much of Bolivia is impoverished, social media has made Uyuni a boomtown. There are not enough workers to fill all the jobs needed to compensate for the uptick in tourism. Much of Juan's salary goes back to his wife and son, who live out of town and whom he sees one weekend a month.

If the flats were once a lake, our SUV feels like a wide boat, cruising across the surface, kicking up a wake of salt. Juan keeps his eyes on the road like a ship captain maneuvering around rocky jetties. He has to. Bumps in the salt or a crater of salty water from a rainfall can easily bend the axle of the strongest vehicle.

We stop along the flats to take some funny photos. We use the lack of depth perception to make it seem like I'm drinking from the world's largest beer bottle. There are about four takes of me jumping and furiously moving my hands, as if I appear to be falling from the sky. Juan cuts a hole in the salt with his knife and picks out a salt crystal. From an angle, my iPhone camera makes the hole look like a huge canyon.

"Grand Canyon! Like Arizona!" Juan excitedly tells me.

We take off for a ninety-minute journey to a desert island in the middle of the flats. No trees or hills or vegetation. No man-made structures or rocks. I've never felt smaller. The magnitude of being so incredibly alone and exposed—this feeling cannot be replicated anywhere else in the world.

The Isla Incahuasi is the top of a former volcano. It's littered with century-old cacti. There are few trails to the top. I'm uncomfortable with hiking in such high altitude. We're already at twelve thousand feet. As I peer up at the top, my hand is taken by an elderly indigenous woman, as round as a bowling ball, complete with bowler hat. I figure she's a member of the island's sole caretaker family.

"Let's go. Don't be afraid," she says.

I chalk it up to divine intervention.

She hops up and down the trail. She's not only fearless but making incredible time. I think to myself that I won't be lapped by a Bolivian grandma, so I pick up the pace and make it to the top. I breathe deeply.

She smiles, locks eyes with me, grasps my hands, and encourages me to stay at the top for a minute. From that height the SUVs driving away from the island look like arrows being shot across the sky with a dust cloud behind them. I climb down the side of a ridge and find a cave. Someone has left a beer bottle and some graffiti. Protected from the sun and comfortable on a flat stone, I take a minute in the cave to process it all: in the middle of the week in early December, I'm in a cave, solo in the world's largest salt flat, 12,100 feet up.

I also owe this moment to Mom. Without her I would never have had the courage to try this. Far from Washington, DC, I begin to see how sheltered I was for so long. In this cave I am living the vision that Mom has so longed for me to see. Though she's thousands of miles away, I tell her I love her.

What she saw in me, I can now see in myself after my week in Bolivia.

NINE

Easter Island

My blinking blue light is smack-dab in the middle of the Pacific. It takes a few thumb scrolls on my iPhone's map to find the next nearest landmass. Easter Island is truly out there, in the best sense of the phrase. A tiny island, five-plus hours by plane, a week by boat, a place humans were never supposed to find. It hits me while the plane taxis to the gate. Nothing has felt this liberating. It's a new year with new adventures. I'm playing hopscotch across the South Pacific. Easter Island, then a drop in Tahiti, and eventually on to New Zealand. A fun way to avoid a fifteen-hour-plus plane ride!

In early February 2017, 2,182 miles out to sea, 4,996 miles from my hometown of DC, with a landmass roughly its size—63 square miles—I notice something about Easter Island before I even arrive. Every person on the plane is smiling.

Interestingly, my visit has coincided with the Tapati Festival: a two-week gathering that promotes the history, culture, and spirit of Easter Island. The center of the village of Hanga Roa transforms before my eyes into a festival ground: a large main stage, dozens of food stands, outdoor bars, music, dancing, art. The entire island shows up for daily performances, and many locals take part in indigenous competitions.

Before long I'm standing atop the Rano Raraku volcanic crater, peering down into a newly minted obstacle course around a large lake. Rapa Nui natives wait to compete. Young men, nearly naked in an ode to their past, with bodies resembling those of action figures, walk nervously in small circles, like bulls waiting to be released from their pens. This is the Tau'a Rapa Nui Triathlon, the most prestigious event of the Tapati Festival. Whoever wins the race is memorialized in island lore. The triathlon consists of a canoe race across the crater lake; a run around the large lake with two heavy bushels of bananas weighing fifty-five pounds strung across each racer's back; and, in the final leg, a belly-down paddle on a small reed back across the lake.

A loud bang sets the men into motion. They sprint to the edge of the lake, jump in their canoes, and paddle with such ferocity that it seems like they're stabbing to death something below. A man reaches the other side and grabs the bananas. My jaw drops when I see the speed at which he carries the awkward weight, like a thundering running back cutting upfield through tacklers toward the end zone. Every barefoot step is measured and precise. The pack begins to gain on him during the second lap. Sensing the possibility of a close finish, the crowd roars for the second-, third-, and fourth-place racers. Yet on the final stretch run, the leader finds new strength. He dumps his bananas and Superman-dives into the water, paddling his reed over the finish line. Pure human accomplishment in a pure human body. He looks like a Greek god as he pants, triumphant.

Outside the bus window I see steep green hills caught between blue skies and blue seas. Cotton-ball clouds dance over the head of the Moai, the ancient stone-head megaliths that have long made Easter Island famous. Carved by hand, with an endless dull stare from their eyes, they're so heavy that many people still don't believe they're the work of humans. Every tourist sees them. Every local abides by them. Almost every archaeologist believes they're the work of the Rapa Nui people, who fled civil strife and arrived on Easter Island from southeast Polynesia sometime around the year 1200. They came upon a pristine, uninhabited ecosystem. For some reason—still unexplained—they dotted the landscape with over nine hundred of these statues.

The average Moai is fourteen feet high. Some are thirty feet. Some rise even higher on a platform. Their meaning has been debated for centuries. Locals say the Moai served as a body for spirits: the ones that looked inward at the community had captured a spirit; the ones that looked outward at the sea awaited a spirit. The locations of the Moais on the island are said to be tied to resources, like water, and the hope of protecting the island from the outer world. Whatever the reasoning, the sheer size and elaborate craftsmanship is beyond belief. The rocks came from a volcano quarry, and once they'd been chiseled, men created an elaborate system of pulleys to move the heavy stones. It sometimes took hundreds of men pulling long straps simultaneously in one direction to make the stone walk.

Just thinking of what went into forming the Moais makes me feel immense pride in the human race. I break off from my tour group and walk farther up the path. One of the Moais is close enough to touch. We stare eye to eye. This face of stone that for hundreds of years has looked off into the sea now gazes into my eyes, poking around my soul. I'm transfixed. Transfixed with the Moais and the mysterious spirits that seem to throw a cloak over you if you stand in a single spot for too long. I smile back at him and let out an enthusiastic, "Thanks for having me!"

My energies are one with the island.

"Hey, you were on my tour the other day." I look up to see who's talking as I turn the corner walking into the town festival. I recognize the kid. He can't be older than twenty-one.

"Yeah," I say. "You were in the back with your parents."

"Dad and stepmom, actually. My name is Franco. Want to grab a beer?"

I admire someone that direct: to ask me to go along with him, me who has ten years on him!

I follow Franco to a guy selling cold cans from a cooler. Franco is a good-looking, lanky Argentine who loves to play guitar. He suggests we hang for the night.

"Sure," I say. I want a friend on the island too.

Franco's eyes light up when I tell him my story about leaving my job for a few months of travel and reflection. Between sips of beer and glances at women onstage dressed like hula girls, Franco says he feels limited in Buenos Aires. School is boring. He wants a sense of adventure. In a few months he'll head to Europe alone, with only his guitar and a dream of playing cafés.

"My dad is worried about me. Thinks I'm crazy."

93

"You've got to go. I came too close to living with lifelong regret."

He ponders my words but finds them too serious. "Let's go find some girls and dance."

We find a *discoteca* not far from the festival grounds. He quickly spots two attractive Chilean women and gets them to dance with us. Franco's hips move like Jagger. I, on the other hand, feel bad for the Chilean dancing with me: I'm too slow in every movement, self-deprecation my only saving grace. Thankfully, she finds my duck-walking funny. While Franco and his new friend passionately make out behind me, I introduce myself.

"Me llama Sofia!" she replies.

She has a robust figure, long black hair, a cute face, and a calming smile. I tell her my legs are giving out and I need more beer. She takes my hand and leads me to the bar. Before we order, Franco and his friend come rushing over.

"Hey, man! You got a place? Let's go back and hang. Play some music."

I see where this is heading. The four of us walk back to my bungalow. I break out some wine on the porch. Soon after it's poured, Franco and his new friend, Claudia, vanish into my room and close the door. *Wow, I'm back in college.*

Sofia tells me she has a secret. She is thirty-four and on vacation with her twenty-five-year-old coworker. I tell her I'm thirty-one and on vacation with my twenty-year-old coworker.

Sofia was engaged once but called it off because her partner didn't like her working. She loves her job in sales at a phone company and doesn't want to be a housewife. I tell her I'm a recovering TV journalist, something she doesn't believe till I speak in TV-presenter voice. She laughs. It's evident we're running away from some sort of responsibility, and I enjoy meeting someone else experiencing the same personal struggle. By society's standards we're too old to be that single and carefree on a porch in Easter Island.

She leans her head on my shoulder. I fall back into the railing.

It's late. We doze.

I awake to Franco's face framed by daylight. The kid is ecstatic.

"Man, that was the best sex I ever had! Thank you, my friend, for all your help!"

I smirk and look at the time. Six thirty in the morning. I find a piece of paper on the counter.

Sofia's written down her number and invited me to the beach.

She texts to say she's at Ovahe Beach, the more secluded of the two sandy beaches on the island. I rent a car to meet her.

The road hugs the rolling hills that blend into the seaside cliffs. Even more striking are the colors. They remind me of places I've seen in my life. The greens of Ireland. The red clay of California. The blues of the Caribbean. The brownish-gray rock of the Greek Islands. All the best of the world's beauty combined. Horses graze freely on both sides of the two-lane road. Occasionally it dips into flat plains with dozens of jagged rocks. Other times it elevates into turns that come way too close to dumping the car into the ocean.

To find Ovahe Beach I hike through high grass, cross a small creek, and make my way down a steep rocky ridge before finding the sand.

I spot Sofia and Claudia sleeping off the previous night. I decline to wake them and catch some rays nearby. The sand is pink, the water a spectacular dark teal. Stunningly beautiful.

Sofia turns over. A black bikini hugs her toned body. She still has not noticed me. I sneak over and give her a bear hug.

She's surprised, and I catch an elbow in the ribs, but then she gives me a wide smile. "You made it!"

We go for a swim and for an hour get tossed about by the waves. Sometimes I look out into the blue, other times at the cliff face, but mostly I just stare at her. During a lull in the waves I pull her over. Our eyes lock, then our lips. She straddles my waist and tastes like salt water, flavored ChapStick, and a fruity cocktail. It's paradise. My grasp loosens when a large wave knocks me off-balance.

She laughs. "Not strong enough to hold me and the wave, Lucas?"

Apparently not. Nor am I strong enough to resist the urge to be with

Sofia, even though there's a precious, dear woman back home, Mary, who cares deeply for me. She's somebody I've told that there's a real future between us, after my months of travel. Someone who's been patient and trusting and likely will be for years. Or at least more understanding than I deserve. She always texts, always calls, wants to believe in me and in us. I do, too, but I'm also capable of hurting her. I hate myself for it. She does not deserve to be dragged along, to get half of me. And yet with Sofia I rationalize my guilt by telling myself, "I could die tomorrow." Perhaps being close to so much death makes that easier. It's still wrong. It's remarkable how men can rationalize most anything. Kind of scary too.

A combination of passion and selfishness rationalizes Sofia before me. *Mary will probably leave me anyway; she's such a better person than I am.* My Catholic guilt knows it's wrong, but the beauty of the island makes it feel right. I convince myself I wouldn't be able to stare in a hospice room mirror, foaming at the mouth sixty years from now, not having acted.

But I don't act.

Not yet.

Sofia hears that the sunset on the west side of the island, close to a Moai by the town cemetery, is immaculate. Franco texts to say he and Claudia can meet us there.

The graveyard sits on the edge of the cliff. Sea spray touches the tombstones with a strong wind. The four of us perch ourselves on a hill with a view of the pink light rolling behind the elevated Moai on the cliff's edge. Sipping beer, staring out to the sea as the light slides down the face of the Moai, I see the sun reflected in Sofia's eyes before she nuzzles herself under my chin. I feel that if God were to strike me down at this very moment, put me six feet under in the graveyard behind me, well, I would be going out on top.

When darkness falls, I hold Sofia close on a bench by the sea. I work up the courage to ask if she wants to head home. She nods. We walk hand in hand and kiss under a full moon. I mentally check off every positive Spanish adjective I know. By the time we're home, I think I've told Sofia she's the most beautiful, stunning, attractive, sweet, kind, delightful woman in the history of Western civilization.

She glances at me with a slight smile, partially curious and suspecting. "You're funny."

There's no AC in the warm room, just a small, shabby fan and the occasional sea breeze through the window. As the door closes, I pull her to the bed. In one swoop I pull her dress off over her head. Her hands push my head into her lips. I'm pulsating. There's a rush, packed with the spirits of this island. The sweat from our interlocked bodies drenches the sheets. We don't sleep much over the night hours.

As the sun begins to rise, she turns over to kiss me. We lie with our arms purposely entangled. I've been up for some time. I'm lying in the sin. But it's done. I'm sure it'll follow me. I fix some coffee that we sip on the porch. Later today we'll be on planes, hers east to Chile, mine west to Tahiti and then New Zealand.

As we walk to the car, an old man sways in his chair. He cracks a wide smile and gives me a thumbs-up and laughs. He knows what this island can do.

I whisper a lighthearted "I'm sorry" to Sofia.

She laughs and says, "He's too cute."

It's hard to unclench my hug when I drop her off. I'll likely never see her again. I wish she could come with me. She'd be so fun to travel with. To hold at night. To fight off any loneliness. Yet we both know the road ends here. No future baggage. A memory that'll forever be enshrined.

"Be safe. Maybe I'll see you in Miami someday. I like Miami."

"See you in Miami, Lucas!"

I drive the entirety of the island during my last hours there. I pass free-roaming horses and cattle grazing on the cliffside, their striking figures bolstered by the teal-blue water. Eventually, I pull off into a field of jagged white rocks, close to the ocean and not far from a dormant volcano. I want to walk the unique terrain. A smiling Rapa Nui woman with her four young children catches up to me; she motions that I follow them. On a small trail our little band crosses small, shallow pools, pink around the edges with coral, made full by the spray of the sea. The woman instructs me to carry her youngest. She places trust in a stranger to keep her kid safe. I guess I come off okay.

After ten minutes, we arrive at a large pool. In Spanish she tells me this is her secret pool. It's the first time I've ever been in one constructed by nature. It is too deep to stand on the large smooth rocks in the center, but by the side you can lean on the ridge and support yourself. The kids dive from the sides and pick up starfish from the bottom and hold them up to the sun. I play games with them and encourage their abilities. Every few minutes a large wave crashes, some water creeping over the natural wall, but mostly it sends spray up over the pool, like a rainfall bringing relief from the heat.

It's purifying. On one side of the wall there is a small gap. I feel the ocean jumping up and punching my back. It's a punch of renewal, like a backslap from a dear friend who missed you. I thank the woman for showing me her paradise. She shoots over a smile.

"Don't tell anyone about this place. It's a secret!"

I'll do my best to keep the secrets of this island.

TEN

New Zealand

In my first days in New Zealand, I move about with a quiet confidence. I sit on white beaches while cerulean surf laps at my feet. I learn to drive on the left side of a winding seaside road and take Instagram-perfect photos. New Zealand, I've decided, is the last leg of the few months of travel after leaving NBC. The country's natural wonders, sharp peaks, dense forests, swift ocean tides, and violently windy roads will serve as my capstone. I've become a hardened solo traveler, high off what I experienced in Easter Island.

New Zealand accentuates that good feeling.

This is living. This is what it feels like to finally do what I want.

New Zealand is my victory lap. I step into the Lakehouse bar in scenic Taupō after a few hours of hiking around the volcanic caldera that is the lake.

A brewmaster with a handlebar mustache points me to a barstool.

"What it'll be?"

"Dealer's choice."

With a simple head nod, he turns his back and pours a pilsner draft. I take out my journal and begin to jot down some notes. "Sulfur smell near Taupō volcanic zone intense. Locals seem to have built immunity." I don't notice the woman at the stool next to me till I look up from the page.

"Strong beer, please!" she says in heavily French-accented English. Her vibe is distinctly backpacker, all baggy drawstring pajama pants with a Himalayan print and an open-neck brown sweater. She's dainty, almost a bit malnourished. Can't be older than twenty. She carefully counts out her wrinkled bills, waiting for a drink. I don't pay her much attention till she begins to write in a leatherbound notebook. I glance over as she twirls her pen near her pronounced cheekbone. I fear being overbearing; women deal with too many nosy and uninvited men. She's not my type, though, and Sofia still runs through my mind. I sense a more fraternal connection with the woman before me now. There aren't a lot of us in this world, after all—solo travelers scribbling away, sipping a beer early in the afternoon. I kind of want to hear her story.

"Writing the next great French novel?"

"How'd you know I was French?"

She's totally serious. I tone down my internal sarcasm. I don't want to come off as a patronizing American asshole.

"Oh, I thought I heard French. So sorry if I was wrong! Eek!"

Through a faint smile she says, "You're right. I am . . . of France."

She smiles playfully.

"Can I ask you what you're writing about?"

Her small, clean printed French words I see from the page contrast mightily with my messy prep-school cursive.

"Just life."

She answers the question with such conviction. No self-deprecation. Just confidence.

Her name is Maggie. She's twenty-two, a Parisian and daughter of a German-French mother who teaches school and a French father who curates museums. She's an accomplished flute player and singer but just got a degree from a technical college for audio engineering because, as she says, "Production is a more stable income than performance."

She shrugs. "But a job is not a life."

Her job, she says, won't keep her from singing when she wants, or playing the flute when she wants, or traveling when she wants.

In fact, she says, she uses her job as much as it uses her: her audio engineering gig gained her membership in a technical workers union in Paris. That union has a yearly quota for working hours for its members. She met it in eight months, and for a reason. It gave her four months to herself. With four months to call her own, she hit the road, alone, exploration on her mind.

"And so now I'm here in New Zealand," she says. For the time being, she sleeps in a hostel. Eight to a room. She lives off a small stipend. When she needs more money, she works the land on New Zealand's potato farms, a week or so at a time to give her the cash to press on.

"You work the fields here? Like farmwork?"

"Aren't you a traveler? Don't you know about harvest season?"

I shake my head.

"If you follow the harvest seasons around the world," she says, "it's easy to find work. That's how many of us do it. Farmers always need an extra set of hands around the harvest."

"Wow."

I'm embarrassed by my ignorance and inadvertent admission of privilege. I'd heard of kids who traveled the world with nothing, but I don't know any.

"How do you get around? Bus?"

Maggie shakes her head. "This." She points to her hand. Her thumb is her ride.

I'm inspired by her courage. Maggie is patient and unworried. She makes sacrifices for life experience and not for some corporate hamster wheel or what society thinks she should do. She's made a calculated choice to live life on her terms.

After six months of travel, I remain the opposite. Sure, I've gone out into the unknown, but life has dictated my terms, and comparing myself to her leaves me unsure of myself. I thought I'd had a few things figured out coming into this bar. Maggie shows me what true poise and self-assurance look like.

"And what about you?" she says. "Why are you here?"

I stumble. It's a big question with no quick answer. "I used to be a journalist. I just wanted a change."

I feel like this small French woman has just checkmated my large American self. I pivot and try to inflate my importance. "Look at this."

I show off pictures on my iPhone of me with President Obama. Old screen grabs of when I hosted MSNBC shows.

"That's nice," she says, not interested. To her I seem just another guy whose identity is his career. And I didn't even answer her question!

A silence hangs over us. Each party waits a few moments for the other to interrupt it. Neither does.

She starts writing again. I take a seat next to her but remain silent.

I keep looking at her as she writes freely. Words seem to flow for her, like calmness personified. She sips her beer slowly. I'm now into number three. My mind begins to reflect. Why have I never had the courage to shun norms and take the road less traveled? Even now, I've put an end date on my travels and self-exploration: six to eight months and no more. Why do I not have Maggie's gumption to hitchhike and do whatever is necessary to get by in a foreign land? That's way more badass than sparring with the Speaker of the House at a press conference or ditching oxygen tanks in Bolivia.

Maggie finishes her beer and begins to gather her things.

"Hey, do you want another one?" I ask.

"I can't afford it." She delivers the line with zero sense of shame.

"I'll buy it for you."

"I don't need a man to take care of me."

"Well, from talking to you for five minutes, that's pretty obvious. Your question, though, I'm a bit hung up on it."

She looks confused, like she doesn't understand my phrasing or even remember her question that derailed me. The truth is, I just don't want her to leave. Not yet.

"I want to understand how you do it all," I blurt out. "Want to get some food? I know you don't need it, but I'd like to hang out for a second. I'll trade you dinner for travel advice?"

I let out a little laugh at the end of the question.

Maggie shrugs and accepts. "Sounds better than hearing hostel stories."

We sit down at a Lebanese place around the corner. On the walk over, I notice the extent to which her baggy clothes hide her angular frame.

"Have your pick of the menu," I say, in the tone of an older brother.

She modestly chooses a small appetizer.

"Please, get more, you need . . ." I cut myself off. Who the hell am I to give directions? Maggie knows what she's doing.

She's unsure but at last orders a lamb platter with extra pita bread. When the dish hits the table, a deep-seated hunger jumps out of her stomach. The small French girl, no more than one hundred pounds, scarfs down meat and bread at a rate that would impress a bodybuilder.

Music starts out as the crux of our conversation. It's nice and light. I tell her how a few days earlier I saw Guns N' Roses play a sold-out show in Auckland. Slash's whaling guitar and Axl Rose's shrieking voice still ring in my ears. I mention I'd seen Jim Morrison's grave in her native Paris and she gushes about the Doors. I tell Maggie how much I love Bruce Springsteen. Maggie says she adores Springsteen's folk song "The Ghost of Tom Joad."

"I love to play it on my piano. I've even performed it on my travels," she says, her fingers moving across the table as if the keys were beneath her.

"You weren't nervous? Performing in front of foreign strangers?"

"Why would I limit myself? Every audience gives me feedback that makes me better. Also, I think that's easier than performing for friends and family!"

We laugh.

I strangle the stem of the wineglass between my thumb and index finger. I look at Maggie scooping up hummus and then down at the faded tablecloth trapped under the base of the glass. Had I only been as tough and confident as this dainty, petite French girl, I'd have been happier earlier. Simply put: I've feared letting down those who expect so much from me. I've feared failing in a job and life that chose me, and I've feared not living up to the family name. I've feared the disapproval from my parents' cohort, the best and the brightest of my hometown. Tim Russert's son is *not* supposed to be some hippie bohemian in search of life's deeper truths. He's been given too much to do too little with it. I am supposed to be, expected to be, established. People are supposed to know me. I am supposed to build a nice career and things are supposed to fall into place. There can be no dereliction of duty.

Sitting opposite Maggie, listening to her, I can't help but ask myself: What has the whole of my life so far been about? Have I chased a legacy, trying to keep ghosts alive? Was that sense of self-validation, following in Dad's footsteps, worth feeling lost now? At thirty-one I want desperately to be Maggie at twenty-two, yet the sad reality is that she is more mature in her young age than I will probably ever be. She is comfortable with herself. She knows herself. I've

103

traveled through Latin America and traversed the South Pacific. I've learned a lot about other countries, cultures, and communities, searching for a sense of who I really am; those trips helped convince me that I'm capable of trekking on, living this nomadic life, yet I'm not sure I know myself any better and am certainly no closer to finding Maggie's inner peace. Hell, I haven't even been able to process the questions that might lead me there.

Maggie forces out hard truths.

Two hours pass and between us no topic is off-limits: politics, travel, religion, culture, always with the implication that we should experience all of it. Maggie is the rare one where youth isn't wasted on the young, where not a single day is wasted.

When the restaurant lights turn up high and the place closes down, I pat Maggie on her shoulder.

"Let me walk you back to your hostel."

She nods.

Up a long hill we go, the lights of Taupō, this city amid volcanoes, illuminating a path through a misty fog. I'm a few steps behind her, keeping a protective watch.

"This is it," she says, pulling in front of a single-story place, decently kept, where inside she sleeps among eight other residents.

"Such a great time," I say. "You taught me a lot. I need to be like Maggie!"

She nods. She knows I'm not joking.

SOUTH ISLAND

I arrive on the South Island of New Zealand, on a new course of self-reflection spurred on by Maggie's wisdom. I'll take a week to drive from Christchurch down south to Queenstown, some seven hundred kilometers using my coastal backroads path. Just enough time to know a place like no other.

Rolling gold fields, spectacular seas, ancient rock formations, glaciers, rain forests, waterfalls, lakes, rivers, and streams so clean they can be drunk from—all this together in such proximity—and the crown jewel at the island's southernmost point, the fjord known as Milford Sound. New Zealand has a singular beauty.

I make my way down State Highway 73 into Korowai / Torlesse Tussocklands Park. Much of this is literally "Middle-earth." The famous *Lord of the Rings* movies were filmed here, some scenes shot not far from Castle Hill, an area where moon rocks are scattered around brown clay slopes as if they're sprinkled seed on pavement. It's beautiful and beguiling country that makes you believe humans can coexist with nature. There are no strip malls, billboards, fast food joints, or ugly signs of commercialism, just winding roads into the heart of the wild. Hills and mountains enclose me on both sides. At times snow or clouds cover their tops while their slopes shade green, brown, white, black, or gold.

Along the way I see hitchhikers, commonplace in New Zealand. Here, camper vans and people living for months off the land are the norm. The government actually invests in campsites with showers and stoves. It starts to drizzle and then storm, and I feel pity for a lanky blond-haired kid holding a sign of destination. He looks cold. His face is dark pink. The rain soaks his clothes. I slow the car.

"Where are you going?" I yell to be heard over the raindrops.

"Hokitika!" the kid responds. I've consulted enough maps to know that's northwest of here some seventy miles.

"You aren't a terrorist or serial killer, are you?" I ask.

"No," he laughs. "Just trying to get back to my van."

I give him another once-over from head to foot. I've never picked up a hitchhiker. But why travel if you're just going to live life as you always have?

"Let's do it!" I say. "But I may stop along the way to take some photos."

"All good."

In pops Felix, a tall twenty-two-year-old blond surfer from Germany, chasing waves and dreams of wanderlust.

An hour into the drive I can tell something is wrong. His eyes stare blankly out at the endless wilderness. I ask him about it. In thick German-accented English, he explains how he has a girlfriend, a Hawaiian girl. They'd met surfing in Westport, New Zealand, and spent a month driving the coast in his van, surfing at will, sleeping in the car, their only concerns the next beach and

LOOK FOR ME THERE

how many peanut butter crackers they had left. For a while it was wonderful, and Felix shows me proof: his forearm tattoo, a memento of his love of surfing and his girlfriend.

"But she had to go back to Hawaii," he says. The couple hitchhiked to the airport because he couldn't afford the gas to get there and back. He's just dropped her off at the terminal, and now he's hitchhiking back to his van in Hokitika.

"You miss her already?"

Felix moans. "I'm a hopeless romantic," he says.

"Bahaha. Yeah, you are!" I can't help but love the kid.

When we come upon the beach town of Hokitika, Felix tells me, "Right turn here."

We drive in circles through small town streets, and then a maroon Honda minivan at least fifteen years old comes into view. Inside are surfboards, blankets, shoes, clothes, and groceries: Felix's ride.

"That has to be you, Felix!"

"It is. It is," he says.

I park next to the minivan. He thanks me for the lift and adds, "Want to walk to the beach?"

"Sure, man."

The beach turns out to be the last spot he surfed with his girlfriend. We look at the water. The waves crest rough and choppy.

"It was calm, with smooth barrels on our last day together," Felix says, a bit wistful.

He snaps a few pictures of the surf. These waters, tough as they are today, are the final place the two were one.

"I'll text her some shots," he says.

Is it wrong for Felix to hope his love might endure time and an ocean of separation? As we walk amid the driftwood, I think about my relationships. They're much less passionate and spontaneous than Felix's over the last few months. Minus Sofia on the enchanted isle, the women I'd ever given a chance to were deliberate and fraught with thought. Could she handle official Washington, with its formal events, celebrations, and galas? Could she shake hands correctly? Could she live up to family expectations? Could she handle the media spotlight? If so, what about the pressure put on her by a DC society that ranked power couples like sports teams? How would she deal with the ever-prying eyes? Eyes, eyes, everywhere, connected to toxic people who, once your back is turned, will happily rip you and your loved one to shreds.

Standing next to Felix I realize how sad it is to think like this. Love should come in the form of someone who gives you the same feelings that sent Felix hitchhiking to the airport and getting a tattoo.

"Keep living for me, Felix," I say as we walk back to his van.

He shoots me a look: *What do you mean?* We hug it out and I wish him luck instead of explaining.

I drive off, contemplating how two people barely out of their teens could teach me more about myself than I care to admit.

RSA

I would say my travels continue, but the reality is the next day, a Monday in early February, the locals celebrate a national holiday known as Waitangi Day, which commemorates the treaty between the Māori people and Great Britain that birthed modern New Zealand in 1840. Coincidentally it is also a national holiday in America: Super Bowl Sunday. Years of watching the Super Bowl with my parents and friends, with buckets of fried chicken, pizza, and ice-cold drinks: Super Bowl and "Russert's house" have always been synonymous. Some traditions must be maintained.

A bar showing the Super Bowl is nowhere to be found in rural New Zealand. Around kickoff time I begin to panic. A sympathetic barkeep has a suggestion: the Returned and Services Association, or New Zealand's version of a VFW or American Legion. The local RSA keeps a large satellite TV for foreign sports events, usually European soccer games. The barkeep kindly calls ahead and gives me a thumbs-up; the RSA guys will put the game on for me so long as I have a few drinks.

I find a large well-lit space with a long bar. The carpet smells of stale beer. About a dozen older men, dressed in khakis and polo shirts with white sneakers, mill around. Some play pool. Others gamble over card games. A few drink at the tables around the bar and watch cricket. When I walk in, the bartender, a young guy, immediately says, "You're the American, right? You wanted to watch the final football match?"

"Yes!" I yell.

I offer my many thanks and settle in.

Soon I'm nursing a beer and watching a foreign feed of the Super Bowl without announcer commentary. At first my arrival barely registers, as the veterans invest themselves in their drinks or gambling. When Lady Gaga appears in one of her eccentric outfits for the halftime show, old men's attention veers toward the TV. A group jeer and laugh.

One says, "They said you were watching a game. What the hell is this, lad?!"

I explain that in America halftime entertainment is as much a spectacle as the game.

They all scoff. "Spectacle all right. It's when you're supposed to get more beer."

They're endearing, these old guys. I could be in some Buffalo American Legion Hall with my grandpa and his buddies, minus the picture of Queen Elizabeth presiding over the entry door—that would be sacrilegious to the Buffalo Irish.

Once Lady Gaga finishes, most of the vets retreat to their cards and cups. Ian, a tall white-haired man with a stout stomach, settles into the chair next to me. We chat. Ian's son lives in Annapolis, Maryland, and has married an American girl. Ian's grandkids all love NFL football. Ian doesn't get it.

"The game seems too slow with too many time stoppages," Ian says. "And the pads make it too weak. Why don't they just make this rugby? It's a better game!"

Ian is a good man. His decency shines through when he asks if I have safe housing on the island. "Some of these places don't have working smoke detectors. Not good."

When my pretzel bowl is empty, he insists on fetching me more, even though walking takes him considerably more effort than it does me. As I look into his creased red face, cheery and at ease, I see my grandfather, Big Russ, who passed away not long after my dad. Big Russ preached many things, but the most important was that you were well fed and well cared for. Far from home and a bit lonely on Super Bowl Sunday, I feel like a grandson again. I gravitate toward Ian's familiarity, his and his friends' wholesome goodness, these gentle veterans on the closing chapter of life.

Like Big Russ they've lived courageously, humbly, in the hope that successive generations might live better. Big Russ returned from the war and raised a family of six on two salaries, one as a truck driver and the other as a garbage man. He went to Mass, laughed often, never cried, and served for years as the commander of a place much like the one I'm sitting in today, American Legion Post 721 in South Buffalo.

I watch the second half of the Super Bowl and think about Big Russ's life as I share beers and jokes with the vets. Did Big Russ ever entertain thoughts like mine over the last few days? When his B-24 Liberator crashed in England in October 1944 and he was pitched clear of the bomber and engulfed in flames, did he worry about dying without knowing his inner truth? After V-E Day, did Big Russ ever think of finding the English nurse who'd helped to heal his burned flesh and making a new life in Europe, away from his family and their attendant expectations in Buffalo?

No. Big Russ didn't do any of that. He enlisted at nineteen, fought a war, defeated fascism, and then came home. Because *his* father expected him to. So Big Russ fulfilled another duty: making a life for himself and, ultimately, for his wife and son and daughters, in the place he'd known since childhood. Duty, optimism, family: Big Russ passed that on to Dad. Tim Russert lived a life arguably larger than Big Russ, and Big Russ was fine with that. "Take care of your family. It's your most important job," he liked to say. You should grow the pie, for the betterment of God and country.

What am I growing? Or is everything in New Zealand—Maggie, Felix, and the whole four months of travel that led me there—indulgent? Taking advantage of the privilege given to me and not giving back anything in return? Why must I know who I am? Has this trip just been an exercise in vanity?

In the backroom, the RSA guys set up a buffet table of Thai food. The veterans ask if I'd eat with them; in fact, the RSA guys insist.

I pull up a chair, and they discuss everything from ferry service to local politics. They speak with a different accent, but these RSA guys really do remind me of men from my life. They're earnest but carry a cutting sense of humor, a cheerfulness about the approach to one's days. Every few moments, I sit up at the table and look toward the front door, convinced I'll see them walk in—Big Russ puttering like a penguin in front, Dad gently guiding him with a hand on his shoulder. They would be at home here.

When the meal ends, I give Ian my contact information on the chance he is ever in Annapolis to visit his son. He promptly passes it back.

"I'm closing in on eighty, lad. I don't fly twenty-five hours anymore. If they want to see the old man, they come to me."

"I understand. Well, thanks for taking care of me. Let me get you a beer."

"No, no, no. It's all paid for. Be gone with yourself. Enjoy your time and—" Ian cocks his head a bit, as if he's noticed my introspection, as if he's intuited my emotions from the way his eyes lock with mine—"and be well, lad."

"Absolutely."

"Getcha go to Ōkārito tomorrah." Those are the words of a drunk dairy farmer at a roadhouse bar in Whataroa where I spend the night some days later after an aggressive schedule of sightseeing. Why I trust a drunk's recommendation could define a lot of my reasoning: I have a gut instinct that if he is that passionate about a place in his altered state, he couldn't be lying about it. So the next day I drive forty minutes out of the way to Ōkārito, even though I need to be on the road from dawn to dusk to get south to Queenstown before nightfall.

Ōkārito is a tucked-away coastal village near a sandspit on the Tasman Sea. The road to get there runs through a dense rain forest with large ferns. Behind the sandspit, brackish waters form a small bay that rises with the tide. Snowcapped mountains sit to the right, and to the left spreads the ocean. The drunk was right—it's a breathtaking place. I take a stroll to the beach that shoots out beneath a cliff and think about what I should do next. *Has this whole trip just been some merry jaunt?* For not the first time in my life, I feel guilty about the gifts Big Russ and Dad and Mom bestowed. I even feel unworthy of them. New Zealand is beautiful, but these thoughts are not.

I check the date on my phone. It's Valentine's Day. I sent Mary some flowers and chocolates, a hollow attempt at being decent, without explaining what I've been doing. Even without my guilt, Valentine's Day has always been odd for me. The day carries outsize importance because the person I loved the most, my father, would jokingly make a big deal out of it. He showered me with chocolates, king-sized Twix bars (my favorite), and called me his valentine. I think it grew of genuine fatherly love as a backup in case I wasn't a crush's valentine. One year when I was fifteen, he gave me a poster of Britney Spears with a word cloud that said, "I Love You, Luke. Be My Valentine. Go Bills!" When I got older, the valentine came with beer money, often in FedEx packages shipped to my college apartment. A note would read, "Be good to your valentines Miller and Bud! Love, Dad." These simple gestures meant everything to me.

I realize how much I miss the man. Not just Dad's love, his presence, his care to see me succeed, but all the things that were a scheduled and set part of my life. Nine years later, I still long for those valentines.

I stick my feet in the Tasman Sea. I always feel a calmness near the water. As the waves lap at my ankles, I look to the sky toward the cliff. A small rain falls and a large, shining rainbow stretches the length of the beach.

Dad loved rainbows. All the doubt and self-loathing I've subjected myself to—does Dad hear it? Could that reflecting light be Dad now? It seems ludicrous and childish to think like this, but it also seems the only answer in my state of mind. I start to jog toward the rainbow, hoping to touch it. My feet, almost on their own, move faster. My legs pump harder. Suddenly I'm running and then sprinting—absolutely sure that rainbow is Dad. I carry on like this for maybe a quarter mile, and when I get just below the streaming colors, I'm out of breath, panting, and trying to suppress the emotions that get in the way of taking in oxygen.

I get down on a knee and hold my hand up to the sky. For a second the colors of the rainbow are inside my palm. This is Dad! He's shaking my hand! I'm sure of it.

I sob. It's a full-on breakdown, raw and cathartic. I'm so far from home, so far from the life he envisioned for me, but nevertheless he's come from the other side to check in on Valentine's Day.

I understand amid the crying that there's something else Dad wants to tell me. In the same way that I heard his voice as I delivered his eulogy at Holy Trinity—"You're doing great, Luke!"—I can sense Dad now, sitting next to this rainbow.

"You're fine, Luke," a voice inside me says. "This is what you should be doing right now."

All the self-doubt of the last few days, the uncertainty—they're serving a purpose.

"This is what you should be doing," the voice repeats.

I should be traveling. This journey *is* worthwhile. I break down again, this time in gratitude.

I get up and stack seven rocks, Dad's lucky number, on top of each other and write his initials, TJR, in the sand.

I know he sees it.

New Zealand proves I have to extend my travels. I am not finished with the road. I've barely begun. I will take the time to do what I can to fulfill a need. The world I see and the self I see reflected here—they scare me and scar me but nourish me too. I write in my journal as I prepare to leave New Zealand and map a new and extended course of travel:

> My spirit is fiercely free today, whatever I do in the future must allow for this
> type of feeling more often than not . . . I shed demons here and came to my
> own mountaintop of understanding. There is a better way to live, one of not
> just belief in the self but of embracing what's in front of you. Of learning,
> appreciating, and being. And if what is in front is beautiful and worthwhile,
> it just makes it easier.

By exploring New Zealand, I begin at last to truly broach the inner reaches of myself.

PART 3

ELEVEN

Cambodia

My ride is late, but I don't care. I wait for thirty minutes at the Siem Reap International Airport in Cambodia for a Volkswagen van from the hotel. A few months ago, this may have rattled me, but now I just see it as another adventure. When it never shows, when I can't get through to the front desk on my phone, when the day proves way too hot and humid to keep waiting, I flag down the only thing I see: a guy throttling a motorbike with a two-wheeled carriage, an authentic Cambodian tuk-tuk.

The whole thing looks unstable. I throw my luggage in anyway and adjust my large American frame into the center of the carriage seat. The seat wobbles to an equilibrium. Am I that fat or is this thing that small? The driver, whose helmet says "Lucky" on the back, seems unfazed. "Hey, how much to here in Siem Reap?" I show him the address in the Khmer language on my phone. He nods, then holds up ten fingers and sticks one in my chest: "Dollar, not *riel.*" Not a bad price. I agree to it.

Money isn't too tight, but it has to last for this year of travel. I'm relying on funds, sufficient but not inexhaustible, that now come my way because of how Dad structured his will. So cheaper countries like Cambodia aid in my effort to stick to a budget.

We leave the airport and putter onto a two-lane highway. Buses, vans, and sedans whiz by at a tremendous speed. Curious tourists behind semitinted glass look out at me; I give them a wave. It's free and easy on this road. I am lucky, and I'm with Lucky. The tuk-tuk hugs the shoulder. It moves at just fast enough of a clip to cool my body. The air pounding my face feels so good.

I've come to Cambodia to see part of the world I've sought. To set my compass for adventure and intrigue after my moment of clarity a few months back in New Zealand. Adventure and intrigue start in Angkor Wat, the largest religious monument in the world.

Mom saw it first. In fact, a photo hangs in the hallway at the family home: Mom doing a headstand at one of the Angkor Wat temples. She balances upside down, a woman in her sixties, a reminder of her ageless athletic ability. However, my eye has always been drawn to what's in the photo's background: carved gray stone with elaborate portrayals of various Hindu and Buddhist holy figures. All of the carvings are beautiful, and some are even sensual. It's been impossible not to get lost in the detail.

I must see them for myself.

I stay for a day in Siem Reap's city core. It's flat, damp, and full of foreign money. Luxury hotels sprout up like dandelions next to graffitied and abandoned buildings. Local homes have been swallowed up by the tourist boom and speculative buys of Chinese and Korean investors. I walk the blocks across the river into town. The French controlled Cambodia for a long time. Their architecture remains. Paired with the heat, the low-lying wetlands, and the cheap beer for sale everywhere, I feel a hint of the worst of New Orleans. Hastily constructed bars and restaurants cater to any taste near the appropriately named Pub Street. If you want to buy a knockoff NBA jersey and then eat a scorpion, you can do it at the night market.

I walk past the Hard Rock Cafe, where a group of Mormon missionaries sits at an outdoor table. They eat burgers and drink milkshakes. Some bop their heads to the Journey songs coming from the speakers.

I stop and lean against the patio fence. My inner Irish wiseass won't let this moment pass.

"Are you guys allowed to be here? This is a little risqué, isn't it? There's rock music and booze in there, boys!"

The leader, a young white kid with blond hair, flashes a big grin.

"No, sir. We're off hours. We'll be back at it early tomorrow! You bet!"

I admire his earnestness.

I'm not beyond the bars tonight. A siren lures me, a cover band blasting '80s hits from a second-story terrace. Up the stairs I'm shown to a small table with a large velvet swirling chair. It's clear I've been intentionally seated next to the only other white guy in the bar. He happens to be an American, probably in his fifties.

"Hi, I'm Eric, from Ohio. I used to do some work in this area. Here on business."

I grab a beer and pretzels and use the swivel chair to take in the surroundings. Various Asian tour groups, all with drinks and all fixated on the band. The lead singer is a middle-aged Cambodian man with aviator sunglasses and long, flowing black hair. The female backup singers wear short black shorts and long black boots and attempt to dance in unison.

Before I can talk to Eric, the band lays into the first chords of Billy Ray Cyrus's "Achy Breaky Heart."

Each table's tour group rushes to the dance floor to sing and dance along.

"Holy shit!" I scream. Eric leans over and, with the confidence of a veteran, points: "You see, that table is Korean; that one is Japanese; and that one is Chinese."

"And all dancing to 'Achy Breaky Heart,'" I say. "USA, man—what a country!"

It's quite a scene, perhaps no better representation of America's superpower status as exporter of pop culture. We may not unify the world with our foreign policy, but our music sure can. I laugh as I head down the stairs and off into the sticky night. Billy Ray Cyrus was not on my Angkor Wat bingo card.

ANGKOR WAT

"You need to wear pants that cover the knee. Temple rule."

It's early morning and already the heat is stifling, but I retreat to my room to change out of my shorts. I don't want to show any disrespect, especially in a place revered by two major religions. Constructed in the early part of the twelfth century as a tribute to the Hindu god Vishnu, Angkor Wat is an elaborate complex of stone temples, palaces, and shrines set across four-hundred-plus acres. Over time much of the stone became intertwined with nearby trees, whose roots have wrapped themselves into and around the intricate carvings of faces, animals, and religious iconography. When Cambodia transitioned to Buddhism toward the end of the twelfth century, Buddha replaced Vishnu as the honored deity. The space stayed the same.

When I emerge from my room, the heat is scorching, so intense that I check my manhood and use an umbrella to shield myself from the sun. But Angkor Wat, which means "Temple City," transcends my earthly concerns. Approaching the main temple palace, its five iconic carved towers loom against the horizon. With swampy greenery and exotic trees, a pond serving as its moat, the temples are the apotheosis of grandeur. And all date back nearly one thousand years.

The guide leads me through dozens of ancient ruins. Up old stairs constructed of worn-out sandstone, everything weathered, everything somehow very much alive. It must be that it's a result of the trees growing into and out of the rock. A mix of nature's eternal qualities and man's eternal attempts to control it. Around each corner is a new treasure, something that defies logic: large faces made from stone protrude from a temple fence; an ancient gong in front of a wall of what looks like hieroglyphics. How could people create such grandiose beauty with such primitive tools?

The guide jokes, "Cambodians used all their energy building this. We have none left. That's why our country has had to deal with so much. We're forever tired!"

The throngs of tourists annoy me. They represent the worst of contemporary culture. Pushy, greedy, disrespectful. I'm watching a relic being destroyed in real time. A white guy with a bandanna climbs an old tree, motioning for his friend to "get the perfect shot for Instagram."

I seek a route out of the crowds.

Tucked behind a corner in a nondescript smaller temple is a Buddhist altar, made from an ancient stone structure. Buddha stands tall in an orange robe atop yellow stairs. Candles and incense burn in front. For reasons I cannot fathom as a practicing Catholic, I feel an urge to meditate or pay respect to the Buddha.

I place coins in the plate, cross my legs, and just breathe. For a half hour I sit in a trance. I'm able to block out the surrounding world and focus inward. I push out the worries of the day—travel logistics, the need to check in with loved ones, what I am doing on this journey. I breathe in a sense of purpose, of being present, without concern for the ups and downs of the day. In this space I am unaffected by the anxieties of the mind. There's clarity inside the chaos of the most visited tourist site in Cambodia.

I motion to the guide. "Can you take me to a Buddhist temple? I want to go to a quiet place, away from the Angkor Wat."

Even though there's two hours left on the tour, he doesn't act surprised. He simply nods.

WAT PREAH PROM RATH TEMPLE VISIT

Wat Preah Prom Rath is a Buddhist monastery and temple complex smack-dab in the middle of Siem Reap. Despite its proximity to the debauchery of Pub Street and its tourist traps, Wat Preah Prom Rath maintains zen. Once inside the gate, the outside world mutes itself.

I do not see another person on the grounds.

Around the complex are well-kept gardens. The paths between them are dotted with painted Buddhist sculptures. There's a main pagoda in the middle, with others scattered about. As I walk slowly around the perfectly manicured green bushes, life-size Buddhas, and colorful pagodas, I think of my own faith. Catholic churches full of life-size statues mean to convey a story, but instinctually I associate them with joy, grief, and penance. The joy of a wedding or baptism. The grief of a funeral. The admission of sin, shortcomings, and failure. These are a wide variety of emotions. The comfort of the church rests in beauty and familiarity. Still, I seldom go inside without feeling a deep sense of atonement. An expectation that I must beg for the forgiveness of sin and ask for mercy.

Those feelings aren't present here.

The sense of calm that came at Angkor Wat embraces me again as I walk into the main temple. Here, my thoughts begin to order themselves. Questions come to mind. *What did I learn today? What can I do with that knowledge to feel more purposeful and fulfilled? How can it be measured effectively in a mindful way?* Again, I do not know why these feelings come in front of the Buddha, but they are welcome. I realize I'm engaging in a version of the Jesuit Examen, the daily meditative exercise that encourages Catholics to draw closer to God by engaging in the following steps:

1. Become aware of God's presence.
2. Review the day with gratitude.
3. Pay attention to your emotions.
4. Choose one feature of the day and pray from it.
5. Look toward tomorrow.

Something that had been taught by the Jesuits yet was never acted on now comes out in the presence of the Buddha: the importance of understanding our small stature in this grander world. I also realize something that's been gnawing at me. This year, for the first time, I did not visit Dad's grave on the anniversary of his death. I was in transit through China a few days ago. However, I did light some incense at a Buddhist shrine there when I could not find a Catholic church. This moment in Cambodia feels like a confirmation of that action.

Dad always had a curiosity for other religions. I guess I picked up on it too. An old saying comes to mind: "We're all getting to the same faithful ending. We just take different roads." Amen.

Parts of the pathways underneath the portico attached to the main temple are adorned with painted walls. These walls tell the story of Buddhism. In their chronology, they are reminders of the Stations of the Cross. They tell the story of Prince Siddhartha, who would become Buddha.

The plaque starts out: "The prince longed to see more of the world, realized that he never stepped outside of the city limits. Early one morning he got into his chariot and asked his chariot driver to take him as far out as possible . . ."

To paraphrase the story further, the prince's father wanted to shield him from suffering. Around age thirty, he left the palace grounds and encountered the four realities of life: old age, sickness, death, and renunciation. The prince yearned to learn the cause of suffering. He renounced the palace and lived an austere life in the forest, trying to ascertain the cause of human pain. But trading in years of "self-indulgence" in the palace for "self-denial" in the forest did not lead to clarity. Enlightenment came between the extremes. He realized that life is, in fact, a form of suffering, and to embrace it is to understand life.

Suffering is eternal. Acknowledge you can't escape it, and peace will be within you.

I find deep meaning in the story. Then two young monks in orange robes stroll by. Skinny, with shaved heads and sandals, they walk to the temple. I follow behind and then ask to pray with them. I see they're kind of confused. I raise my hands into a prayer sign. They smile and instruct me to sit between them.

One rings a small bell and chants out prayers in Cambodian. I take deep breaths and meditate. At the risk of comparing myself to Buddha, I focus on how I, too, am privileged and was sheltered from the worst suffering of my village by my father. While my parents took time to bestow on me the ways of the world and the importance of love, charity, empathy, and compassion, I felt secure on the palace grounds of comfort for a long time. This journey, away from what I've known, fits within my own quest for enlightenment. I occupied the self-indulgent world and now see how a life of self-denial is a way toward peace. However, I see more purpose in the middle. The middle way, the idea that human suffering can be eased by understanding the mind, its impulsive nature, and calming its worst desires, rings true. Selfishness, ego, discomfort, anxiety: I will fall victim to those traits, but I realize that being aware of them and letting them be in control stifles happiness. I turn to the monks: "So embrace the suffering!"

TWELVE

Vietnam

I am here for my parents.

Vietnam shaped so much of their lives. They both lost childhood friends to the war. Dad went to John Carroll University, forty-five minutes from Kent State. When the National Guardsmen killed four anti-war protestors there, some Kent State students fled to John Carroll and described the tragedy for Dad in great detail. It haunted him. He joined many anti-war protests. Because of Vietnam, he volunteered for RFK's presidential campaign in 1968. Because of Vietnam, he went to Woodstock in '69. (The musical lineup didn't hurt either.) Because of Vietnam, he spent the whole of his political and journalistic career questioning politicians, at times deeply skeptical of "what the suits sold," he said, the so-called best and brightest.

For Mom, Vietnam reinforced what she learned in the Peace Corps in Colombia: America's greatest might is its soft power. Bread, not bombs. The war inspired her first foray into documentary film, when she was part of a team covering the 1972 GOP convention. There she was tear-gassed and watched veteran and war critic Ron Kovic, whose life Tom Cruise later portrayed in Oliver Stone's *Born on the Fourth of July*, get pushed around in his wheelchair and spat on by delegates. As it had for Dad, Vietnam shaped Mom's journalistic career: reporting from the set of *Apocalypse Now* and, decades after the war, informing almost every question she asked of authority figures, a writer who remained forever skeptical of official narrative.

Vietnam shaped my childhood too. The music I heard at home was centered on that era: Dad blasting on his stereo Springsteen's "Born in the USA," Edwin Starr's "War," and Neil Young's "Ohio." So many of the movies and documentaries I watched centered on the war. So many of the dinner conversations Mom,

Dad, and I had spun out of Vietnam. The all-familiar phrases when explaining something: "It was during Vietnam" or "Still coming out of Vietnam."

But neither Mom nor Dad had come here. Dad and my uncles got student deferments or got married. Mom, the world traveler, never wanted to come. "It just permeated everything for so long—I never felt an urge." I am the first Orth or Russert to visit, and as the rice paddies come into view out the plane window, I play Creedence Clearwater Revival's "Run Through the Jungle" on my headphones, just like in all those Vietnam movies, a corny homage to my upbringing and my parents.

But instead of getting off a plane and whisking away to some canvas-tent-laden outpost, where shirtless men in green fatigues and dangling dog tags lug equipment, I go through customs in a modern, well-lit, air-conditioned Hanoi airport. There's a friendly driver from my hotel holding up a sign with my name. He puts me in the back of a Hyundai minivan with cold bottles of water from a cooler.

American soft rock comes through the speakers. Sitting there in the mini-van, with Vietnam passing by the window, I scoff at all the notions I had of this place.

A lot has changed in fifty years.

HANOI OLD QUARTER

The Old Quarter is forty blocks of delightful madness. Many of the buildings are French inspired: two or three stories of colorful concrete with wooden shutters over windows and balconies. Much of the culture is outdoors. Restaurants and shops open to the street and spit out tiny little plastic stools and tables for seating. When I sit for a beer, my knees are near my ears, but it works just fine. Throngs of people walk on pedestrian-only thoroughfares. On the larger avenues, armies of scooters whiz by in controlled chaos.

The scooter is king in Hanoi. Families ride scooters; the elderly ride them. Even Uber operates via scooter. I drop off my stuff at the hotel and immediately take to the street-festival vibe, the only downside being the stifling humidity where sweat stains expand across my clothing within thirty seconds. The Hanoi locals somehow don't sweat.

The shops are a mix of local pottery, silk or tailored clothing, and trendier boutique coffee, craft beer, modern art, and vinyl records. Many businesses play American music from their computers through YouTube. On one corner local hip-hop dancers perform. On another, a traditional Vietnamese string quartet. This is Hanoi: one foot still in the past, the other planted in the here and now.

Since economic reforms in the late 1980s, Vietnam has pursued a "capitalist-communism" path similar to China's. It's a manufacturing powerhouse, making everything from clothes to appliances and smartphones. One man goes to great lengths to show me how the Under Armour shirt he sells for five dollars here comes from a Vietnamese factory that then sells the shirt for eighty-five dollars in America. "Same, same, same. Why pay more? They just mark up to be greedy."

I'm wearing an Under Armour golf shirt. I rub its quality and then the one in the store. There is no difference.

Eating in Hanoi is an exalted glory. Charcoal or wood grills sit just a few inches above the street. They're tended by squatting locals. From your feet, up comes gourmet-caliber banh mi sandwiches stuffed with meats, fresh veggies, and spicy sauces, and bowls of pho so filling I could get by on one for a day.

At night I glance out at the vortex of hysteria that is the Old Quarter. Street sellers, drunk Aussies, supermodels selling tobacco, outdoor dance parties, clouds of smoke from cigarettes and cooking, beeping scooters: despite the tight confines, I don't feel claustrophobic. There is too much fun. I swim through the crowds, using large beer bottles as buoys till just before sunrise. It's similar to being caught in an undertow: best swim sideways for a while; it's the only way you'll get back to shore.

HANOI HILTON

At dawn, I'm on a mission, one that needs context, a bit more personal history.

The first political campaign to truly inspire me was John McCain's 2000 presidential run. His no-bullshit "straight talk" maverick approach appealed to me. McCain was not a usual politician. He spoke his truths and did not back down from a challenge. As a fourteen-year-old kid, I admired his willingness to take on the establishment of his own party on issues like the national debt and campaign finance reform. Back then, he seemed the closest thing to a pragmatic independent. During that run, Dad had him on *Meet the Press* and took me to Michigan for the interview. There I got to ride the "Straight Talk Express," McCain's well-known campaign bus, and watch a rally. When he found out my name was Luke, he nicknamed me "Skywalker" because he needed help taking on the "Evil Empire," which was then the Bush 2000 campaign.

Years later when I covered the Hill, I developed a relationship with McCain. He still called me Skywalker. We grabbed coffee a few times to trade barbs about sports teams and politics.

McCain had a wicked sense of humor. I once ran into him on a flight to Phoenix on my way to a bachelor party. When he found out the reason for my trip, he pulled me aside on the jet bridge and whispered in my ear, "Skywalker, if you get arrested outside a Scottsdale strip club—I'll fucking kill you!"

I cried when he died.

McCain didn't just campaign on his principles. He lived them the best he knew how. That's what inspired me the most about his life. So, on my second day in Hanoi, a bit hung over from all the fun of the night before, I walk to the Hỏa Lò Prison, known by Americans as the Hanoi Hilton, where McCain spent five years as a prisoner of war.

McCain arrived at the Hanoi Hilton with two broken arms and a broken leg after his plane got shot down over the city. Prison officials set two of his fractures without anesthetics. He had been bayoneted in the balls, and the Hỏa Lò staffers chose not to treat that wound or his other fractures. For his first year and a half at the prison, McCain was routinely tortured. The interrogators cracked his ribs, starved him, hung him from a meat hook, threw him in solitary.

The prison drove many men to the brink of suicide, including McCain.

How did he persevere?

The government razed most of the prison in the 1990s to make way for a shopping mall and apartment building. What remains is an entry guardhouse and part of the barracks. They've been converted into a museum. Built in the early 1900s by the French, the prison originally held rebellious Vietnamese. Their story makes up the bulk of the museum's presentation and gives a window into the atrocities of colonialism and anti-communist containment policies. Till 1954, Vietnamese suspected of engaging in seditious acts were chained to a log, beaten, and even beheaded. The prison's original guillotine holds a place of prominence in the museum's center. I'm creeped out by it.

A small portion of the museum is dedicated to the experience of American POWs. The history here is extremely propagandized. Pictures of American POWs playing basketball, eating Christmas dinner, drinking beer, and getting medical treatment hang on the surrounding walls. One plaque reads, "Americans were humanely treated while Vietnamese suffered." History is written by the winners.

A preserved cell housed Americans and Vietnamese. Cramped, dark, and damp, without a sliver of light, an affront to human rights. My admiration for John McCain grows. Shortly after being captured, when McCain was emaciated and weighed one hundred pounds, prison officials discovered McCain's father was an admiral in the navy. They offered McCain the chance to walk out of the Hanoi Hilton. The VC wanted the propaganda hit of showing mercy to an American naval officer's son. McCain refused. The American military's Code of Conduct stated the POWs should be released in the order they were captured. McCain believed in that code so much that he said he would rather die here.

The Vietnamese were not pleased. They tortured him all over again. Knocked out his teeth. Rebroke his arms. Cracked his ribs again. The prison's commandant then asked McCain a second time if he wanted to leave. McCain refused. So they threw him in a punishment box, a cell much like the tiny thing I'm staring at now. McCain stayed here for years.

What thoughts ran through his head? Where did he find the will to live?

After five long years, when it was at last his turn, McCain stumbled out of the Hanoi Hilton. Not only did he walk out after honoring the Code, but he went on to have a long and storied political career, raising a family rooted in public service and maintaining grace after two crushing losses as a presidential nominee. But even these accomplishments pale in comparison to his ability to forgive. In an interview McCain said, "There's certainly some individual guards who were very cruel and inflicted a lot of pain on me and others, but there's certainly no sense in me hating the Vietnamese . . . I hold no ill will toward them."[1]

The Hanoi Hilton is an odd place to find hope, but staring at that tiny hole and later walking out of the prison's gates, I feel strangely optimistic. I stroll over to Trúc Bạch Lake not far away, past some modern cartoon propaganda posters encouraging happy patriotic Vietnamese, including a child in an "I Love Vietnam" shirt. This lake is where McCain landed after being shot down. A small monument memorializing the episode stands on the lake's bank. Close to it, a group of kids play a Vietnamese version of hopscotch using wooden bamboo poles while their parents eat ice cream. It could be Central Park on a summer day. One of the parents smiles as I walk by the kids' game. It hits me. I'm from the country that napalmed innocent Vietnamese civilians, including kids just like this.

The strength to move on—what a gift.

HẠ LONG BAY

I seek out some beauty. Something lighter than a painful prison. Hạ Long Bay, a five-hour trek from Hanoi, is a place I've wanted to visit since I saw a poster of mossy islands in pristine waters at a Vietnamese restaurant when I was a kid.

I'm on the top deck as an old junk boat trudges on through the calm green waters. Around the boat, women in shade hats with bamboo oars push along their narrow canoes, which are packed with fish and grain. Rock formations spring up from the sea like tree stumps in a green grass field. Many are covered in moss. Birds perch at their tips. The topography identifies as Southeast Asia. There is an eerie-quiet vibe here, as though a monster lurks underneath, ready to pounce. The sun is so hot, but the guide says no swimming. Bacteria levels this time of year can be high.

The sun begins to set. Green water bleeds into an orange sky at dusk. The tiny islands we passed earlier appear dark, nefarious, and forbidding. Dinner is a rowdy affair, made all the wilder by the fact that the boat offers no Wi-Fi, so the boat's group of world travelers must, you know, talk to each other. There are Americans and Aussies and Turks and Qataris and maybe seven other nations represented on the boat. Over cheap French red wine and cheaper Vietnamese beer, well lubricated, I propose the world's worst toast: "There are small ships and tall ships and ships that sail the sea. But the true ships are friendships, and may they always be!" From there, the conversation unravels into countless stories of travel. Sojourns through Oman. An ankle break on a scooter in Thailand. After dinner the smokers walk out on the main deck. Everyone follows. The reflection of the moonlight spreads out like a white bedsheet over the bay. Smoke hangs in the air; there is not much wind. Sounds from other anchored boats skip across the surface as the clock approaches midnight. The bay feels alive. Most everyone is having one of those conversations to solve all the problems in the world. Without Wi-Fi, forced interaction has spurred a camaraderie and togetherness. That night the effect of Wi-Fi's power comes into being for me. If we live only within our own curated digital worlds, control our exposure, and limit what is culturally comfortable, we are not living in a real world at all.

On the five-hour trek back to Hanoi, I'm pitched against the window of a cramped van, swiveling through miles of waterlogged rice paddies. Some roads are smooth, most are not. An Irish accent breaks the silence, a middle-aged mom traveling with her grown daughter. She asks why some of the farms we're passing have stone tombs in the fields behind the home. A young guide answers from the front seat: "Two reasons: Children often take over the farm from their parents; they want the spirits of their moms and dads around for guidance. The dead also believe that if they are buried in the middle of their land, they'll come back to help raise the crop." I instantly relate: We all need our parents to guide. We also need them to help us grow anew. I'm carrying my parents with me. Perhaps I'm the new crop, being raised to comprehend what happened here.

SAIGON

To see Saigon is to realize the city doesn't want to linger among the country's ghosts. I saw some of them.

The nearby Củ Chi tunnels where the Vietcong resupplied nearly all their military efforts underground are still well intact and a reminder of the scale of the conflict. "How can you defeat what you cannot see?" is a question posed by the guide. You can't.

Or the Mekong Delta, the waterway not far out of town, where former Secretary of State John Kerry heroically commanded his Swift Boat under enemy fire among sampans and riverside villages. I always admired Kerry, and seeing how unforgiving the Mekong Delta was during war made me an even bigger fan. For a privileged Yale grad to subject himself to the water's danger was a patriotic affirmation of love for country. Ironically, the place that earned Kerry a Silver Star haunted his own presidential campaign. I felt these ghosts. But in Saigon, not so much.

It's a gleaming modern metropolis, lush with investment cash and sleek high-rises that signal a new era of Vietnam as a global financial and manufacturing powerhouse. Saigon has grown considerably in recent years. Young people from the countryside looking for a piece of economic salvation, coupled with a large influx of tourists and expats, has led to a near-constant standstill of traffic. Like any booming city, it has its problems. The metro system under construction is over budget and behind schedule. It adds to the gridlock: full city blocks across town are shut down as tunnels get dug out. Construction is a theme. From my room I see dozens of cranes moving steel beams, bricks, and mortar. A city being built before my eyes. There's a red star across the Saigon River. I think it's the red star of communism, that prominent symbol for the Vietcong. But looking again, it's the red star of Heineken Beer and part of a large collection of billboards announcing Heineken's presence in Vietnam.

There is no better metaphor for Saigon.

I walk bottom to top out on the pedestrian-friendly Nguyen Hue in District One, the epicenter of Saigon's twenty-four districts, and it's almost like walking through history. At one end is Saigon City Hall. Built by the French around 1900, it was modeled after city hall in Paris. Its regal stature, balconies, and a veranda with a bell tower make it seem more at home in Europe than Southeast Asia. In 1975, when the city fell to the communists, it was made into the People's Committee Building. Here, a statue of Ho Chi Minh holding a small child is placed out front and the street transforms from French opulence to proletariat meeting space. At night it's beautiful, lit up with shadows of the palm trees reflecting on parts of the building.

Farther up Nguyen Hue, Saigon transitions into its new financial identity. Towers emblazoned with the logos of global banks, posh hotels with lounge bars, where through the windows I see tall, striking women in miniskirts waiting on foreigners, some American, who are smoking cigars and sipping cocktails. Children run in circles, begging parents for ice cream or balloons. By a fountain a band covers American rock music. I take a seat on a bench, buy a beer for twenty-five cents from an old man out of a foam cooler, and take a listen as the band jams to the Cranberries' "Zombie." It's a song written about the Troubles in Northern Ireland, yet here it's not about that at all. A Vietnamese woman, in perfect English, belts out the lyrics about tanks and bombs but the fighting living in your head.

Prior to this walk I have only known Saigon as the place where America lost its sense of conviction. The infamous photograph of a helicopter evacuating the remaining American personnel from a Saigon rooftop in 1975, an endpoint for the tanks, bombs, guns, and death. An ending that was the site of America's most embarrassing defeat. What I've just seen is far from expectation. If America lost here, the Hue proves that the capitalist system clearly won. I know this not just because of the skyscrapers but because of the people window-shopping in Dior, Versace, and Louis Vuitton. Not exactly a traditional "People's Republic."

I think about the war, the communism-must-be-stopped ideology. All the protests in America, the lives shaped by the conflict, all the time my parents dedicated to it and how it defined their generation. All these years later, there is a fucking Versace store selling $900 shirts in the communist city of Saigon? Good old boys are slinging back whiskey on the rocks and rubbing waitresses' backs in lounge luxury hotel bars? I feel not just the futility of war but also the inevitability of self-interest. If capitalism is allowed to flourish, it will flourish anywhere.

There's a poster for chicken wings and cold beer in the window of a joint called Phatty's. The waitstaff are all young, female, and wearing tight mesh jerseys. A Buffalo Wild Wings knockoff with some sex appeal. I settle into journaling, glancing up only when I want another beer. I catch my waitress trying to read my words. Her name is Rose. She is extremely interested in my journal and the act of writing. Whether this is a flirtation to get a tip or genuine interest, I'll never know, but she hovers around me to practice her English.

"What are you writing about?"

"You, Rose!"

She half laughs.

"Where are you from?"

"Washington, DC, USA. You?"

"From a farm three hours away. What do you write about?"

"I write about my travel and what I see."

"What do you see here?"

I describe the room: The group of Brits drunk on beer yelling at a soccer match. A tall, well-dressed Aussie, standing at the bar, eating a full steak and drinking a bottle of red wine by himself. Waitresses always smiling and quick with a light for a cigarette for eager men. In a corner table, some Vietnamese young people in suits and cocktail dresses.

"Who are they?" I ask.

"Those are local kids. Very much money. They go to school in Hong Kong or London. Come here after work at the banks."

"You like Saigon?"

"Yes, my home is very boring."

"What do you want to do?"

"I want to travel. Take me with you!"

She isn't kidding. She picks up my journal and tries to make out my cursive. "Your writing is ugly!"

After a few tries to sound out a paragraph I've written, she says, "I really want to travel!"

132

I quip that there's no space in my suitcase. I tip her a lot. Her look of gratitude will sustain me for days. I don't want to leave this place.

I next walk by Saigon's Notre Dame Cathedral. Radiantly lit up at night, it really makes the city feel like "Paris of the Orient." I take a seat and reflect. Despite all of my past and all of America's—my country dropping millions of pounds of bombs on Vietnam and torching villages—the Vietnamese people could not have been nicer. I feel nothing but genuine love for them.

This country is far more than I expected, more layered and complex, and should not be avoided by any other American.

Or any other Orth or Russert.

THIRTEEN

Japan

THE STOP BEFORE HIROSHIMA

I feel like a traitor. For the first time in my life, I'm not in the United States for the Fourth of July. I'm in Bangkok. Fresh off a week around Thailand, where I avoided full-moon parties on tropical islands, walked sinful city streets, and survived the backpacker haven known as the Khao San Road. My trip was temples and Thai boxing—Muay Thai.

I was supposed to be in Hiroshima, Japan, but it felt improper to be there today, for obvious reasons, so I've extended my time in Thailand by a day. This is my first Fourth of July alone. As a kid, I spent the Fourth on Nantucket doing the fun stuff: the watermelon-eating contest, the BBQs, and then, as I got older, the bikinis, the crashing surf, and hanging with my good friend Mr. Miller from Milwaukee. The Fourth was a big day for my father and his sense of patriotism. "A celebration of the American ideals. Never forget how lucky we are to be here," he would say.

So it's all the more out of step to spend this Fourth in a constitutional monarchy where the king still exhibits great power. The day's challenge: find the United States in Bangkok.

I hit the streets and eventually spot a large Old Glory, swaying slowly in the sticky humid afternoon of the city's Nana neighborhood. Above it is a faded red, white, and blue sign that says, "THE TAVERN: A Small Slice of the States."

As the door closes behind me, I observe a great dive you might find in Buffalo. By the entrance stands a plastic table with a red plastic tablecloth full of free food. Sliders, chicken wings, nachos, hot dogs, ribs, and some Thai dumplings. On the walls are American license plates, posters of Cubs great Ron Santo, Elvis, Marilyn Monroe, George Washington, Abe Lincoln, and the Apollo 11 astronauts. Underneath the plastic coating of the bar, old base-ball cards and *Sports Illustrated* swimsuit pictures stare back at you. Dad took me to bars like this growing up, in DC and around the country. Beer for him, Coca-Cola for me. He'd let me feed a jukebox or play pinball if they had it. I think the dives made him feel connected to South Buffalo; they grounded him a bit or at least served as a haven where nobody bothered him. You don't pry at a dive.

"Welcome, kid!" yells a large older man in the back office.

I assume he notices me from security camera footage. He's the owner. Behind the bar are three Thai women with American flags affixed to their hair. At the stools are a hell of a cross section of American characters.

Across from me is a heavyweight of a man who hasn't shaved in weeks and whose backward khaki hat covers his red hair. A large USMC tattoo stands out on his sleeveless arm. He does not smile or nod when I wave.

Next to him is a fit guy in his forties from Long Island, who speaks quickly, drinks like a fish, and gets up only to use the restroom or play Whitesnake on the jukebox. My gut feeling tells me he's definitely an American in Thailand for the hookers.

On my right is an Indian man who works in Bangkok but lived in Minnesota for fifteen years. He loves the States and every year takes today off to do something American.

On my left is an army veteran, a Hawaiian born in Samoa and proud of his Samoan tattoos. He regales me with stories about being based in Texas and Florida in the late 1970s. "Rules did not exist like they do now. We did some crazy shit!"

I needed this moment. The eccentric quirkiness, that unity through dif-ferences that is distinctly American, shines through in a Bangkok bar. Our melting pot where we all came to find one another.

The Samoan army vet tries to ask the marine about his life, where he's from.

The marine speaks softly and lets out what is now his familiar refrain: "I wouldn't know." The army man asks about his service.

"Lot of time in the sandbox. Iraq."

The marine is coping with something. I try to signal to the Samoan to give the marine a break.

The Samoan won't have it. He grabs the marine and they go outside for a cigarette.

Whatever he says works. When they come back inside, they share a quick hug and the marine gets more engaged.

"Is he okay?" I whisper to the Samoan.

"Yeah," he says. "I told him about help he can get from the embassy here for veterans' affairs. Those benefits are available overseas."

An incredibly sweet gesture. God bless America.

HIROSHIMA

I leave Bangkok on an overnight red-eye to Hiroshima. Set to arrive on the early morning of July 5, deep in thought, I look out the window at the faint white clouds strewn through dark night sky.

It's important to go to Hiroshima first. I want to reach my own conclusions about what happened here.

Big Russ, my grandpa, the former World War II airman, never doubted the use of the atomic bomb. Neither did his buddies in the American Legion hall. They thought highly of Truman for doing it: *Why sacrifice more American lives when the war could be ended from the air?* Big Russ saw Truman as a hero.

My father's view was more nuanced but ultimately the same. His former boss, the great statesman Senator Daniel Patrick Moynihan, told Dad that the bomb saved his life. Had it not happened, Moynihan would have found himself on the front lines of an endless bloody conflict, as evidenced by how hard the Japanese fought over small Pacific islands and the emperor's promise that every man, woman, and child would fight for Japan's homeland. Dad once told me, "If any country was going to use it, it should be us. We're the only one responsible enough to use it."

But were we?

"I don't know!" That's what my Boston College history professor Seth Jacobs screamed out during his lecture on the bomb. It's odd for an academic to not have an entrenched opinion, but this was not an easy question. Like many scholars of the time, he could never make a definite conclusion because the arguments on both sides carried so much merit. President Truman felt an American invasion of Japan could lead to the deaths of millions. But General Eisenhower felt that the Japanese were ready to surrender and looking for a way out that could offer them the ability to maintain as much dignity as possible. In due time, the Japanese would have been starved of resources and ready to negotiate. Such an extinguishment of innocent human life was not necessary. From my own research as an undergrad, I was more closely aligned with Eisenhower but, like my professor, I didn't know.

I do know what inspired me to come to Hiroshima. During a dull day in May 2016 on Capitol Hill, I watched a speech given by President Obama, the first sitting president to visit Hiroshima since the US dropped the bomb. In my cubby of an office, I turned the volume up on NBC's raw live feed. His opening statements struck a nerve:

> Why do we come to this place, to Hiroshima? We come to ponder a terrible force unleashed in a not-so-distant past. We come to mourn the dead, including over 100,000 in Japanese men, women, and children; thousands of Koreans; a dozen Americans held prisoner. Their souls speak to us.[1]

I could not shake the last line. I knew I needed to hear from the people— those souls—referenced by President Obama.

I walk a few blocks from the train station to a local Hiroshima hotel. The Japanese are notorious for maximizing every square inch. My room is the size of a suburban walk-in closet. A tiny bathroom in which I cannot stand fully upright tucks itself behind a single bed. When I lie on that bed, my ankles dangle over the edge. From this position I can also touch the wall on the other side of the room. If I stand and jump, I hit my head on the ceiling.

Despite its prison-cell structure, I find myself sitting in the room longer than anticipated. I'm avoiding this city. I'm avoiding the Hiroshima Peace Memorial Park that I intend to visit. I feel the eeriness of being here, sitting in a hotel less than a mile from the bomb's epicenter. Seventy-two years ago, someone would have been sitting in a room like this when a white light flashed. It's almost as if I can still see that light seventy-two years later.

Curiosity eventually pushes me out the door. Within ten minutes there's the "A-Bomb Dome" or the Hiroshima Prefectural Industrial Promotion Hall. It's famous for being the closest building to the blast still standing. There isn't much to see. It's a hollowed-out frame of an edifice. But on a plaque outside is a picture of the dome, taken a few days after the bomb fell. In the 1945 photo, there's an endless wave of waist-high debris, as if death were swept up in the fragments of what was a bustling city.

A bridge leads to the Peace Park suspended between the banks of the Motoyasu River. I make my way to the main museum.

Considering the devastation, I'm surprised by the evenhandedness of the Japanese presentation. While certainly critical of America's decision, the museum's curators do not lack self-awareness when it comes to their nation's imperialist motivations during World War II. Still, most of the focus is on the bomb and its aftermath.

Three things stand out.

One is a miniaturized replica of the city as it stood at 8 a.m. on August 6, 1945, fifteen minutes before the bomb fell. Through a multimedia presentation, the diorama comes to life. Suddenly a white light flashes. A wave of destruction flows out over the replica city. Everything is decimated. Wiped away like a countertop after a meal. The quickness of the bombing stuns me. I see 92 percent of the city's 76,000 buildings destroyed. Like that.

The second thing is the account of twelve-year-old Naoki Mikami, his story memorialized by a pair of his ripped trousers, which today is one of the museum's exhibits, encased within glass. Mikami was in his schoolyard when the bomb fell. He managed, despite his serious injuries, to walk a few blocks to his home and find his mother. She had miraculously survived. His mom's words, printed in English, stare back at me from behind the exhibit's glass:

> He had nothing but his underpants on and was bleeding from his shoulders and back. His hair was completely burnt, leaving a pitch-black lump on his nose. The skin of his hand was peeled off to the nails, hanging as long as 15 centimeters. His appearance was too dreadful to be seen twice . . . all we could do was wait for his death. . . . Having difficulty breathing, he repeated that he wanted to go home.[2]

Seventy-two-year-old bloodstains, still on the trousers, hint at the horror of the story.

The third thing is a decayed tricycle. A three-year-old named Shinichi Tetsutani was riding it in front of his house when the bomb hit. His father buried him with it in the backyard of their home, knowing how much his son loved the tricycle. In 1985 the father felt compelled to dig it up and donate it to the museum. It shows the uncompromising capacity of the bomb to kill. Nobody and nothing were spared.

That's as much as I can handle.

Outside, I walk past a memorial cenotaph, a hall of remembrance and a peace flame, lit in 1964, continuously burning, scheduled to be extinguished when the world is free of nuclear weapons. So probably never.

This event happened so long ago, and it still hits at my raw core.

I find a bench in the small Honkawa Park, just across the river from the memorial, bury my head into my hands, and softly weep. I'm not naive enough to think that the Japanese were the good guys, done wrong by the Americans. I paid attention to the school lessons on Pearl Harbor. I've heard about Japan's evil imperialism—its subjugation of Korean women, its numerous human rights violations. Still, the majority of us on this planet are often collateral damage for decisions made by flawed men. Leaders possess the power to eliminate billions of people in a single day. Sure, I knew it from history books, but seeing it here—I understand the precariousness of existence. If eighty thousand could be killed instantly in 1945, what's possible today? Stories about unsecured nukes in Russia and Pakistan take on a deeper meaning, as do the men who have their hands on the codes—the impulsive, aggressive, egotistical men. There's a sense of deep uneasiness.

I become forever opposed to nuclear weapons. Hiroshima did not need to happen.

THE CARP

On my way back to the hotel, my eyes dart from one unreadable Japanese sign to the next. I see a couple. The man, gray haired and in his seventies, wears number fifty-one, for a player named Suzuki. His wife wears number nine, for Maru. Spontaneously, I tug on the man's sleeve.

"Baseball game?"

He looks at me, puzzled. His wife understands.

"Baseball, yes."

"Is there a game tonight?"

"Yes, game."

"Thank you!"

Their jerseys say "Carp," so I google "Hiroshima Carp." I discover that the local team started in 1950, five years after the bomb, as a means of giving the citizens something to brighten their day. Baseball had been introduced to Japan by American teachers in the late 1800s. A professional league started in the 1920s, and the country has been mad for the sport ever since. The Carp, long underfunded and lovable losers, have recently put together some solid seasons. By luck, they have a game tonight at their home park, Mazda Zoom-Zoom Stadium, against the Yomiuri Giants.

I have to offset the weight of the day. Baseball has always been a release for me. Each year on the anniversary of Dad's death, I try to go to a game. Often alone—sitting in the stands, sipping beer, and getting lost in memories of the countless games we went to. I like to think I remember all of them, dating back to when I was an infant.

I follow the couple in front of me, and soon we're surrounded by a procession of red hats and red jerseys. It reminds me of my beloved hometown Washington Nationals and their red hats.

Up in the distance, a gleaming new stadium rises. The gray skies of the afternoon give way to a soft pink dusk, the perfect backdrop for baseball. This is divine. The old lady I spoke to earlier looks back, points to the ticket counter, and leaves with a smile and a wave.

A few seats remain in the left field bleachers. I buy one.

As the turnstile clicks, the concourse is an exercise in jubilation. Everyone is enthusiastic and happy. The beauty of baseball. It buoys me. I run to the clubhouse store, buy a T-shirt, jersey, cap, and two large noisemakers. It's almost like I'm a kid again. As I walk the concourse, I high-five random strangers and yell, "Go Carp!" The Carp fans take it in stride and smile at the large, sweaty white guy grinning ear to ear.

I've watched baseball in America, the Caribbean, and Latin America. After an inning here, it's obvious nobody does baseball better than the Japanese. Fans cheer and chant all game. The chants are all positive. There is no heckling or boorish drunken behavior. Fans stay in their seats during the game and get up to move only between innings. Positivity cloaks itself in this park.

The stands are immaculate. There is no trash. Every fan is expected to pick up their own waste and dispose of it in its proper recycling bin on the concourse. Concession stands run smoothly; lines are rarely longer than two minutes. The bathroom is safe and sanitary. I get a bowl of warm noodles with beef and a tall, frosty beer, and when I try to tip the vendor, she looks puzzled. A man behind me explains in heavily accented English that there is no tipping in Japanese culture. Good service is expected.

Once back at my seat, it's humid and I begin to sweat, enough to have to dab my face with a napkin every thirty seconds. A mom in front of me notices, reaches into her bag, and gifts me a Hiroshima Carps paper fan. She even fans me off for a little bit before handing it over. The kindness is beyond measure.

Darkness settles in around the seventh-inning stretch. It's now a comfortable summer night. On the jumbotron, a crazed man in face paint implores fans to start singing. On cue, all thirty-two thousand Carp fans stand up and start waving red balloons that look like large inflatable condoms. I'm laughing so hard—but I'm also upset I did not get a condom balloon myself. In unison they sing the team fight song. It is so catchy that I'm able to hum along after one verse. After the third chorus, all the fans release the air from the lower part of the balloons, and they go flying into the sky to thunderous applause. Immediately, a volunteer in each section picks them up. They are then sanitized to be used again.

In the ninth inning I walk the ring of the concourse. Though the Carp play rather listlessly, down 5–0, not a single person has left early. At a railing that overlooks center field, four little boys in their Carp shirts and hats hold their gloves and yell for a ball. I think back to the kids mentioned in the museum exhibit earlier, the kids who died in the blast. They were just like these kids, probably baseball fans too. But the Japanese people have the ability to move forward, rebuild, forgive. I leave the ballpark with gratitude.

KYOTO

A dream is about to be achieved. Nobody knows it but me.

My dream dates back to a video I watched in science class in sixth grade about the physics of speed. Less air resistance means more momentum. The example the video cited was the bullet trains of Japan. From that day on, I've always wanted to ride one.

The long Shinkansen train with the platypus-style beak pulls up to the platform on time. Instead of nonsensical garbled noise that is the American train intercom, soothing music emanates from overhead speakers. The Japanese, neatly dressed, line up in an orderly fashion to board. Seeing that I'm a foreigner, a conductor with white gloves personally guides me to my coach seat, hoists my bag into a luggage compartment, and bows. My excitement is to the point where I'm laughing with glee.

The floors are clean enough to eat off of. There are no quiet cars because nobody would do something so disrespectful as make a phone call.

The train speeds toward Kyoto at up to two hundred miles an hour. So fast that when I stand up, I hold the railings above the seats and move my feet like I'm trudging through snow. It takes a few tries before I master the art of walking safely. How I wish my dad had been able to experience this. He'd love it so much. Dad knew how much I adored trains, mostly because I hated flying, and he promised one day we'd go to Japan to see "the real ones."

We used to ride the old Amtrak regional trains to New York City. We'd rarely sit in our seats. Dad would instead direct us to the café car, where he'd sprawl newspapers over the table and read them cover to cover while eating a microwaved hot dog. I'd lean my back up against the window to spread out my legs and read the sports section. Those trains were rusty, grimy, and dilapidated, but I loved the time with Dad. We got excited when the Acela higher-speed train came online in the Northeast Corridor—but it isn't comparable to this.

As the Japanese countryside whizzes by, I think about the old man. I find the café car and sit down behind a table. I sprawl out a Japanese newspaper I cannot read. Thankfully, they don't serve microwaved hot dogs, though I kind of wish they did.

Kyoto is the cultural capital of Japan, full of countless shrines and temples. It was set for the same fate as Hiroshima, but Henry Stimson, the secretary of war, had honeymooned in Kyoto and implored President Truman not to destroy such a beautiful city. Stimson said blowing up Kyoto, with its religious significance, would forever push the Japanese away from the United States. Thankfully, Stimson's view won out.

The majority of the country practices Shinto, a worship of nature that's tied in with indigenous spirituality and nationalistic undertones. The most famous Shinto temple is in Kyoto: the Fushimi Inari, named after the god of rice, the backbone crop in Japan.

At the temple's main gate at the base of a mountain, with stairs stretching to the top, I start out.

It's about a ninety-minute trek in the excruciating summer heat. I pass through thousands of toriis, orange gates that mark an approach to a shrine. Individuals, families, and even corporations can purchase a gate as an offering. The toriis at Inari arrange themselves over a stone path that goes to the top of the mountain.

The vertical mountain face becomes brutally difficult. Drenched in sweat, I finally get to the top and see the rows of toriis, appearing like orange dominoes below. It feels like, in exchange for the trek, I've been given an audience with Inari. I've read that Inari grants wishes. At the base of the mountain is the main offering hall and a section where you can write down your wish to Inari and the other Shinto gods. The process is called "dedicating an ema." For a few dollars, I get a wooden board with a string attached. I write my name, my address, and my wish.

"May the Buffalo Bills win the Super Bowl in my lifetime. Luke Russert. Washington, DC." An attendant takes it and hangs it up on a wall.

My dad's wish, now my own. I wish he could see Kyoto too.

Maybe he can.

TOKYO

"Go!" I excitedly yell to myself. Two thousand five hundred people move at once when the light turns green. I'm at Shibuya Crossing, believed to be the busiest intersection in the world. I've emerged from a train station that serves 2.4 million people a day. I walk into a mosh pit of humanity. It's somehow incredibly orderly. I'm having too much fun, filming it on my iPhone in a 360-degree circle like a goofball idiot. I come into the neon-sign-laden streets. Anything I could ever want and would never need is at my fingertips. KFC, beer, clothes, crafts, sushi—all of it flashes onto my retinas.

After a few turns to try to find my small hotel, the pressure from all the light releases considerably. Off the main drag are narrow pedestrian streets. Small green trees sprout from gray concrete as a reminder that true nature does still exist. This is Tokyo, chaotic and zen.

The main streets may be lit up like Times Square, but the side alleys and back ways are local, nondescript, empty of unnecessary light and full of culture, little urban villages strung together to make up this megacity of nine million.

I fall in love fast with Tokyo because it's a city I can't quite figure out. From the dockside tuna markets to the gardens outside the Imperial Palace to the trendy cool kids in Harajuku hanging outside superchic shops and Airstreams that sell craft beer—there is no *real* Tokyo because Tokyo can't sit still long enough to figure itself out. It is everything and I love it.

There is nothing I have to see and nothing I can't miss.

There is one thing I would like to see, though. Mary has a fascination with otters. She considers them the undisputed cutest animals in the world. She turned me on to following otter Instagram accounts, the majority of which come from Japan; some Japanese keep small otters as pets. Yes, it's pretty silly—a grown man in his thirties following pet otter accounts on social media. I wish I could chalk that up to a relationship making me do crazy things, but I really like them.

While scrolling through Instagram over breakfast, I use a translation feature to read a post about an upcoming otter art exhibition in Tokyo. It's showcasing the work of Instagram user Ponchan918.

Ponchan918 is one of the most popular otter accounts in Japan. I've followed it for years. The person behind it is a woman named Ayako. She's the caregiver of a famous small-clawed otter named Takechiyo, which translates to "bamboo." Ayako posts daily videos and pictures of Takechiyo and has more than two hundred thousand followers. Mary would often send me videos or pictures of the otter as a pick-me-up during the workday.

I have to meet this otter.

I hop a metro to the warehouse district of Asakusabashi, home of the otter art exhibit. Unlike other parts of Tokyo, this one isn't well marked. It takes thirty minutes of walking in circles to find the gallery. The exhibit is quiet, but I barrel through a small wooden door and nearly knock over the petite curator.

"Are these the otters?" I yell.

Her befuddled, bewildered expression shows itself for two seconds before Japanese modesty returns. She nods.

Bulletin boards are covered with pictures of famous Japanese Instagram otters. I recognize most of them because Mary or I follow them. But I can't seem to find Ayako. I approach a desk.

"Excuse me. Where is Ayako?"

The curator takes out her phone and uses Google Translate.

"Ayako has gone home. An hour ago."

I'm devastated. I missed my chance.

On the train ride back, there's a new post from Ponchan918. It details Ayako's time at the gallery opening. Without thinking, I write on her comments wall about how I had gone to great lengths to see her and was upset that we didn't connect at the gallery. The weirdness that I, a grown man in my thirties, can complain to a person behind a Japanese otter Instagram account doesn't really set in. I truly feel I know Ayako because I've seen so many of her videos of Takechiyo. I know the rooms of her apartment; her other animals, like the tortoise named Ratasu that she sometimes posts about. I know she likes golf; dotes on her adorable daughter, Reina; and rarely shows her own face in accordance with Japanese customs on modesty.

That evening a direct message comes through on my Instagram. It's from Ponchan918!

"Do you want to meet Takechiyo?"

I reread it four times before I know it's real. Immediately, I respond that it would be my honor.

Ayako then apologizes for missing me, a crazy fan. Using a translator app, it takes her twenty minutes to explain that we can meet tomorrow morning at her apartment. Her friend can serve as a translator and I can have a half hour with Takechiyo the otter.

I can't believe it.

The next morning, I hand the cab driver Ayako's address. Japanese taxicabs are the best in the world. The driver wears a full uniform with white gloves. He's diligent, meticulously detailed, and honest. Within ten minutes, I see Ayako standing on the street with her iPhone.

"You are Luke."

Next to her is a tall man named Damian. He'll translate in flawless English.

Ayako lives in a luxury high-rise. In space-starved Japan, she is very well off. I remove my shoes in the mudroom and walk through the second door. To my left I notice Ratasu the turtle, a common fixture on her page. Then I see Ayako's kitchen, her couch, her TV, and her daughter's toys. I know where everything belongs because I've seen it so many times on Instagram. It's like seeing the set of your favorite TV show.

Down a hallway, Ayako calmly knocks on a door. After four small thuds, a set of little webbed hands sticks out under the door. Damian tells me this means that Takechiyo is ready for visitors.

The odor of the otter is repugnant, but I don't care. Takechiyo bolts past my feet and out the door into the kitchen. He hops up on a chair, then a table, and finally motions for me to come over. The otter knows how to impress a fan. I extend my hand, and he grabs it between his webbed claws. Ayako motions for me to play tug-of-war with him using a towel. This goes on for ten minutes.

It's obvious this otter knows he's a star. He exhibits many of the same egocentric mannerisms I saw in some of my colleagues in TV. He knows when to pose for a photograph, how to position his jaw. After exactly a half hour, Takechiyo looks me square in the eyes, nods, and scampers back to his room. He even knows when he's off the clock! Ayako speaks to him in Japanese and closes the door. Soon, his webbed hand emerges below the door frame. Ayako tells me to give him a handshake goodbye. I obey. She thanks me for coming and escorts me outside.

I've just lived the height of our new social media reality. A connection with an otter in Japan over Instagram becomes a connection in person. The absurdity of it all! The world feels smaller today. It also feels kinder. Maybe the connective tissue of social media could be real. What came through technology and those small social media screens really was attainable in life.

It's hard to leave Tokyo. It's hard to leave Japan. I've fallen in love with the country's decency, its honor, and its order. It's odd, I suppose, to travel the world, cutting ties with the demands of the past, seeking a free-spirited existence and yet craving the orderliness of Japan. But it's more than just an orderliness. It's the respect and decorum of the country. At the airport, a fellow American tells me how he lost his phone and wallet on a public bus in Tokyo. Somebody returned it. They saw his plastic room key with the hotel name on it and took time out of their day to bring it to the lobby. Not a single thing was missing.

That's Japan.

It's provided a window into such a promising world. Mom has never been. I promise on my train ride for the flight home that I will bring her. For now, it feels like my own personal benchmark—will I feel this good about myself or a place ever again? My time in Asia is a true accomplishment. I made peace with some complicated history and came out a more understanding person. Forgiveness goes so far. I know I'm blessed, but Cambodia, Vietnam, Japan—they've truly made me feel it.

FOURTEEN

Ephesus

The baseball hat sits over my left knee, just as it has through every country. It was there a few weeks ago in Asia; it'll be wherever I am. I look down at it as the bus cruises through the eastern edge of the Turkish port city of Izmir. "CG" stares back at me from just above the bill. It's reassuring to see a piece of Corey Griffin always around. The charitable foundation named in his memory made up the hats. A small batch at first, but they grew in popularity until they were a hot item. Anyone who ever knew him wanted one.

The hat shows its wear now, the pristine navy blue faded to an almost grayish color after months of sweat, sun, salt water, and crude washes in hotel room sinks. The "CG" still shines through in an off-white color, undeterred and ready for adventure—just like Corey.

Like Dad's, Corey's spirit has guided my travels. In particular, Corey's spirit has guided me to Turkey, and specifically to Ephesus, a place where many believe the Virgin Mary lived out her final years. A place where people come for intense reflection and powerful prayer. I close my eyes and remember.

Corey was a devout Catholic, the friend who always nudged me to go to Mass on Sunday morning, even when we'd barely slept off Saturday night. We met at BC; he was a year behind me. Smart, loyal, humorous, he was acutely aware of his blessed life. A highly regarded hockey player, he found success as a venture capitalist. His charitable heart was renowned too: a founding member of the "Ice Bucket Challenge" to fight ALS, Corey raised hundreds of thousands of dollars. He once said to me, "If you're not giving, you're taking."

We grew even closer after graduation, spending summer days together on

151

Nantucket and linking up in Boston and New York. We'd text, we'd phone. Corey was good about checking in. He was never down, always sunny. His personality was infectious. Guys wanted to drink with him. Old men wanted to fish with him. Women wanted to marry him or chase him around town. I was convinced for a time that my own mother preferred Corey over me!

Corey lived to experience everything the world had to offer.

He regaled me with stories from his travels. Flying helicopters in Montana, surfing off the coast of Portugal, shark fishing in the Caribbean. One trip very special to him was his visit to Medjugorje. It's a small village in Bosnia where many Catholics believe the Virgin Mary appeared as an apparition in 1981. When one of Corey's dad's closest friends was diagnosed with terminal cancer and given months to live, Corey's dad took his friend and made a pilgrimage to Medjugorje. His friend was cured, a real miracle. Corey went back to the town with his own family. He felt the spirit of the Virgin Mary. "It was unreal, such a powerful place," he told me.

I knew in my own travels I wanted to feel that religious ecstasy Corey had described. Ephesus in Turkey was my first chance to do it.

"Do you think she lived here? You're Catholic," Ecrin, my guide for the day, asks me. She's a slender Turk, a Muslim with dyed blond hair, olive skin, and dark eyes. A beautiful woman with an inviting face.

"I have to feel it out first," I say. "But I have faith."

The bus we ride in hugs the curves of the windy road up Bülbül Mountain. I've always accepted the mystery of faith. The resigned acceptance that you will never be able to prove that your God or your savior was ever here on this earth. Or if they were, that they were more than mere mortals with an evocative story. On this bus ride I think about the comfort that comes from connecting a spiritual figure to an ordinary world. Right now, it means seeing the Virgin Mary's final earthly refuge.

After the death of her son and prior to her own heavenly assumption—what the Catholic Church hints at but will not take an official position on—Mary spent her last years on earth a few miles outside the ancient Greek city of Ephesus. Ephesus today sits near modern-day Selçuk, ninety minutes from Izmir. Mary lived in a simple stone dwelling on a peaceful hillside, with a mountain behind it and the Aegean Sea in front. Here, the mother of God stayed safe from persecution and reflected on the enormity of her life.

"Why do people think Mary was here?" I ask.

Ecrin's smile lights up. She recites the story, told so many times that it is like a musician singing a hit.

Anne Catherine Emmerich was a bedridden German nun. During her life in the late 1700s and early 1800s, it was alleged she was stigmatic, meaning Christ's wounds on the cross appeared on her body. Emmerich also claimed to communicate with the Virgin Mary. Many were skeptical, but the rich detail of her visions combined with the stigmata persuaded church officials and noblemen to visit her.

One visitor was the famous German poet Clemens Brentano. He spent many days by her bed, transcribing her visions. He later published two books about them, one about the Virgin Mary. In *The Life of the Blessed Virgin Mary*, Emmerich describes a major port city in Asia Minor, which was Ephesus. The Virgin Mary lived three and a half hours away on foot, on the side of the hill overlooking the Aegean Sea. Her house was built from stone, different from the others around it. An apostle visited her and looked after her. This apostle was, according to Emmerich, John.

In the late 1800s, inspired by Brentano's books, a group of French priests set out to find Mary's house to test the validity of Emmerich's claims. Using Emmerich's details, they found a mountain overlooking the Aegean Sea, a three-and-a-half-hour hike from Ephesus. On a wooded, rocky slope near a stream was a house unlike any other, as it was made of stone. Locals, both Christians and Muslims, called it "the door of the holiest." This, combined with John's documented presence in Ephesus, and Jesus' request of John to take care of his mother after his crucifixion, proved enough for the French priests to say the Virgin Mary lived out her days on this mountain.

As Ecrin finishes her account, I feel a warmth that I felt whenever I was around Corey. Like I did three years ago when I was seated next to him, just laughing and living.

Within minutes of emailing him an invite to my birthday dinner in the summer of 2014, Corey said he'd be there. It was the night before an annual event on Nantucket Island named after my father, to benefit the local chapter of the Boys and Girls Club. My birthday on Friday, Dad's charity event on Saturday, recovery on Sunday: the plan was for Corey and me and a few other guys to make a weekend out of it.

For a month we texted back and forth about how excited we were. Any "planning" was just an excuse to gab.

On August 15, 2014, Corey arrived in Nantucket in the early evening. I could smell his cologne before I saw him. His date for the weekend had canceled due to her work, so he was solo. He proudly announced that after dinner he planned to go to the local music bar, the Chicken Box, to find a date for the next night's event.

I laughed, not because it was absurd but because in all likelihood he would pull it off.

There were seven around the table that night: three couples and Corey. Steaks, lobster, wine. A feast. Everyone put on the stupid birthday hats and sang for me when the cake came out. I glanced over at Corey. Pure joy as he sang.

"Luker, you coming to the Box with me?"

"Nah. I need to rest up. Have to give a speech tomorrow night. You have fun."

We shook hands and hugged. He climbed into a friend's convertible and went off into the warm summer night.

My mom burst into my bedroom and flicked on the lights.

"Luke, something serious happened, get up. Corey drowned!"

"What?"

I rubbed my eyes and looked at the clock. It was around 4 a.m.

"He drowned! Not at the beach, down at the pier." In shock, she barely made sense of the words she was speaking. The finality of a young life not fully registering.

I picked up my phone and noticed a barrage of text messages. "Oh shit,"

I murmured. But maybe this was a mistake. Maybe he'd just passed out and had been brought back with CPR.

When I connected with my friend Reilly, who'd called the house and told Mom, I knew right away that Corey was gone. Reilly's voice was crushed.

"Luke, he drowned. He died. He died. Oh my God."

I didn't cry right away. It was too unreal.

I reached out to some friends who had been with him that night. After the bar closed, a group made their way down to the town pier. They jumped off a building roof and into the harbor. It was a Nantucket summer rite of passage. The landing spot was deep—where the ferries came in. Thousands of people had made that jump without issue.

I was told Corey had his wits about him. He had always been an adventurous guy. He jumped into the channel.

Yet something happened upon impact with the water. Corey injured his neck in such a manner that it caused him to drown. Resuscitation efforts were fruitless.

Corey was dead at twenty-seven.

A policeman knocked on our door to confirm the terrible news. I called Corey's father and told him I'd head to the hospital. Friends who were at the dock and had tried to save him were there, sobbing, shaken, and bewildered. I hugged them all close.

Since I was not family, I was not technically permitted to see Corey. I pushed past a nurse anyway. She tugged on my shoulder while I was blocked by another. I caught a glimpse of Corey's feet. My friend, the one I'd hugged just hours before, dead beneath a white sheet.

As the sun began to rise, I drove home. I was broken. Emotions I hadn't felt since Dad had died six years earlier flooded over me. I screamed out, "Why is this happening again?! Why? Please make it stop. I can't do this again!" A pain in my stomach became debilitating. My hand shook as I tried to grip the wheel. I needed to get off the road. I stopped at a little beach by the harbor and waded into the water.

I was the only person there that early in the morning. A beautiful sky pinkened the horizon, the sun shining through in a mix of orange and blue.

I'd never seen a sunrise like this. It was simultaneously beautiful and reassuring, the promise of a new day. I felt it was Corey telling me he was okay. I cried. Not tears of pain, exactly, but something approaching gratitude. I was thankful that my friend was at peace.

My stomach pain went away.

It's a warm Turkish summer morning and, as mornings go, almost as beautiful as the day that broke after Corey's death.

I chat with Ecrin as we walk into some woods.

"You know I travel a lot, too, Luke."

"You do?"

"Yes, every foreigner I give a tour to, I pick up a little piece of them and their country. I've given tours to over seventy-five different countries! I feel like I've been to them all."

It's a good point: Sometimes you travel through conversation. Sometimes you learn from the world by giving a bit of yourself.

"What should I pick up from Turkey, Ecrin?"

"The tree branch should be bent when it is young."

I'm confused. "Explain."

"You're young, Luke. Like me. You're learning things. You're learning things in Turkey. It's good to learn young because when you're grown up, your mind is harder to bend."

"I'm stealing that, Ecrin!"

"Turkey gives it to you for free!"

If you're not giving, you're taking.

The sun rises overhead. Streaks of yellow cut through the green canopy of the Taurus firs. The morning dew beneath the shadows of the trees keeps the path to the house temperate and cool. A statue of the Virgin Mary tells me I'm close.

The air is crisp and pure on this hillside. My eyes lock onto a large tree trunk, slightly elevated atop a flower bed. Its branches hang over a stone house, almost fanning it in a way.

"That's the house, right?" I ask.

"Yes," says Ecrin. "Remember, it has been reconstructed. Only the foundation is thought to be original. But that's what it looked like."

As I walk to the entrance, a feeling of serenity takes hold. Any noise is blocked out. Inside is a red Turkish carpet, laid out in a welcoming fashion. It leads to the shrine of the Virgin. Beneath a stone archway is an altar. Atop it, the familiar statue of the Virgin mother. The small scale of the house, the total quiet, the mystical energy lurking in its foundation: it gives off a unique feeling of intimacy. Intimacy in the sense that what I feel inside this home is between the Virgin Mary and me. Everything else disappears.

I say her prayer, the Hail Mary, and bring my mind to a deeply reflective place. I reach a state of clarity and feel a sense of purpose. A voice in my head takes over. *I'm supposed to be here. I'll know how far to go, I'll feel it.*

I then see Corey's face, his light blue eyes and his boyish smile. He stares back at me, a soft sunny horizon behind him. He doesn't say a word. I know he walks with me.

"Luke, you must see this!"

Ecrin marches me over to a section of the grounds dedicated to Mary's relationship with Islam. A plaque explains how Mary is the only woman to be named in the Quran. Muslims dignify her as the mother of a prophet. Some passages about her righteousness and purity are referenced, such as this one from chapter 3, verse 42: "Mary, God has chosen thee, and purified thee, he has chosen thee above all women."

Close by are stands for votive offerings. I light a candle and give thanks. When I open my eyes, I see a group of Muslim women in hijabs, their heads bowed, deep in prayer.

"This is a holy site for them too," Ecrin says.

I walk in step behind the women toward the wishing wall, a large fence where visitors write down their prayer requests. I see prayers in numerous languages from people of many different faiths. I add mine to the collection. I take a moment to walk by myself, into the trees away from the other people. Through breaks in the branches I can see the Aegean Sea off in the distance. I think about the reasons to believe. I have a sense that this is all too obvious.

The apostle John was tasked with keeping Mary safe. What better place than a hill far from Jerusalem? A place with ample fresh water and in an area known for relatively peaceful pagans at the time? Then I think of Mary's earthly life, from the virginal birth of Jesus, to watching her son die on a cross, and to the final ascension into heaven. Nobody here would know Mary's story. She was free to be herself, to reconcile her experience. A light breeze comes through the woods, softly rattling the branches. I picture Mary walking among these trees, staring out at the sea and into the sky, serene and safe. I'm a believer in Ephesus.

I turn back to the main path and find Ecrin.

"Hey, Luke, what does the CG on your hat mean?"

FIFTEEN

Senegal

"One's destination is never a place but rather a new way of looking at things." I come across the quote from the famed writer Henry Miller somewhere after Asia and Ephesus. I point my compass toward Africa, a continent so involuntarily intertwined with the American experience.

"Welcome to Senegal, the gateway to West Africa!" It's the sign in customs as I rub the sand out of my eyes after the transatlantic overnighter. It's fitting. I am entering from where so many left. This Senegalese coastline, the starting point, all those centuries ago, of America's original sin. Back then a trip where the reward for surviving the disease-ridden ships was a tortured life of bondage.

There are other reasons to be here—the National Geographic videos I watched as a kid showing wildlife scampering across African grasslands, the natural beauty, the democracy that flourishes here in Senegal and has for generations—but before I see much else, I feel I owe it to my nation's history to see where its most evil chapter began.

This is why I'm in Dakar.

Oumar knows that. He is my guide today: six foot, three inches tall, two hundred pounds, reassuring smile, dark skin, with an optimism that makes him instantly likable. He will take me to Gorée Island, he says, when he picks me up in his white sedan, but will drive me first through modern-day Dakar.

"Are you in the service, Luke?" he asks.

"What do you mean?"

"Your beard. You are a big man. We see some American military here before they go to Mali and fight."

Senegal, an oasis of democratic stability in the region, has also served as a gateway to US counterterrorism operations in Western African nations.

"I'm not military. I'm just a traveler."

"Good! Then I can be more honest!"

I laugh.

The Dakar he shows me on the way to Gorée Island is a city in transition. Only some roads are paved. Modern high-rises and walled-off homes share streets with tin-roof shacks and steel skeletons of projects left unfinished. Locals cram onto the backs of dingy minibuses that spew black soot. Oumar remains upbeat about all this, excitedly pointing out landmarks, office buildings, and restaurants.

He spent ten years living in Chicago. He says he enjoyed America and worked his way up to managing a Subway restaurant, on his way to living his own slice of the American dream.

"You know Subway restaurants, Luke?"

"Of course. Why?"

"Important man like you, I did not think went to Subway restaurant."

"I eat anywhere, man."

I smile back at Oumar, but my mind lands on a conversation I had with Dad one summer when I worked on a delivery truck in Nantucket moving freight. It was backbreaking work, but it paid well. I was a driver's assistant that summer, seasonal help to speed up the job. I still recall so much.

"How was the day?" Dad said as he looked up from his news clippings. A ball game was on the TV in the den.

"Not bad. Worked a shift with Mike, the army vet who fought in Somalia. The guy that can parallel park the twelve-wheeler like a golf cart. We moved in an entire living room. But this lady didn't tip or even let us use the bathroom. That sucked."

Dad looked disgusted. Disrespect toward working folks was an affront to everything he valued. "Remember how you felt. Small, right? What has she done that warrants that? Nothing! Probably some blue-blood asshole." The man didn't curse much, but I could tell his own red American blood boiled.

Later that week Mom, Dad, and I went to a cocktail party. Pure torture for Dad, who found it full of silly pomp and predictable questions, including the eternally stupid, "Hey, Tim, what do you really think about politics?" But Mom liked to socialize, and I could usually sneak a drink from a sympathetic bartender. By happenstance, the lady who denied me the use of her bathroom came over to say hello to Dad. She then gushed over his "handsome son." I half smiled back, the contempt readable in my pupils.

She didn't recognize me. Maybe because I had on a polo shirt and khakis instead of my cargo shorts and work boots. Or because only now was I proper and presentable.

When she left, I told Dad who she was. "Hmmm," he responded.

He glared over at her as she made small talk with a man in a blazer with a pocket square and loafers with no socks.

"Well, she's dead to us. Don't ever be that person. Let's get the hell out of here."

My mind comes back to Dakar. I sit up in the front seat and engage Oumar.

"Why did you return to Senegal?"

"I missed my son. I could not get him papers to come to America, and I felt guilty letting him grow up without a dad in the house. I was one of twenty-three kids, so I did not get much attention from my father. I did not want that for my son."

"You were one of twenty-three kids?!"

He laughs. "Luke, that was common in Senegal long ago. A strong man would have many children with a few strong women."

Like 95 percent of his nation, Oumar is Muslim. He does not consider himself to be pious. It's Friday today and he's missing prayers to give me a tour. He explains that his Sufi sect is more mystical. "It's about direct spiritual closeness with God. About tolerance and acceptance. We hate extremists like ISIS. I like to go dancing at night!"

We pass a popular nightclub. Oumar nudges my shoulder. "If you come back tonight at eleven, the most beautiful women in the world will be inside. I promise!"

A short time later we move on to Gorée Island.

GORÉE ISLAND

The sun burns my face as the ferry presses on toward the island. We're both sweating on the top deck. Oumar has no hat or sunglasses. He shouts over the loud hum of the diesel engine: "This is where we will see the Door of No Return!"

Local history says Gorée Island was the last piece of African land that millions of men and women stood on before sailing into a life of slavery, often in the Americas. Though today some scholars peg the number in the thousands. When we disembark from the boat, Oumar hands me an informational pamphlet from UNESCO:

> Ruled in succession by the Portuguese, Dutch, English and French, its architecture is characterized by the contrast between the grim slave-quarters and the elegant houses of the slave traders. Today it continues to serve as a reminder of human exploitation and as a sanctuary for reconciliation.[1]

Without the weight of its history, Gorée Island would be a charming place. No cars, a sparsely populated island, teal-blue water lapping lightly on clean beaches. We start off at an informative museum that explains the history of the slave trade in Senegal and West Africa. The level of brutality and sheer volume of the trade come to life through artifacts and depictions of the time, including sketches of shackled, grossly overcrowded slave ships. The physical and psychological pain inflicted on the enslaved is well demonstrated and well documented. It all happened right here. It feels immeasurably real in the moment.

"Hey, Luke! Is that you? Haha!"

I glance over. Oumar points at a portrait of a bearded French slave trader.

My heart sinks. I see the resemblance, especially the oval-looking eyes. I grow a bit defensive.

"Not me. I'm Irish, Italian, and German. My ancestors were migrant laborers. They didn't like slavery because it drove down their wages."

I immediately catch myself and realize the gravity of what I've said. My people disliked the practice almost entirely because of wage stagnation, *not* morality. It's an uncomfortable truth too many white folks ignore.

Oumar's smile fades.

We walk out of the museum and down a path to a large house. The stone exterior is colored pink. Two matching staircases connect a lower courtyard to a second level. It's extravagant in appearance.

"This is the House of Slaves," Oumar says. "It's where men and women were processed prior to the Middle Passage."

Oumar becomes emotional as we walk underneath the stairs and into a dark basement below the house. Though he has shown people like me this tour before, it does not feel like an act. He rubs his forehead to loosen his facial muscles. "In this pit they were beaten, chained, shackled. Then processed like cattle." We walk over to a hall with tiny holding cells, no larger than seven feet by five feet. They remind me of the prison in Hanoi. Dark, cold stone, decrepit and cruel, with little headroom. "Dozens of Africans, locked in here, cramped for days before the voyage," Oumar says.

Haunting.

Around the corner, at the corridor and past the holding cells, lies the infamous Door of No Return. A blue door is tied back to the wall, its frame in the shadows. Through it is the ocean lit by the sun. Oumar's hands run along the door's frame. "Can you imagine stepping through this and knowing it was only going to get worse? Some jumped off the dock and drowned themselves."

This beautiful water, a haunting grave. Oumar tells me to take a minute and stare out. I see the limitless sea. It's something I have long associated with total freedom, yet at Gorée Island it symbolizes the worst of what one man can do to another. Never has water seemed so sinister.

At the door I feel the pain of the past; I'm not the only one. Presidents Clinton, Bush, and Obama visited the door during their administrations. Pope John Paul II grew emotional when he came to this very spot and apologized for the Catholic Church's role in slavery.

I'm near tears. The years of strife in America related to slavery. The Dred Scott decision, the Civil War, segregation, the lynchings of the Civil Rights Era, the continual need for movements like Black Lives Matter. The modern-day manifestations of racism, which bind themselves to slavery: systemic inequality, race-baiting in politics, voter suppression, blackballing an NFL quarterback who took a knee to protest injustice. In some sense it all traces back to this door.

"How do you feel?" Oumar asks.

"Ashamed."

When we're back in Dakar, Oumar looks my way and tries to lighten my mood. It's not lost on me that a Black man is trying to make a white man feel better about slavery.

"I want to show you a real Senegal market. Not one full of fake Chinese things. Real Senegal!"

Oumar will get a cut from the vendors for any goods I buy, and I appreciate that. I'm happy he is finding ways to motivate tourists to experience more than the country's difficult colonized past. Which is a good thing: the country *is* on the upswing.

I cheerfully follow him.

Soon Oumar and I are talking about the modernity of Senegal. And to talk about that is to talk about China. The last decade has seen massive amounts of Chinese investment.

"They do a lot of good for us. They build roads, stadiums, and buildings," Oumar says. "But we think they take a lot too."

The crafts market sits near a harbor. Brightly colored wooden fishing boats stand at attention on a beach terribly polluted by plastic bags. Oumar makes it a point to walk me to an outdoor area where men sit hacking away at wood that they will eventually carve into souvenirs.

"You see, Luke, they are making it themselves. This is not Chinese. This is Senegal wood."

Many Senegalese, as do many artisans around the world, feel the Chinese flood their crafts market with cheap knockoffs and hurt their livelihood. On the way out, Oumar strikes up a conversation with a young man. It grows animated but ends with a hug.

Oumar is out of sorts. "You okay?" I ask.

"That is my nephew," Oumar says. "He is a good boy, but it is hard for him to find work. He may try for Europe." Oumar then explains how some of his nephews have migrated to Europe looking for jobs. Then his voice grows quiet. "One of my nephews—he died at sea trying to get to Spain."

I gasp. "Did the boat sink?"

"No, he got sick. The boat was overcrowded. They threw him overboard so it would weigh less and move faster. I don't want that to happen again. It's not fair that these boys have such trouble finding work. Many of the best jobs go to people who are connected. It doesn't matter what degree you got. Sorry. That's why I get sad."

I sit in stunned silence.

I need some grace.

"You ever been inside a church before, Oumar?"

"No."

"Can we stop at that cathedral we passed on the way to the ferry?"

"The French one?"

"Yes."

Oumar follows me out of the market and then, a few blocks away, through the cathedral door, albeit with some hesitation. It's a lovely church. The white walls and marble inside match the white stone exterior. I find a stained-glass window of my namesake, Saint Luke, here referenced as Saint Luc.

"See, Oumar? I am named after that guy."

"Who was he?"

"He wrote one of the important stories about Jesus."

I find a votive candle before a Virgin Mary statue. With the light of a match, I pray for healing. Oumar stands behind me, silent and respectful.

When I rise, Oumar looks at me anew. "Want to see the central mosque?"

"Of course," I say.

It's a short drive. The mosque is empty. There are large violet carpets spread out over the floor. Oumar drops to his knees and kisses the ground. I stand back and watch him pray. As we walk back to the car, he slaps my shoulder. "It feels good, right?"

"It sure does."

On the ride back to the hotel, we share a few laughs and lament the end of our daylong friendship. I contemplate inviting Oumar to dinner. Senegal is playing for a spot in the World Cup this evening. Maybe he'd like that. But I don't want to pressure him to abandon friends or family. I thank him for walking me through such painful history. We've both shown enough vulnerability to exchange not only a handshake but a hug.

Oumar leans out of the driver's window. "Don't forget what I told you: the Senegal women are the best looking in the world! Go see it!"

A light end to a heavy day.

He winks, smiles, and drives off.

DAKAR AT NIGHT

I stand behind twenty-plus men in a semicircle, staring at a TV set up in front of a bodega on a dirt road. The TV is the old rabbit-ears style. The image is grainy but clear enough to see Senegal defeat South Africa 2–0 to guarantee a spot in the World Cup for the first time since 2002. As the clock hits zero, the men run into the streets and dance. Car horns go off. Flags wave. Euphoria.

A few blocks away at an outdoor café, well-heeled locals, dressed in colorful silk kaftan tunics, smoke hookah and sip tea. Time for a beer and fries. When I pull out a cigarillo for a victory smoke, a dignified man promptly asks if it is a cigarette.

"No, it's a mini cigar. Like a real cigar, just smaller."

The man motions for it, his arm emerging from underneath the kaftan. He's tall and well filled out. From the cut of his clothes, fine leather shoes, and gold rings, I gather he is a man who has never been told no. I hand the cigarillo over along with another from the pack.

With a smile, he pats me on the back and smokes them both at his table.

My ears pick up the pulsations of mbalax, the local rhythm music that is a violent clash of steel drums, horns, keys, and percussion. It drapes over the main drag called the Ngor Strip, a wide, modern thoroughfare. There are bars, clubs, and lounges and a healthy amount of locals blasting mbalax from their car stereos. In a Muslim country, alcohol is everywhere. A red carpet leads into an open-air lounge bar. Intimately lit, full of plants mixed about bistro tables, the place is populated with aging French men and women, NGO workers letting off steam, middle-aged locals dressed to the nines, and an assortment of—and here Oumar was right—stunning younger Senegalese women.

With smooth, unblemished skin and tight-fitting skirts, the women hover around like floating goddesses. Strobe lights go off, a bass kicks so hard I feel it in my sternum. Talking is not possible. Dancing is the only language. A young Senegalese man stands up, hoists a bottle of champagne, and toasts the soccer team. He motions for everyone to come onto the dance floor. It's a melting pot, hundreds jumping up and down in unison, bound by love for Senegal.

As the sun rises, I take off on foot through the streets. Dakar is not pedestrian friendly. Rubble from construction buildings spills out into the sidewalks. Everything is under construction but nothing feels close to done. There are vendors seeking shade under trees, selling food and drink. Some speak French. Many offer a handshake. It's friendly but also feels like a test of sorts. Will I engage? Or am I too high-and-mighty to touch? I feel the undercurrent of race at play.

I shake every hand and smile.

A seaside road houses many waterfront restaurants. Bars with million-dollar views and ten-cent plastic tables and stools. Some places are upscale and rival anything in the US. I half expect stars like Leonardo DiCaprio to come walking in. It feels like some high-end, French-château-inspired place in Malibu. These restaurants and surfer bars with their fried food cluster together along the shoreline between vast stretches of open space. Brown dirt or yellow grass pushes up against the rocky coast.

On an outstretched cliff, I see local surfers below. Their muscular bodies stand out against the spray of the waves. Fearless, they navigate jagged reefs of rocks with ease. These are badass dudes. After riding a large wave into shore, one of the surfers catches me taking his photo. He shoots me the *shaka* hand sign, the worldwide symbol of hanging loose. The waters that yesterday represented so much evil today begin to restore themselves into a more hopeful and progressive present, for a world where we not only atone for our sins but understand each other.

I flash a shaka sign back.

SIXTEEN

Zimbabwe

I miss the first call at 5:30 a.m. Twenty seconds later, my iPhone buzzes again. The same number. This time I pick up.

My friend Johnny's voice sounds a bit anxious.

"Tanks are rolling through the streets," he says. "The airport is going to close."

Johnny works for the American Embassy in Zimbabwe. I'm supposed to see him later today in Harare, the capital. I'm currently a flight away in the tourist town of Victoria Falls.

"You better not come here," Johnny says. "Military is moving on Mugabe. Try to get a flight to South Africa or cross over to Zambia on that bridge if the border opens. I got to go."

On the TV, an intimidating Zimbabwean general in camouflage fatigues says the events unfolding are not a coup but an attempt to rid the presidency of criminals. Robert Mugabe, Zimbabwe's longtime dictator, is being forced out. People should stay home. I check the American Embassy website in Zimbabwe.

"Shelter in place immediately," reads the alert on the home page. "Avoid demonstrations."

This is uncharted territory. I did many things as a journalist; being a war correspondent was never one of them. Whatever the generals on state-owned TV might call it, what is happening now in Zimbabwe sounds like a coup. I take a deep breath and immediately book the earliest flight to Johannesburg. It's set to take off at 10:45 a.m.

It's now 6 a.m.

My adrenaline pulses sky-high as I pace back and forth, pulling back the shades every few moments. The street looks normal. *Perhaps people are just waking up to the news?*

I walk briskly down to the front desk. A picture of Mugabe hangs on the wall behind the clerk. It's titled "His Excellency."

"Do you know what's going on?" I ask the clerk.

"Everything seems normal, sir," she says.

I know she's lying, but she is not going to make a guest more afraid.

"Seems normal. Right."

I head back to my room and scroll through Twitter for updates. Western news outlets and people in Harare are using the word *coup*.

Raw fear creeps in. Yes, it's unlikely anything catastrophic would happen in a tourist town like Victoria Falls, away from the capital, away from the power center, away from the military. But what do I really know?

I know nothing. I'm consumed by a vicious, almost primordial energy. Will the airport be open? Can I cross the bridge to Zambia? If so, will there be roadblocks? Are police going to fight the military? Will people riot?

As the sun rises, I plot my escape. If I can get to the airport, I'll be fine. I text Mom what's happening. I'm supposed to meet her for a safari trip in Tanzania in a few days. She's packing in DC when she calls.

"Just be calm," she says. "Stay in touch with Johnny. When you venture out, stay as safe as possible."

Dad never took a chance and went to a war zone as a journalist. He did not like risk. I feel a sense of anger from his spirit. "Why the *hell* are you there? What's the point?"

I'm in Victoria Falls because yesterday I went to see the largest waterfall in the world. Double the size of Niagara Falls, a magnificent wall of ferociously falling white water. Unlike other waterfalls I had seen that emptied into a wide river, Victoria Falls nearly jumped over and touched me. Amazing. There were few safety rails. I walked close to the edge. Due to the narrow canyon space between the cliffs, sprays of mist whacked my face like an uppercut to the jaw. On the other side, in the country of Zambia, I could see the Devil's Pool, a small pool, right on the edge of the falls, where tourists took pictures. It was not for the faint of heart. A slip and strong currents could send you over. Through binoculars I saw white women in bikinis taking selfies. It was low tide. At high tide, in the rainy season, I was told the currents moved so fast that elephants could be knocked over the falls.

I had walked the length of the Victoria Falls Bridge into Zambia, mostly because it made sense to count another country. A long line of tractor trailers sat idle on the left side of the road. I had expected to dodge cars, but instead roving bands of baboons patrolled the road on a quest for food and mischief. I'd seen a few meandering around the town of Victoria Falls, but in a pack they were terrifying. I carefully crept along the shoulder and watched as they went inside the cab of a poor driver who had forgotten to roll up his windows before he noticed that a baboon had stolen a loaf of bread and some apples.

The beasts were meticulous in how they found food. When they weren't stealing it, they were knocking down garbage cans and separating trash from scraps. They feared no man. They flashed large teeth. They let out obnoxious, loud piercing screams. Taunting was a sport for them. With my head down and quick pace, I avoided playing. After a passport stamp and a jaunt to Livingstone, the Zambian tourist town, I went back to Zimbabwe.

Hyperinflation, hunger, and human rights abuses make Zimbabwe high on the world misery index. The country is a by-product of contemporary corruption. British colonialism and its subsequent apartheid system allowed a white minority to rule until the 1980s. Robert Mugabe was originally a freedom fighter. Over time he fell victim to autocratic corruption that enriched his cronies and left millions of ordinary citizens to suffer. I was under no illusions when I booked the trip that things would remain peachy. On my first walk through Victoria Falls, a young man offered to sell me "funny money"—old Zimbabwean $100 trillion bills, relics of terribly high inflation.

I wanted to help the guy as much as pocket the souvenir, so I paid him ten US dollars for it. He was ecstatic and then asked for my potato chips. I forked those over too. Almost all the locals were slender. It did not seem by choice.

From Twitter I'm able to pick up enough of what is happening; instantaneous citizen journalism is saving the day. In the hotel room, I get instant updates of a coup by following hashtags. Fellow Twitter users become my eyes and ears. Through their posts I get a read for the streets in real time.

I learn Mugabe has been detained inside the presidential palace. The military is in charge now. It's unclear if Mugabe loyalists in the police force or on the streets will strike a counterblow.

It's 7 a.m. and not only is the breakfast buffet downstairs open but the hotel is full of bewildered tourists, many of them older, who are content to ride it out at the hotel. Some are even still arranging tours and excursions. Because of my Twitter feed, I do not share their nonchalance.

On my ride in from the airport, I had used a driver named Owen. I call him now for a ride out.

"Owen, you think it's safe to drive to the airport? Or maybe the bridge to Zambia?"

"Mr. Luke, let me check with my family who is police. I will call you back."

Local suits gather in the driveway of the hotel. Beyond the gates everyone out in the streets listens to radios and watches TVs. If there is a cohesive tie, it is the lack of clarity. I ask a man in a suit, who looks like he's in charge, if he's nervous.

"I am nervous but excited. If Mugabe leaves, it is a great day for Zimbabwe."

Another lady is more cautious: "We need to see."

Owen calls back. "Mr. Luke, the border to Zambia is closed. The airport is open. It is the best chance to leave. There may be a checkpoint. I will see you in twenty minutes."

The white sedan pulls up and Owen gives me a wave. He is cool and calm and smells like aftershave. He takes off down the highway. Speed limits are arbitrary today.

"Are you worried, Owen?"

"I don't think things can get much worse, and I don't think most people would fight for Mugabe. Not here at least."

We pass a burned-out car off the road. It says "Judas" on the side. A bad sign. One mile from the airport we come across a checkpoint. Two policemen with guns roam the shoulder.

Panic sets in. Owen tells me not to worry and to get out of the front seat and into the back seat. While the car is moving, I climb in the back.

The police motion for us to stop. They keep their hands on their guns. My knuckles are white. The cops point at me. Owen puts down the back window and rolls to a brief halt. He smiles at the cops and yells something indistinguishable in a local dialect.

Without much more than a flinch, the cops wave us through, motioning their guns like brooms.

"What did you say?"

"Driving an important diplomat!"

I laugh, smile, and slap his shoulder. Owen is tipped well.

The airport is chaos. Tourists keep arriving, but flights to Harare are being delayed or canceled. For every person trying to leave, many enter. These tourists appear unconcerned. Am I overreacting? Maybe not. Local airport security is down to a single lane with a scanning machine and a magnetometer.

It takes forever, but I get through. Then an agonizing ninety-minute wait by the gate. The TVs in the airport show tanks in Harare. There are reports of small-arms fire. Another embassy alert says to shelter in place. Nevertheless, airport employees remain calm. Johnny texts: "Definitely leave if you can. What's it like on the ground there?"

I write up a paragraph of my morning and hit send. He texts back to say it's going in an official security situation report.

That makes me laugh. I ask how he's doing. He has a wife and kids in the hot spot.

"This is what I do," he texts.

I begin to feel the importance of the day, the value of the rule of law and the fragility of order when government is corrupt and ignores the basic needs of its citizens. I'm standing in a place where a strongman of nearly forty years has been swept out of office overnight. Will violence follow? I'm acutely aware that I don't have to wait to find out. I can exit. Too many people can't leave and have to live in oppression or perpetual uncertainty.

On a flight-tracking website I see my plane is close. When it comes into view, a sense of relief comes with it. The flight boards quickly. On the PA a British-accented pilot implores people to find their seats, as he does not want to stick around longer than needed. The safety briefing is the CliffsNotes variety.

The plane backs out from the terminal toward the corner of the runway. Within seconds the engines flare up, and the plane jumps off the ground. Dusty farmland and groves of trees disappear below as the bird ascends to the clouds.

I exhale.

I'm out.

Rwanda

Our car rambles northwest, from Kigali to the Virunga Mountains, Mom and I in search of the endangered silverback gorillas. We move through beautiful fertile valleys, up into lush green forests. We drive along the tops of ridges where we can see mountain ranges that extend to the horizon. We pass coffee farms and tea plantations, children playing soccer below a green canopy. It's a different country from what you would expect: the surroundings secure and tranquil and removed from the wrenching genocide of thirty years ago that pitted neighbor against neighbor in a tribal conflict, where eight hundred thousand people died in a little over one hundred days.

Rwanda today thrives on tourism and a burgeoning modern tech economy. Its topography is also different from where we'd just come from: Tanzania, on safari. I met up with Mom there shortly after the Zimbabwean coup. I was in good spirits. On the way to see her, at the airport, I'd encountered a group of United Nations–sponsored refugees heading to America to be resettled in Buffalo, of all places. I taught them "Go Bills!" and gave the oldest kid my traveling Bills koozie. It was a good omen that I needed after Zimbabwe.

I could tell that Mom had a sense of pride knowing I'd gotten out of Zimbabwe okay. I hadn't withered. Like her, I was a person of action. Mom saw this as a valuable learning experience. If you can keep calm in a coup, you can keep calm anywhere. Thankfully, it was relatively nonviolent. After some tense days, Mugabe was officially overthrown. My friend Johnny even danced in the streets with elated locals.

The Tanzanian safari was Mom's "trip before I die" request, a week glamping with the lions, cheetahs, hippos, elephants, and wildebeests. The grasslands of the famed Tanzania National Parks Authority—Tarangire, Serengeti, and Ngorongoro Conservation Area—felt so vast they seemed limitless.

This part of Rwanda is denser, held together by thick vegetation.

After three hours we're in the village of Kinigi. It's the gorilla-tracking base camp, with stunning views of Rift Valley and the mostly dormant volcanoes that make up the Virunga mountain range in Rwanda. Even though we're around eight thousand feet above sea level, Mom walks quickly about the markets and finds an authentic wood-carved hiking pole with a gorilla for a handle.

I'm having flashbacks to Bolivia and labored breathing. I don't let on about my discomfort, though.

Mom has trouble attaching gaiters to her boots. These gaiters are mandatory for our hiking, needed to keep debris and water out. I adjust her fit. She tightens the top clasp and looks down at her legs. We look like we've just pulled up our shin guards preparing for battle, like Greco-Roman soldiers.

"This is far out!" she says.

It all is. Just a few days prior we shared a Thanksgiving meal of chicken sandwiches in the Tanzania grasslands off the hood of a Land Rover. Our entertainment wasn't an NFL game but a wildebeest migration. It was something Dad would have never done. Hell, I can't think of many in our cohort who would've done it either. But that's Mom, and now that's also me.

Mom's in her seventies, and we're both preparing to climb into the fog to find gorillas. It's invigorating to feel her passion for exploring.

"High-end, low impact" is how local rangers describe the gorilla-tracking tourism industry. There are fewer than a thousand silverback mountain gorillas in the wild. Tourism, ironically, helps them. Once Rwanda realized how much money could be made by keeping gorillas alive and safe, the country moved to protect them with strict controls. Private tour operators can arrange a visit, but every trek is government run and regulated. Permits are expensive—$1,500, which is around the average yearly wage in Rwanda. (Thanks, Mom!) Of that money, 10 percent goes to the local community and the rest into nature conservation and the salaries of park rangers, gorilla trackers, and porters. The gorillas and tourists are guarded by rangers wielding AK-47 rifles. Many of the porters are former poachers; the government's commitment to paying them an honest wage helps to cut down on the lure of nefarious activity. The same can be said for nearby farmers. If the gorillas venture into their fields, any eaten crop is reimbursed. Lately, they've planted closer to the gorillas' land to get more subsidies. Tourism is limited to ninety-six people a day. People are split into groups of eight. Everyone undergoes an hour-long safety and education briefing. If your group and guide find a gorilla family, you are limited to one hour of observation and interaction.

Finding gorillas is not guaranteed. "Mountain gorillas live as families," says our guide, Keza. "Each family has an undisputed silverback leader. The leader can be backed by a subordinate, usually a son aged eight to twelve. There are numerous females, infants, and adolescents in a family. Some families reach thirty members. It's possible to see multiple silverbacks in a single group, but usually the younger ones seek to make a power play and split the family." These animals share 98 percent of our DNA. Their familiarity extends beyond blood, though; it goes all the way to the young male who needs to strike out on his own.

Mom and I and six other tourists are given a gorilla family to find—the Muhoza family, a newish group formed the year prior. The patriarch is a young silverback named Muhoza. His family of seven moved into the thick brush of a nearby mountain last night. Our job is to find him today.

We eight tourists face a long and grueling hike, and the others in our group opt for a less strenuous experience. They want to see another gorilla family at a lower altitude. Mom and I agree to find Muhoza. We will be on our own, with a ranger guide, a guard with a rifle, and two porters who carry supplies.

Keza, the guide, is a tall, good-looking Rwandan woman in her midtwenties.

"Remember to make way for the gorillas. If they look at you, they're mostly curious. If you feel frightened, grunt and growl. They should back off."

I'm more excited than afraid, to be honest. Keza carefully leads us through a maze of strangling vines, communicating on a radio with a gorilla scout who's been following the family throughout the night and early morning. It begins to rain, and the hiking gets tough. At times, the vegetation is so thick we forget we're on an African mountain and not deep in the throes of a rain forest. Mom shows unbreakable courage for her age. Despite being nearly nine thousand feet high, she perseveres through gunky mud, slick terrain, and narrow ledges. Still, at some points, I carry her or pull her up. She does not like it, but we need to make swift time.

After two and a half hours up a steep incline, we find our family.

A female gorilla comes into view. She gathers branches and bark from a tangle of vines and small trees. She places them to the side and doesn't pay us much attention. Two of her adolescent sons are wrestling nearby in a small clearing. One rolls into her space, and she shoos him away, annoyed that their roughhousing got close to her. After collecting herself, she disappears into the tangle; a few minutes pass before she emerges with an infant gorilla. The infant is playful and engaging. He gets close to our group to show off his climbing skills on a tree. From the top branches, he breaks off twigs and throws them toward us. He smiles excitedly, just like a kid. I wave at him, then I hear a large crack.

Ten yards away, Muhoza breaks through the thicket and makes his way toward his lady and child. The adolescents scatter—they want no part of Dad. Muhoza is huge. Extremely broad in the shoulders and stocky, he easily clears 450 pounds. Keza says he's still a young silverback, which means he's still learning the dynamics of being in charge of a family. We pull back and give him space to pass as he comes into a clearing. Muhoza promptly sits down in front of the female. She picks bugs off his back. Soon the infant jumps down from the tree and does somersaults to grab his father's attention. Uninterested, Muhoza stretches out for a nap. There is something so innocently human about the interaction. Or is it innocently gorilla? I guess we copied them. Once rested, Muhoza gets up to pick bamboo. At Keza's behest, I crouch and crawl to get within four feet.

I'm not afraid. I feel a strong connection with this young fellow trying to start his own way in the world. I absorb his energy. As I look at him, Muhoza rather unexpectedly turns around and walks toward me. The ground vibrates beneath my feet. His deep, dark eyes come into focus; the frown lines of his forehead are clear and distinct. We stare at each other. Close enough to shake hands. He can kill me in two seconds if he desires. That's of no concern, though; I'm mesmerized by his presence and his power. A few feet behind me, Keza whispers to crouch lower, push out my chest, and join her in a soft growl. This tells Muhoza we mean no harm.

Mom, next to Keza, is a bit startled. She lies down flat on her back. As Muhoza keeps staring at me, sizing me up, I let out a tepid "Grrrrrrrrr." He smirks, flares his nostrils, and moves on, brushing Mom's leg in the process—it feels mockingly brazen. He knows he's the unquestioned master of his domain. After his inspection of us is complete, Muhoza summons his family with a yell and leads them up a steep hill and back into the thicket. They don't look back.

Mom and I take a moment near the top of the mountain, just a few yards from where the gorilla family had sat.

"I think that was the most incredible thing I've ever done."

"Definitely, Mom. That was it."

We're both at a loss for words. We stare at the forest around us.

After a while I say, "I'm glad you made it up here, Mom. It wasn't easy."

"There's no way I wouldn't. That was too special."

I see the tenacity in her face. She's proud of doing it. I am too. I also know she needed my hand to get to the top. That counts for something.

Maybe, like Muhoza, I'm gaining that independence. I planned the trip. I took care of Mom. I made her happy and fulfilled.

I walk off the trail on my own a little bit. There's too much fog to get a sense of the view of the valley. A year and a half ago, I was upset about how my congressional coverage had been bumped by Donald Trump's reaction to Harambe, the gorilla killed at the Cincinnati Zoo. Now, I'm tracking real-life silverback mountain gorillas on a mountain in Rwanda—and leading my mother to the summit.

It *feels* like I'm on top too.

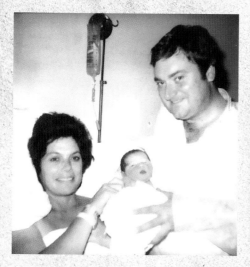

Debuting at nine pounds, thirteen ounces, Thursday, August 22, 1985.

Early memories of Dad were synonymous with the NBC peacock.

Grandpa, the sweetest man I ever knew. A World War II vet, he was a man whose glass was always half full and whose heart was fully open.

As Dad said, "Being a Buffalo Bills fan really isn't being a fan. It's a way of life."

Cheering on Team USA as a family
at the 1996 Olympics in Atlanta.

Last baseball game I ever saw with
Dad. Opening Night at Nationals Park
March 2008. I hold the memory close.

Last family photo, taken at the Vatican,
June 11, 2008. Dad would pass two days later.

Watching the rainbow over Washington, DC,
the day of Dad's funeral. That was him.

Behind the desk for MSNBC.

My favorite arena: a Capitol
Hill press conference.

J. SCOTT APPLEWHITE

Interviewing Democratic leader Nancy Pelosi.

Listening in as House Speaker John
Boehner holds court with reporters on
the Speaker's Balcony—Merlot in hand.

ALEXANDRA MOE

The trip that started the journey. With Chamberlain the pug and my truck in the backwoods of Maine.

Enjoying a cold one after seeing my first-ever glacier in Patagonia.

Mom showing me the ropes at a local market in Paraguay.

No depth perception in the Bolivian salt flats. Looks like I'm falling into my trademark CG Corey Griffin hat!

The Moai of Easter Island—absolutely surreal.

Felix, my hitchhiking surfer friend in New Zealand. He taught me a lot.

At peace after meditating with Buddhist monks in Cambodia.

With Takechiyo, the famous Instagram otter of Japan!

"The Door of No Return," Senegal. An enduring symbol of the sin of slavery.

Mom snaps a picture of silverback gorillas in the wild in the mountains of Rwanda.

With the Sadhus holy men in Nepal, a group that renounce the worldly life.

The infamous Mr. Namir, Sri Lanka.

Catching a ride in the Mekong Delta, Vietnam.

A rainbow in Iceland on the tenth anniversary of Dad's death. There are tears behind the sunglasses.

Russian soldier selfie during World Cup, just outside Red Square in Moscow.

With Mom ahead of her big Emmy win for *The Assassination of Gianni Versace: American Crime Story.*

Lost in West Texas.

Renewed and refreshed by the Bay.

Post-soccer fun with some
Palestinian kids in Hebron.

Praying at the Western Wall. Notice
the Buffalo Bills yarmulke!

First and last pictures of father and son. The delivery room and the Vatican.

PART 4

EIGHTEEN

Kitchen Table Convo

The pug barks when I pull up the driveway to Mom's house. I see his small, dark face pushed against her kitchen window. It's the second month of 2018. I've been on the road most of the last eighteen months. I'm north of thirty countries visited now and have amassed a decent social media following of my travels for Instagram. If the road calls, I answer. It's more than a lifestyle; it's life. I've returned stateside for a few weeks to check in on Mom and get a sense of what needs to get done at her house: stock up on Duraflame logs and ice-melt salt for the DC winter.

But I'm also here today because I have been summoned.

"I think it's time to talk," Mom said.

In the past, a phrase like that could portend something bad, or picayune, or great, or some combination of those three.

Mom sits at the kitchen table when I open the glass door. Newspapers are spread out before her, a fresh cup of tea is in her hand. She motions to the pot on the stove.

"Make yourself a fresh cup if you like."

I do.

When there is tea, there is usually a serious point to be made. We fast-forward through the small talk.

"So what I'm wondering is, how long do you plan to keep going, Luke?"

It's a judgmental tone. The pug nuzzles his face into her thigh, as if where the conversation is heading makes him uncomfortable.

I take a sip of green tea. It's a cold, dreary early February day in Washington, but my skin is golden brown, a tan left over from a recent jaunt to Brazil. Another country counted. I've been expecting Mom's question. Mom hinted at it soon after Africa in various conversations: "Time to get focused." "Life is not all fun and games." And, at her most direct: "You need to do something."

"There's some more places I want to see. People are into it too; they learn from my posts. I'm not ready to stop."

I know the response needles her. It's all over her face. She used to look at me with cautious optimism. Now there's more worry and disapproval behind her fretful eyes.

"You can't do this forever—wandering aimlessly. You need to settle down at some point. Not just drift."

But I don't feel like I'm drifting, and the past eighteen months have been anything but aimless. I've learned so much about living and about other cultures. My mind has been reframed into a more understanding and empathetic angle. I've worked to shed the narrow worldview often projected by Washington and America. If this education is not going as fast as she wants, well, I lived at the pace of others for a long time. I'm not ready to quit traveling. I'm not ready to quit on myself.

I'm also, frankly, a little skeptical of the person who's looking at me like that. I push back hard. "Mom, respectfully, you were the one who encouraged me to travel. You said I needed to see the world. You left your family behind in California at my age. You got married late. I'm following your lead, right? Also, what the hell? A third of the places I went, I went with you! Places you wanted to see. Places you wanted me to carry your bags. To see you through!"

Her face grows strained. "Yes, I appreciate your help. It meant a lot to me. I enjoyed our time together. I hope you did too. But don't act like it was some grand sacrifice. People would die for opportunities like you've had. You've had plenty for the last year and a half. I'm not supporting this anymore. You're privileged enough. No more trips with me where I pick up the tab. You're completely on your own now."

It's not a death sentence for my travel. I can afford to lose Mom as a backstop. I've paid for every trip she wasn't on, anyway. If anything, it's motivation to keep going. I have more to prove now. *Mom can't win!* In fact, the ways of the past can't win. That conformist thinking of "you *need* to do this" will not win. I'll tighten my budget further, stretch those dollars Dad bestowed me in his will. Accrue all the travel points I can get. Who cares where you sleep when you just want to see? I'll sacrifice anything for the road. Anything to not be stuck in Washington living out "what's expected."

"Fine," I say. "I can do it myself; hell, I've been doing it myself! I can make it work, and I will."

She lets out a pained sigh.

I get up from the table and push the chair in, then pour the last of the tea into the sink. I look around at the kitchen, the pug, my mom. My old truck is parked on the street outside the house. Dad's umbrella is still in the holder by the door, below one of his old sets of keys. Almost ten years since his passing, they're still there. This feeling of family, home, and hearth, it does not have the same appeal it once did. I don't find it comforting. In fact, it's limiting. I'm not ready to come back to this life or to build my own version of it. The physical personification of my parents' life work, this beautiful, inviting house, this one my father cried in when my grandpa walked through its doors the first time—right now feels like settling. I need to leave.

"So what's next, then?"

I shrug. "We'll see."

"We'll see, then. Are you keeping a journal of everything? Are you even writing or just playing around on Instagram?"

She knows how to push my buttons, but today I won't let her. I'm thirty-two, a grown-ass man, and getting lectured like I'm twelve again. I want to explode but curse myself for getting into this woeful situation—a place where Mom views me as so dependent that she can talk down to me. I bite my tongue.

"Just stop, okay. I keep good notes. I was a journalist for eight years and a history major before that. I didn't forget how to write."

I give the pug a pet and walk out the door.

I'm on my own, where I want to be.

NINETEEN

Nepal

Seeing Mount Everest is not nearly as difficult as climbing it. Still, seeing it is not simple either. I'm going for the same reason George Mallory climbed it: "Because it's there." Maybe that personifies this leg of the journey. Why not?

I arrive in Nepal with the plan to see the tallest mountain in the world. It feels like a flex in a way. I can conquer this mountain, show Mom and everyone else I'm worthy. I'm out there doing *big* things! Living!

My itinerary involves a sightseeing flight on Buddha Air not long after I land in Kathmandu. I leave my dusty, drafty boardinghouse with a half-asleep porter at the wheel of the run-down family car. It's 4:30 a.m. Due to weather conditions that change drastically within minutes, it's imperative to be ready to board the plane at sunrise.

For the first time in my life, I walk into an airport terminal where nobody has a bag. We're all sightseers, not travelers. The waiting room is an unorganized mess: Chinese, Japanese, German, French, Hindi, Arabic, Spanish, Portuguese, Nepalese, English—every language screamed at once. None of us can make out the garbled words from the aging PA system. It is as if a chorus of languages keeps shouting the refrain, *What did they just say?*

The concourse is a run-down high school cafeteria. The smell of bleach emanates from the bathrooms, so strong that if you stood by it for too long, you'd pass out. The coffee is lukewarm water with dirt. A fleet of prop planes lines up in a row on the tarmac. They depart like buses every few minutes. It's unclear which one I'm supposed to get on, so I meander to the desk. A stern woman tells me to wait with group six. After an hour we walk to a plane. Soon after the safety briefing we're told to get off. There's weather, and Everest is not visible.

A moan, again in every global language. Two hours go by in the waiting room. I pace. We board a plane again. It begins to taxi. God, I hate prop planes, and now I'm going in one around the world's highest mountain range? I dabble in some gallows humor, unlike the usually superstitious me: "If I die trying to see Everest from a plane, do I count as a climbing victim? Planes climb, too, right?" I calm my nerves with deep breaths. While in line to take off, the pilot says, "The weather is bad again. We are not flying today."

A third moan in every language.

Back in the terminal, I'm handed a voucher. "Repeat attempt tomorrow."

Guess I'll go see Kathmandu.

"Beware of the Kat-Lung."

That's a message from a mountaineer friend of mine. He's not wrong. The smog is so thick in the city that the dust can't settle. Pollution just engulfs me. Kathmandu still reels from a 2015 earthquake that killed nine thousand people, decimated nearly six hundred thousand buildings, and uprooted hundreds of thousands of lives. Many roads are still littered with ash particles. It's not uncommon to see the charred remains of a crushed car. Compounding the earthquake's effects are the dirty conditions of any developing country—the brick kilns, the industrial waste, the unchecked auto emissions—my eyes, nose, and throat burn. Dirt soils my clothes. The air, even with a gleaming sun, is a constant beige haze. There's a good chance a driver cannot see more than a few feet in front of his car. On the sidewalk I start to cough heavily. Soot plaques the back of my tongue. A kind Nepalese woman hands me a tissue and a face mask. I'm able to cough out some phlegm and wipe my nose. The white tissue turns jet black.

My new goal is to fit most all of Kathmandu into a day. There's an emphasis on speed, not just because of the pollution but because I want to see as much as I can. If a place that demands four hours gets fourteen minutes, that's fine. I now feel most compelled to feed my Instagram feed; it grows by each picture post, each geotagged location, each hashtag of somewhere new.

After a cab ride I find the Swayambhunath Stupa, known as the monkey temple. The Buddhist holy site is also revered by Hindus. It sits atop a tall hill on the edge of the city, accessible via 365 steps to that hilltop, dodging holy monkeys along the way. I've never seen a stupa temple; it looks like a white dome with a steeple. Connecting the spire to the dome is a gold box painted with stern, intimidating eyes. These signify the "eyes of Buddha." They are always on you. Many locals meditate around the structure and receive holy dust on their foreheads in the surrounding temples. *This is why I travel*, I tell myself. *This is what I want to see.* I text Mom some photos of the stupa and an old Nepalese couple sitting on a porch. In a way it validates me: *See, Mom, there is still a lot left to find.* Why be stuck when you can move?

I cross over to another part of town to see Pashupatinath, a Hindu holy site in the predominantly Hindu country. Perched alongside the Bagmati River, The temple's primary importance is hosting funerals. As a non-Hindu, I'm asked to cross over to the other side of the river. Up a path and on top of a flat hill are gray stone shrines, housing various Hindu deities. There are men clad in orange togas, wearing dreadlocks, with white ash rubbed into their skin and orange face paint, praying. I approach one of them; he sticks out his hand asking for money. I'm confused. Why is a holy man asking me for money? A friendly Nepalese man tells me the group are Sadhus. I google "Sadhus" and learn these guys are considered wandering Hindu holy men. They smoke hash for meditative purposes, are free of all earthly possessions, abstain from sex, practice intense yoga, and live off the charity of others. To become a Sadhu, one has to attend their own funeral, a symbolic ceremony distancing them from their families and hometowns. The old man in orange shoves his finger into my rib cage. I've taken some photos, and he wants money. I hand him a ten-dollar bill, more than the local suggested. The man shakes his head. I back off: "No more!" He's angry but lines up his friends to take a picture. There I am, in the middle of these Hindu holy men, looking like Indiana Jones. I love it, and I post it immediately. The likes rack up like numbers on a slot machine.

Across the bridge there are large bonfires set on platforms hanging over the water. Shirtless men in white wraps tend to the fire. Groups stand around the platform, deep in prayer. Some people cry.

The holy men in white bring a deceased woman to the platform; she is wrapped in white cloth with hints of orange. They pray over her. This must be a funeral. Then a family member lights wood and kindling under her body. *Oh my God—a real life cremation!* The holy men place wet straw on top of her to shield people's eyes from the burning corpse. I'm one of dozens of people spread out watching the ceremony. It's not uncommon and is even encouraged by some families. The local Hindu custom is once the body turns into ash, it's swept into the river, where the Bagmati links with the holy Hindu Ganges River. Hindus believe that the Ganges can rid believers of sin and lead to rebirth. If the ashes come from the Pashupatinath Temple, the rebirth will be as a human. From dust thou came, to dust thou shall return.

The woman's family begins to weep as the fire takes hold. I can hear the cackle of the flame engulf her flesh and bones. An entire circle of life, burned out and swept off. I'm not feeling the enormity of the moment the way I should. My faith is shallow. I somehow don't feel present. I'm a bit off. I walk out as the black smoke rises from the corpse.

I tell myself I need to see something else, like Everest.

It's day two, and the early morning airport process repeats itself. The shower had no warm water today; the cold substitutes for the jolt of a morning coffee. I poke the poor porter who groggily gets behind the wheel at 4:30 a.m. Upon arrival, a lady from Buddha Air says there will be a three-hour weather delay. Again, a room full of tourists scream in many tongues for many minutes. After three hours, the ATR 72 twin-engine fifty-seater prepares to board.

We idle on the runway for another hour.

Finally, nearly five hours after its scheduled time, the plane takes off.

Everyone has a window seat. Everyone has cameras at the ready, eager for Everest.

Sagarmatha. That's what the Nepalese call Everest. It translates into "peak of heaven." It's a much better name than Everest, an Anglo product from colonialism and the British surveyor and geographer George Everest, who worked in the region.

The plane cuts through the Kathmandu smog and lifts into the clear blue mountain air. For the first time I see the Annapurna range of the Himalayas. The height of these hills is wild. We're flying amid the clouds but still well below the peaks. As the plane levels off at around twenty-four thousand feet, the flight attendants begin speaking. I'm homed in on the Himalayas: my forehead presses against the window, slowly committing a mental picture to memory. I'm shocked that people try to climb these things. Unforgiving is an understatement.

"And that tall one?" the flight attendant says. "That looks like it is smoking a pipe? The cloud coming out of the rock like pipe smoke? Yes, that is Sagarmatha. That is Everest."

I summon the kind woman over and stick my index finger on the window, just below the peak, just where the cloud smoke starts.

"That's Everest?"

"Yes, sir, that is Everest."

"How far away are we?"

"About twenty-four kilometers."

The tallest mountain in the world, 29,029 feet, is only fifteen miles away from me. Ten times taller than the world's tallest building. Ten times greater than anything man could build. Giddily, I snap more pictures and pump my fist. Eat it, haters! Here I am, flying in the heavens, looking at the highest point where man can touch God. How will I tell the story over social media? Will these pictures and videos do the mountain justice? I'll upload them as soon as I land. I feel such a sense of satisfaction when I "drop a bomb" on Instagram. Another monumental moment.

TWENTY

Sri Lanka

He's late and I'm agitated. I cannot stand tardiness, especially if I'm paying somebody to do a job. I'm also battling a stomach issue, a going-away present from Nepal. It's so bad I had to wear a diaper on a plane. Different parts of the world have different standards of what constitutes tardiness—for me, a minute late is too long—and I pace in the lobby of my Sri Lankan hotel. After a half hour, I ask the deskman to phone my driver.

"What's his name, sir?"

"I don't know. He's a driver for Luke."

The man in a sharp suit dials. There's no answer.

"Why don't you try again?"

"Can we wait five minutes, sir?"

"No, try now."

This time there's an answer. The two men speak in Sinhala and share a joke.

"He'll be here soon."

"Sure he will. Okay, I'll be out here."

Here is the back patio of the Galle Face Hotel in Colombo. It dates back to 1864, complete with a classic British style and refined history. Che Guevara, Gandhi, Pope John Paul II, Emperor Hirohito, Yuri Gagarin, and Prince Philip, whose old car resides in the lobby, all stayed at this hotel. Waiters in white coats mill about. The Indian Ocean laps at the retaining wall. There's some well-cut grass in between a vibrant pool deck and the lapping sea.

Yesterday I was supposed to go to Jaffna, a less-refined relic of British colonialism and a town on the northern tip of the Sri Lankan island, where the minority Tamil people, mostly Hindus, live. The city has only recently opened up to tourism. During the Sri Lankan Civil War, which killed tens of thousands and ended in 2009, Jaffna was a main base of the government opposition rebel group—the Tamil Tigers. Yet to get there meant waking up at 5:30 a.m., taking two trains, and finding a guide—and so I chose sun over slog. I was missing out on a unique experience, but I was also unmotivated. Another recovering war zone and study in humanity. Authenticity was beginning to feel tiring and trying, and so I chose to play tourist. There was plenty of history at my hotel. I spent the day eating a burger and sipping beer outside, not acknowledging any possibility of burnout.

My one meaningful interaction came after I noticed something odd down the coast: large machines shooting sand into the air.

A waiter told me, "Sir, they're reclaiming the land. China is building a city."

"China is building a city! Damn."

A manager who witnessed the encounter escorted me, shirtless in bathing trunks, to see a well-dressed saleswoman. In her office she showed off a brochure for "Colombo Port City," a "New Dubai!" Part of China's investment-oriented Belt and Road Initiative. When done, the city will double the size of Colombo, house eighty thousand residents, and host hundreds of thousands of people daily. I was seeing history made, from the confines of a well-manicured resort.

"Would you like to invest, sir? Get in on the ground and retire at the top?"

As chlorinated water dripped on the woman's marble floor, I joked, "I guess I'm already retired."

"Hello, sir, I'm Mr. Namir!"

Dark-skinned and bald, in his early sixties, about six feet tall with a paunchy gut, Namir has wide black eyes that glimmer under the spectacles of his smiling face. He does not apologize for being an hour late.

"Hi. You're late. I hope it's not a pattern for the week we have together."

I sound like an asshole. I'm pissed. Namir keeps smiling and says nothing. I've concocted an aggressive plan to see as much of the island as possible. Many miles in few days. There's a list that needs to be checked off.

For tourists, getting a driver for a week is a common affair. It's not considered a luxury in this relatively cheap country. Hotels include driver rooms in the overall bill for a stay. For an island with bargain prices to begin with, a driver is a necessary and affordable cost. I question whether Namir is worth it. His smile seems condescending.

Before we begin the drive to Sigiriya, an ancient rock fortress, Namir wipes the steering wheel of his modern Honda with the heels of his hands three times and then bows his head in prayer. This goes on for five minutes.

"Namir, what the hell is this? We're already late."

"Sir, this is a Buddhist car blessing. It's very important to ensure good luck on our journey."

"Okay, well, tell me about it next time so I can offer up some words of my own and not sit here twiddling my thumbs." I mutter "Jesus" under my breath and slowly exhale.

Once on the road Namir frequently jerks the wheel. He drives too fast or too slow. An hour into our trip into the interior of the country, he's lost. He refuses to use Google Maps.

"I know where I am going, sir."

"You clearly do not."

When I make him use a navigation app, Namir pouts. He loudly smacks his lips while trying to clear his throat. He refuses to speak. I'm so turned off by his demeanor that I shut up too. Gone is the curiosity that was so prevalent in other countries; my inherent desire to learn has been suppressed. Right now, I couldn't care less about Namir's story, his take on his country or its culture. He's annoying as hell, and it almost feels like he's testing me. It's better to ignore him and waste away time looking out at the passing scenery.

Women on the side of the road in colorful saris sell bananas against rolling greenery. Palm trees line the shoulder and soft, wavy yellowish-green high grass flows gently with the breeze. Men labor about the terrain, some driving cattle. Occasionally I see specks of modernity: fuel, food courts, and a small strip mall. Eventually the topography changes. Less humidity, crisper mountain air. The five-hour journey takes nearly eight. We make it to Sigiriya close to sunset.

"Sigiriya cannot be missed!" That's what my travel research said. I spent eight hours driving here, got a room for the night, and this morning I don't even know what I should be looking for. Whereas in the past I may have taken a moment to prep for the day so I could get more out of it, now I'm more focused on just getting it done and taking the needed pictures. Pictures are my muse. They provide content and, on Instagram, give people an idea of what I do. They somehow make me feel that I matter.

Namir is pouting again. After not answering my texts, I found him behind the hotel, drinking coffee and yukking it up with other drivers near their bunkroom. In the past I may have joined them and made a bond. I don't have it in me today. Namir drops me off at the ticket office and points to a section of a parking lot where he'll meet me.

A pamphlet tells me what I'm seeing. Sigiriya is an ancient rock fortress and palace dating back to the fifth century. It cuts an imposing figure against the Sri Lankan interior. Sigiriya means "Lion Rock" in the local dialect, and, apparently, this rock has become a point of national pride. It's an early example of urban planning with meticulously laid out gardens and water pools, complete with a lion's paws carved into the nearly seven-hundred-foot-tall freestanding stone.

There is some speculation that the Lion Rock is actually an ancient king's pleasure palace. I like lions, too; I'm a Leo, after all. I'm amused. Dodging literal hornet nests and hordes of tourists, I see old paintings of nude women inside the rocky caves. The hypermasculine strength and spirit of the lion reflect the king's sexual prowess. When I reach the top, I have no doubt this is a pleasure palace. I stop reading or caring about any other interpretations. "Welcome to Mount Orgy!" I say to myself. I laugh a bit and think about a playboy king and his concubines shacking up on top of this rock. *This* is why I spent a day in the car with Namir?

Thank God it photographs well.

Namir is surprised to see me back in the parking lot so quick. "You're done already?"

I tell Namir that I tweaked my hamstring on the hike and need to sit in the back of the car to stretch my leg. This is a lie. I don't want to sit next to him. My nerves are frayed by his idiosyncrasies.

After an hour on our drive south to Nuwara Eliya through the inviting town of Kandy, it becomes too much for Namir. He's upset and senses that I'm avoiding him. He asks that I ride shotgun.

"No! I need to stretch my leg. It's all good, Namir. You just drive. Do your job. I'll sit where I want. Okay?"

It's odd behavior and I recognize it, even as I fail to stop myself from acting this way. Mom would say I'm being a disingenuous snot. Maybe I am. I don't know why.

Namir pulls over and turns to me. "Please sit in the front. It's not nice for you to be back there. Do you have respect?"

"Whoa! Okay. Okay. Okay. We good."

From Kandy we drive to the heart of tea country, the village of Nuwara Eliya. Another place to check off the list. The tea plantations are stunning: layered rows of green tea leaves with red clay built in for farmer access.

Soon the Honda hooks around blind curves, more dangerous than usual as dusk approaches.

"Slow down, Namir!"

He smiles stupidly. It's aggravating, the lack of care or concern. The sun begins to set over the hills. I ask Namir to pull over so we can take a picture. He refuses.

"We're taking the goddamn picture, Namir!"

He sighs and slams on the brakes. More pouting.

I snap a few gems for Instagram and think of a caption: "Didn't spill my tea," or something corny and stupid like that. As I open the car door, Namir asks, "Do you drink?"

"What? Um. Yes, I do, Namir." Especially on this trip.

"Poya holiday, big Buddha day, starting tonight and tomorrow means no alcohol will be sold. You should buy some in town."

"Well, Namir, we're getting somewhere now! Let's get to town before the store closes!" I sarcastically pat his shoulder.

On the main strip of Nuwara Eliya, I find the local package store. The booze is kept in a cage behind a wooden counter manned by two men with stone-cold black eyes. I join a line of twenty or so tea plantation workers who have finished their shift, all of them men. All of them muscled, no fat. They are loading up ahead of the dry day. Bottles of arrack, distilled palm syrup, as high as 140 proof, fly off the shelves. Some grab Lion Lager. Nobody pays me much attention; nobody seems to care that I'm there. Kind of like how I feel. Best to ask for a six-pack and crack a dumb joke about hoarding before the holiday. It gets no response from the clerk, who just walks to the cooler and pulls out the beer and drops it onto the wooden counter. He stares at me blankly and states the cost.

I buy a bottle of arrack too.

I eat solo at the hotel after passing through a dinner buffet. Plates of fried rice, chicken and fish curry, Sri Lankan delicacies. Nobody asks me to join them. I scroll on my phone. I might as well be back in the Capitol cafeteria. I walk past an old billiards table. A local bartender, bored and slow on work because of the religious holiday, jumps up excitedly.

"Sir, would you like to have a match?"

He is almost giddy at the prospect. Fifty-something and well-built, his eyes are warm and genuine. I can only imagine the stories he must have. I tell myself I should listen to them. So much could be learned. But I don't have it in me tonight.

"Maybe tomorrow," I say.

That's a lie. I leave in the morning.

In my room I take a few shots of arrack, sip a beer, and fire up Netflix.

"You're not spending time in Ella?"

Namir *tsks* his tongue. Many visitors to Sri Lanka spend weeks around Ella. The hikes through the steep green mountains are reportedly the best in the world. It's even serviced by an old British-era train, referred to as the "most beautiful train ride in the world."

"No, I'm not. That's a lot of hiking, a lot of process. I'd have to find a group, make friends. It's too much. Let's just go to the beach."

Namir gets lost on a hodgepodge of two-lane congested roads with buses, tuk-tuks, trucks, mopeds, cows, dogs, and humans walking on what is supposed to be a shoulder. I say nothing. It's pointless now. I only know we're close when palm trees begin to appear again.

When we get to the beach town of Mirissa, I learn it was decimated by the infamous 2004 tsunami. More than a dozen years later, it's still recovering.

I ask Namir about the tsunami. He grows quiet, eyes still watery. He'd been near the coast on a work project that day; prior to driving he had worked in some construction field. At first, he noticed animals moving quickly and making noises. They had felt the earthquake. The humans had not. Soon, Namir could see water retreating out. He did not know what it meant, but he knew it was not normal. He saw some fishermen move out and begin to scoop out fish in the abnormally shallow water. Then large waves formed and a supervisor yelled out, "Tsunami!" Namir and his colleagues ran inland. He was lucky. He found a tuk-tuk driver and sped out on a bumpy side road. He outran the surge of water. I ask if he ventured back to see the destruction. "No, I knew I had to get home to my wife." The couple lived inland and were spared the brunt of the tsunami; it would be days before Namir came back to the coastline.

"What was it like?" I ask.

I can see the lines of anguish on his face. "I don't talk about that." I nod and don't press. Minutes later he realizes that he missed another turn.

I can't get mad at him for that one.

Mirissa is the perfect town to hide out in, a place you could spend two years and not really know what was happening in the greater world. Namir complains about the driver room at the hotel. I've decided I'm extending my stay by a day; I want to hang out by the beach. It's fine if he wants to go home.

"I don't have to drive you anymore?"

"No, we're good. You can go home."

"I'll go to the beach."

"You just told me you didn't like the room here."

"Yes, but I don't have to drive you. I'll relax."

Namir emerges within minutes in a turquoise Speedo, towel draped over his shoulder. He smiles and disappears in the direction of the beach. I contemplate yelling "Don't get lost!" after him, but I've been more than enough of an asshole already. I had to give him credit: he just flexed on me in a Speedo.

I stay in a half-built motor lodge two blocks back from the water. When I check in, the owner gives me a large bear hug. "My friend! Please give me a good rating on Tripadvisor." If there is a contemporary international greeting, this just might be it.

Much of Mirissa has been rebuilt since the tsunami. The new constructions are modern and structurally sound. I get to the beach. Wave after perfect wave barrels into the shore. My ass sinks into a plastic chair. A pretty local woman brings a bucket of ice-cold beer. I'm flouting the Poya holiday rules. It's disrespectful, but I'm at the beach. There's a friendly mix of bohemian Europeans sprawled out around me. Reggae, surfing, and fun make up the scene. The water is clean, clear, and perfect.

With a full moon overhead, I snack on a burger and some more large beers. I walk the length of the beach. My eyes look over the tables of couples eating along the shoreline. They're having a series of perfect moments. Making memories and soon making love in paradise. Perhaps I'll recognize somebody? But I don't. I stare off into the moonlit ocean. It's light enough to see my shadow in the sand. For fifty yards, it's just us.

Not too far ahead a crowd forms in a half circle close by the water. There's a sea turtle laying her eggs on the beach. It's an exhausting process. She furiously digs into the sand with her flippers. I know that shining a light on a turtle can be disruptive. I also know that, in our social-media-loving world, there's no way a tourist doesn't try to take a flash picture. Wildlife authorities have been called and will eventually set up a perimeter, but they are slow to arrive.

Fuck it, I'll set up the perimeter. I motion people back and then crouch down about eight feet from the turtle and scream at anyone who tries to take a flash picture. Half a dozen times, people try to take the photo anyway. One Frenchman is unrepentant. I tell him to stop. He takes more. I size him up. "Hey, douche! Fucking stop it!"

The Frenchman, a lanky weasel, mocks me and gives off a "what are you going to do about it?" vibe.

That's it. "Fuck around and find out," I mutter.

I knock the phone out of his hand. I've got at least forty pounds on the guy. He backs off but not before hurling more insults. Rage boils inside me. I'm being the Ugly American right now; I should keep cool—this is snap rage, the kind that's hard to channel. Whatever I've been feeling the last few days, this poor bastard just walked right into it. "Hey, come here!"

He walks away, still slinging insults. I chase him away from the crowd and push him over into the sand. He leaps to his feet and takes a swing. I dodge and tackle him hard and cock back to throw a punch. One of my knees weighs heavily on his forearm. He throws up his free hand defensively in front of his face. I know I'll really hurt him if I connect. I get up and throw him off to the side like luggage into a trunk of a car. He doesn't say a word when I say, "Fuck off!" He retreats to sympathetic friends. I walk off alone.

At the Bay Moon Bar, two Swiss girls in their twenties chat me up. They worked in corporate jobs for two years and quit. They're traveling together for five months and have nine weeks in Sri Lanka.

"Good for you!" is all I can muster. Their story seems all too tired, tried, and familiar. I should listen more and make friends, but I don't really care. After a few shots I see them sucking face with surf-bro Sri Lankans whose torsos make washboards look pudgy. I look down at my gut, much larger than a few months ago. A few Spaniards working for an NGO are friendly. They've been working on women's equality issues.

"How's it going?" I ask.

"There's a ways to go."

"No shit? Female equality is lacking in this part of the world? Shocker!"

They don't like my snark and soon walk over to some sun-bleached Aussies. Aussies, always a safe bet, half-drunk and fully kind. I run my hand through my prep-school haircut. Here I am in the world's perfect beach spot and there's nobody to share it with. Hell, nobody wants to share it with me. Why not? They like my photos, but do they care beyond that? Do they like me, or am I just some entertaining enigma? Texts home to friends with pictures dry up quickly. The novelty of my journey has grown old. "Keep living the dream, bro. Take care." They have lives with serious responsibilities. Mom doesn't text so much; she's content to let me strike out on my own.

The hyperconnected digital world gives me Instagram likes, but there's a terrible feeling of anxiety being this alone. That's amplified by these surroundings. This solo travel, the focus is so inward, and I don't like what I see. I can't go back to the lodge. That room will drive me insane right now. I numb myself. More beer under the moonlight till it looks like the sun is getting ready to switch places. I see my Swiss friends, or is it the Spaniards? One of them waves. Another hangover in paradise awaits.

I scowl, put my beer down, and stumble off.

TWENTY-ONE

Boxes

For nearly ten years, Dad's files—his "stuff"—have been stored in the attic of the family home, dating from his early work in politics through the day he died at NBC. And for nearly ten years I've avoided visiting it. This is just the "important" stuff. There are more boxes at a storage facility in Virginia. Dad, a trained lawyer, was a meticulous keeper of records. Everything from preparation notes for *Meet the Press* to signed pictures from presidents to thank-you letters he received from a breakfast diner manager in Des Moines.

At first, I used my career as an excuse: *Why fork over precious free time to such a slow, painful, and daunting process? I don't get much vacation; I'm not using it on this.* But right now, to cool down and ground myself, as a way to give me a reprieve from Mom's "What are you doing with your life?" mantra, I've agreed to momentarily return to DC and sort through them.

My goal is to figure out which boxes Mom and I should keep and which should go to a library or a university, if any library or university has interest. I figure some institution will. It's been ten years, and they still talk about Dad on TV. His ghost haunts more people than just me. I chuckle when I see his name trending on social media. He'd have no idea what to make of it. I grab a box and rip off the tape.

"NBC GULF WAR 1991." I quickly realize there is only one way to leaf through this box—or any other. Take a folder. Carefully lay everything out on the floor. Go through each folder.

I can't do it standing, so I grab a small step stool that puts my knees near my ears and set to work.

There is little natural light in the attic space. Even when I turn on the bulbs overhead, there's a melancholy darkness in the room. It matches the attic's quiet. It's almost as if these boxes would prefer to be left alone.

Instead, I am alone with them.

There are so many boxes, at least forty or fifty. I find some dark humor and belt out, "Legends never die! Because they leave hundreds of fucking boxes to sort out, baby!"

Mom hears me from downstairs and peeks her head up, puzzled. "Did you scream something?"

"No, it's all good."

This is legacy management. Something I did in my twenties and swore off in my thirties—or at least I told myself that. It never goes away, though. I can run from it, and believe me I have—I've got a marked-up passport to prove it—but the box pile remains. The man remains.

Remains are heavy.

I run through a gauntlet of emotions. Seeing his handwriting is particularly hard. Each time, I pause and run my fingers over the dark ink. Photos get me too. Dad with dignitaries, colleagues, family, and so on. I spot a good one and laugh-cry. Me in Dallas, ten years old. I'm wearing a Ross Perot mask, featuring the Texas oilman who ran a competitive race for president in 1992 and was a fixture in American politics for most of the 1990s. I'm standing between Dad and Perot after an interview. I can hear Dad's voice from that day: "Luke, have Mr. Perot sign your mask. No, the bald spot on the back—that's a good place for the marker." After the interview Dad took me to drive go-karts and then to an arcade. We ate greasy BBQ and even caught a Texas Rangers game at night. Met the great Hall of Fame pitcher Nolan Ryan in the parking lot. I remember the grip of his handshake; it nearly broke my fingers.

I'll keep this one. On to the next.

What would he want seen? How would he like to be perceived? That's my mindset as I flip through endless binders and folders. When I find older files, dating back to his years in politics, I start comparing myself to the man. This is a sin I swore I'd quit committing. But I have at it anyway.

A clipping from the *New York Daily News* in 1982: "Moynihan Wins Resounding Victory . . . by over a Million Votes." Dad was thirty-two then. My current age. I skim through the piece and read how Tim Russert took a leave from being chief of staff to Senator Moynihan to run his campaign; Moynihan then would win with the largest majority in a midterm election in the history of the Senate. I find a profile piece in *Rolling Stone* on Dad titled "A Man This Good Is Hard to Find"; it's from February 1985, six months before I was born.

The dinner was in honor of Brokaw's friend and colleague, Timothy J. Russert, the newest and youngest vice-president of NBC News. At thirty-four, Russert—who resembles the puckish, chubby altar boy that he in fact was—had spent the past two years as counselor to Governor Mario Cuomo of New York and several years before that as chief of staff for Senator Daniel Patrick Moynihan, all the while building a nearly legendary reputation as a street-smart, media-wise political operative . . . Knowing Russert was a prerequisite for anyone in the know; if he had been any more plugged in, he would have been electrocuted. Inevitably described as shrewd, he was the opposite of slick. Among journalists and media people, there is a veritable Russert fan club, composed of members of every political stripe. Liberal columnist Mary McGrory: "He's the best I've ever seen." Conservative columnist George Will: "He is a superb professional, who understands the Democratic party beyond the Washington Beltway, where most of it—thank God for small favors—lives." Democratic political consultant David Garth: "He's the best guy at working the press I've ever encountered." Republican political consultant Roger Stone: "He's the best strategist in the Democratic party."[1]

Jesus, what am I? Clearly not on a path to being a legend. Hell, it doesn't feel like I'm on any path. At thirty-two Dad was making electoral history! At thirty-four he was the VP of a network news division! All this while he was the son of a garbage man who worked himself through college and law school with no connections beyond Buffalo. And then there's me, as privileged as can be, with every advantage available, and I can't compare. I make no impact. I do no good. I can't come close to him. Can't even bring myself to try. Pathetic.

It takes two months to go through it all. Monday through Friday, nine to five. Each week, each day, each hour is an exercise in discipline. Each box is a wild card. Every file needs to be examined thoroughly so nothing of importance is lost. Some boxes take a few hours. Others take a full day or even two. Any single item can bring out emotions.

Take the box about me. Inside is a collection of all my report cards, dating back to nursery school. I knew he was saving them to show me someday, and I am immediately flooded with tears when I see a Post-it attached to one of the cards with a good grade: "So proud, buddy!" I tape it back up fast. I don't want to relive it now, alone.

When I finish the boxes, there's no sense of satisfaction. Every single one was such an emotional journey. I'm relieved to be finished.

I need to put some travel on my horizon because something else already looms. In a little more than a month, it will be the tenth anniversary of Dad's death. I'm starting to get requests to be part of remembrances, either online, on TV, or in print. I want nothing to do with it. I've got nothing to give. I need to get out of here. Where can I go where people won't give me crap for missing the anniversary? What would be a worthwhile excuse?

And then I find it: the World Cup in Russia—via Iceland, because its airline is cheap.

"Hey, Mom, I'll be gone all of June."

"What are you doing now?"

"The World Cup. Russia."

"The World Cup? In Russia? That'll be interesting. Will that really be it?"

TWENTY-TWO

Iceland

I tell people close to me it isn't intentional—though it certainly is. The day of my sixteen-hour trek around the southern coast of Iceland, most of the trip out of cellphone range, falls on the tenth anniversary of my father's death: June 13, 2018.

I will not spend the anniversary at my father's grave. I feel a little guilty about this. But being in DC would mean being surrounded by tributes pouring in on TV and over social media. Endless texts and calls. I appreciate them, but I lived them in 2008—and in some sense still do. Thoughts of being defined by pain and loss hurt too much. Plus, I don't want to engage with people. I'm tired of putting on a strong, happy face, feigning enthusiasm and wellness. I'm limiting social media and will use the stunning natural beauty of Iceland as a means to remember Dad, free of commitment.

Groggy, after little sleep at the hostel due to the endless daylight of an Icelandic summer and bunkmates eager to enjoy it, I get on a tour bus. Twenty seats crammed together hold sixteen bodies. A diplomatic corps on wheels: a French lady, a Spanish couple in their fifties, two Chinese families of four, a German couple in their sixties, an Indian couple in their thirties, and me. We're led by a mighty Icelander, Dylan, the driver. Dylan is five feet, nine inches, thirty-seven years old, with a solid build and close crew cut. Nobody in the van knows who Tim Russert is, and with scant mobile service, no one will find out.

This is my global family, and they will take me at face value. I play tic-tac-toe with a Chinese kid in the back of the bus. He needs me for the game, and I need him.

"It is going to be a long day," Dylan says. "We leave the station at 7 a.m. and return around 11 p.m. It'll be daylight for the duration."

"Hey, man, are you driving sixteen hours?" I ask.

Dylan flashes a smile. "I'm trained for it and got these." He opens a lunch cooler of energy drinks and high-protein snacks.

Iceland's south coast is unblemished. A proper comparison is the best of New Zealand and Patagonia with the rolling green hills of Ireland in early summer. Much of the tour is the drive itself. Seasons pass on the ride: rain, snow, spring breezes, and summer sun.

The Skógafoss waterfall is eighty-two feet wide with a two-hundred-foot drop. The water of the Skóga River falls off sea cliffs that now face inland. The cliffs were once pushed a few miles by ancient seismic activity. Perhaps that is what is so striking: the water is expecting to fall into the sea, but after its violent fall and collapse, it calmly flows through tranquil grasslands in a stream. The grass around Skógafoss is a resplendent green. It captures the golden sun from an ultramarine sky.

We have thirty minutes to explore the area. I distance myself from the group and move quickly. As I pace toward the wall of water, I see it out of the corner of my eye. Shooting out from the spray of the wall is a rainbow. Rich red on top, then yellow, bluish green, and purple on the bottom.

I sprint, I need to hug it, feel it. That is my father's spirit—somewhere over the rainbow—just like the day I buried him.

It hangs over the stream. This is such a dreamlike situation. Then I hear a voice in my head, telling me to climb to the top of the falls. "Look for it up there."

I leap up the steps, jumping three or four at a time, constantly looking left to make sure the rainbow hasn't vanished. After a frantic few minutes, I get to the top. I see the flow of the Skóga River, the ocean off in the distance, and the magnificent rainbow. It makes a perfect arch across the banks of the stream, just in front of the wall of water. It stands still as if to smile. Then it's gone, in the wink of the sun.

I look down at my watch. Ten minutes have passed. Ten years after he left, I get ten minutes? I take a seat on a ridge near the top of the falls. I cry. God, I'm so fragile; is this spiraling?

I'm confused. I feel alone. All this time alone with my thoughts. Maybe it was a mistake to be away and alone. I wish Dad could tell me something with clarity. I'm relieved he isn't mad at me for escaping, for avoiding his remembrances. But did I see everything I was supposed to? Am I supposed to keep traveling? I feel Mom's concerns, my own aimlessness. Should I keep traveling? When will I be at ease with myself, knowing how to live the life I chose?

No response.

I see Dylan walking toward me. At first he's agitated, but my eyes endear him to empathy.

"You were due at the bus fifteen minutes ago, mate."

"Sorry, I lost track of . . ."

"It happens."

"Hey, are the rainbows commonplace at the falls?"

"The spray produces a lot of them when the sun is shiny, but that was a big one. They usually don't reach up that high all the way over the falls and river."

TWENTY-THREE

The World Cup: Russia

I move on to the World Cup. I need the sweet, beautiful release of sports. Russia or bust!

From my cramped hostel I follow the packs of chanting Moroccan and Portuguese fans donning their countries' kits on the streets of Moscow. We move to the subway entrance, yelling, dancing, and clapping as the Soviet-era escalator takes us below ground. We're all trekking to the World Cup match at Luzhniki Stadium, but the hostel where I'm staying has been its own trip. Citizens from the following nations under one small roof: USA, Russia, England, Ireland, Germany, Sweden, Colombia, Brazil, Peru, Morocco, Australia, China, Iran, Serbia, South Korea, France, Portugal, Switzerland, Senegal, Mexico, and Japan. We're crammed together in tiny matchbox rooms, almost all of us men, and most of us drinking too much at the 24/7 outdoor bar. We've nearly burned the place down with discarded cigarettes. Walking through the hostel's communal kitchen is an international food competition, various smells and spices vying for supremacy. The bathrooms have been an exercise in tolerance. I haven't seen a single spat, even among the drinkers. We are happy to be here.

I played foosball with a local father and son at the corner bar. I kept beating the dad even as he bought my vodka shots. When I was about to beat the dad again, his son pulled me over and whispered to let him win or he'd flip over the table. I obliged. Russians, baby! Dad would approve that I've found so much bonhomie in the country of an adversary. Together time with my global family; things are okay. The road is leading me where it needs to.

The Moscow subway is a beautiful relic from the Soviet era. The last stop looks like an illustrious opera house: gold ceilings with intricate white trim, large marble columns lining the way, white acanthus leaves that bedeck the platforms. The escalator lifts us into the daylight, the revelry quiets a bit. Russian security forces in light blue uniforms and armed with batons are lined up on both sides of the walkway. They look about a decade younger than me; they stand two deep and scowl. Intimidating, but not scary. Every ten yards a ferocious-looking dog sits at a handler's foot. Some bark aggressively.

From a tennis umpire chair, on the edge of the stadium grounds, a young Russian woman endlessly repeats a phrase in accented English through a bullhorn, meant to help fans navigating their way.

"Welcome to the World Cup match at Luzhniki Stadium. There are places to have questions answered. Have a good time and unforgettable emotion."

Budweiser beer tents and dance clubs. Visa credit card–sponsored interactive zones for the fans. Frolicking among the crowds are sexy young Russian women dressed like cheerleaders, sporting the Budweiser logo on their tight white T-shirts. At the foot of the stadium is a large metal statue of communist crusader Vladimir Lenin, menacingly glancing over the plaza. What he sees must horrify him. Just like in Vietnam, hypercapitalism being celebrated by the world! Dad loved "progress" like this. I remember back in 2003 when Paul McCartney played a concert in Red Square and sang the ironic song "Back in the USSR." Dad played a clip on *Meet the Press*. It was a seminal moment for him. A triumph of Western values. I'm channeling Dad's cheerful optimism.

The match is between Portugal and Morocco. We're here to see Cristiano Ronaldo, the best player in the world. There are lots of young Russian kids in Ronaldo jerseys. I get emotional when I see a Russian father holding his boy's hand as they walk to their seats. The dad wears his pride on his face, grateful to share this moment with his son. Memories of my own sporting events over the years with Dad wash over me. I look around at empty seats, imagining Dad in one. He always had to have an aisle seat, more leg room. I close my eyes and go back to the last game we ever attended together.

"These are the best seats in the house!"

Dad was smiling wide. He slapped the top of the visiting dugout at

Nationals Park, admiring the location of our new season tickets. It was a cold Sunday night in late March 2008. The Washington Nationals were playing against the Atlanta Braves. It was Opening Day in the Nats' sparkling new ballpark, and President Bush threw out the first pitch.

"We're going to have a great summer here," Dad said. "You'll be back for good from BC. This is our spot! Lots of great seasons ahead. A real major league park in our town!" He was giddy as he reached into his pocket and pulled out two twenties.

"Buddy, go find us some beers and dogs. None of that fancy beer. A Bud or something. Nothing light."

I worked my way through the crowded concourse and procured baseball's sustenance. When I got back to our seats, Dad gave me a strong backslap.

"Good get. Let's enjoy these."

The Nats jumped ahead to a 2–0 lead in the first. We high-fived. It was cold, but I didn't care. It was one of those moments I knew was special while I was experiencing it. We had done this in so many ballparks around the league, even had season tickets in nearby Baltimore for a number of years, but to be in DC, in a new park, meant something more.

When the Braves came back to tie the game in the ninth at 2–2, Dad finally admitted the cold was getting to him.

"Let's watch the bottom of the ninth; I don't want to freeze in extras. We'll have plenty of opening days here, including some literally during the day with sun!"

"Works for me, Dad." I didn't fight him, though I didn't want the night to end. I knew Dad had been up since 5:30 a.m. getting ready for *Meet the Press*.

Nationals star Ryan Zimmerman came to the plate with two outs. Dad zipped his coat and was preparing to leave. On the second pitch, Zimmerman launched one to deep left center field. A walk-off home run! Dad grabbed me by the jacket and threw me into the aisle and pushed me up the stairs. We sprinted up toward the exits as Zimmerman began his trot. I looked back. Dad was clapping and shouting as he jumped up each step, full of youthful exuberance. The smile from before was now even wider across his red Irish face.

"So great, buddy! Now, keep moving! Let's beat the traffic."

I rub the arm of my World Cup seat and think about our family seats at Nationals Park. I kept the ones Dad and I sat in on that opening day in 2008. I won't ever let them go. I hope that young Russian boy thinks of this day and his dad whenever he sees this stadium, these seats.

Nobody has sat down since the opening whistle. In the fourth minute Ronaldo flies like Superman to head in a cross pass for a goal. The crowd erupts. We've gotten our money's worth right out the gate.

I'm in awe to be a small part of something the size of the world. I sit between a Mexican and a Nigerian, with a Moroccan family behind me, the women in hijabs. When Ronaldo touches the ball, half the stadiums cheers, while the other chants the name of his archrival, Lionel Messi of Argentina: "ME-SSI! ME-SSI! ME-SSI!" It's been nearly two years since I saw Messi in the flesh at that airport in Argentina. How early on in the journey that was. No chance I would have had the resolve to travel to Russia solo back then.

Now, here I am. Wiser, I hope? I don't ponder the question too long. I'm at the World Cup! My Mexican seatmate hands me a beer with a smile.

RED SQUARE

The next day, recovering from a mighty soccer-hooligans-inspired hangover, I put one foot in front of the other on my walk to Red Square. The plan is to see it and then have drinks at the Spaso House, the American ambassador's house in Moscow, with Mrs. Huntsman. The current ambassador, Jon Huntsman, is the father of my friend Abby Huntsman of TV fame. Mrs. Huntsman insisted I reach out when I got to Russia. It feels like an important duty to see her, something my parents would champion. You've been privileged with a special opportunity. Honor your country and its history, especially in Russia.

My route to Red Square goes through Nikolskaya Street, pedestrian friendly and adorned with the gaudiest stores of Western civilization: Gucci, Prada, and Bentley, where local oligarchs shop. The tourists' action is on the walkway. Street performers and musicians mingle with Russian soldiers carrying machine guns.

Red Square is powerful. The buildings are minatory in nature, to put you in your place. Forbidding and baleful, they look down like giants, prepared to quickly squash any threat. Some gentleness comes through the colorful onion domes of Saint Basil's Cathedral, the iconic landmark of Russia, the backdrop for every media report to ever be seen from Moscow. A place my mother and father both visited as journalists pre- and post-communism. Mom has been emailing me her old *Vanity Fair* stories about Russia. She interviewed their authoritarian war criminal leader, Vladimir Putin, when he came into office. Back then, there was hope he might be a reformer.

One of Mom's basic points I encounter for myself through numerous monuments: the Russians never felt they got enough credit for their role in winning World War II. Twenty million countrymen died. Everywhere, the war is memorialized. Putin has used the "respect Russia" ideology to his benefit.

I try to take a panoramic shot of the square on my iPhone. Mom will like the photo. Halfway through, my eye catches a woman a hundred yards away in a blue dress with tiny red dots. She's walking in step with a well-coifed man. The paradigmatic shot of Red Square frames her perfectly, her shoulders just below the domed onions of the cathedral. Her eyes lock onto me as if I were a camera lens broadcasting her to the world. She moves closer. The squint of her eyes grows more transfixed. Then her head shakes and she blinks, almost as if in shock.

The woman screams, equal parts excited and terrified: "Luke?! Luke, is that you?! No fucking way!"

I'm stunned. It's been three years since I've seen Katherine. We dated for two years. At one point, I considered moving in with her. It never happened because of our conflicting lifestyles. She wanted tetherless adventure. I wanted to stay in DC and move up the career ladder. I had a great respect for history and tradition; she found it outdated. Now, in Red Square, I'm the bearded solo traveler seeking enlightenment and she, I quickly learn, is the stable one, married and on a time-sensitive vacation.

The irony isn't lost.

"You're fucking married, and I'm the wandering hippie."

"I love it!"

Surreal can be overused in our lexicon, but this moment is surreal. I'm speechless for a good thirty seconds; I clear my throat a dozen times before I hug her. Her husband kindly chortles. I don't know if this is real or some elaborate plot set up by the Russian KGB to mess with me. Her hair still smells like Katherine's. The memories flood back: all the good times, the pain of our separation. In the shadow of the Kremlin, I'm staring at somebody at one point I wanted to be my wife.

"How the hell are you, Katherine?"

But what is there to say? The three of us laugh hard and begin to blurt out platitudes about the World Cup being so fun and cool. Katherine and her husband had come to Moscow through central Europe. Like me, they took advantage of Russia's open borders during the World Cup. Soon they would be off to a wedding in Scotland.

I do like her husband. He's well-groomed with impeccable manners, a throwback to an America where people got dressed up to travel. I, meanwhile, am sweating profusely into a tight T-shirt that covers a bit of pudge.

We'd been at the same match yesterday. Katherine had told her husband she wanted to see the beautiful, hunky Ronaldo in person. They'd sat in the lower bowl.

"How was the view up high?" she jokes.

"It was great."

But I can't help but think that the upgrade in seat mirrored the upgrade in man.

We return to mindless chitchat to ward off any awkwardness. We're all still in a state of shock. Finally, I work up some courage.

"We need to take a picture," I tell her. And then I hold out my phone to her husband. "I'm sorry, man, would you mind?"

He obliges.

I bring her in close for the shot. I hold on to her waist longer than I should. Damn, this could've been us. This could be some random American guy, kind enough to take our picture. Then in a day we'd go off to Scotland or Greece, or wherever in this big world. Isn't today proof we could have worked through our issues? Hell, we may have been too perfect for each other. To have such a beautiful traveling partner . . .

It hits me: I'm so tired of traveling alone. I think about a young German couple I met in Bolivia. They were only twenty-three and traveling through Latin America with their two-year-old. He went where they went. They made an adventure out of it and never slowed down. What if Katherine and I had channeled that same kind of energy?

My mind snaps back to reality as the husband hands my phone back. Katherine will not go off with me. I will go off by myself. Part of me wants to offer up a drink at a nearby café, to try to prolong the encounter. I can't do it.

I'm too shaken.

"Take care of yourself, Luke," she says.

They fade into the crowd, her blue dress following his white linen shirt. I keep an eye on them till they are swallowed by the sea of humanity.

I scrap plans to go to a war museum. Instead, I find the nearest outdoor café that serves beer. I order a tall mug and sip in the heat. I send the picture of Katherine and me to my mother, who is flabbergasted.

"Wow! I hope you take good notes on that one."

Maureen Orth . . . ever, and always, the journalist.

The torment of the Katherine encounter throws me off the rest of the day. I'm supposed to go to Spaso House to see Mrs. Huntsman, but I can't find the will. The guilt of letting down my country doesn't move me. I'm rattled. I'm fragile. I light a candle at a nearby Orthodox church, but it brings no peace. I can't hobnob or maintain a proper sense of decorum. When I message Mrs. Huntsman and tell her I can't make it, I'm honest about what happened and she's kind and understanding. She's the motherly console I need in the moment.

I then sit at a nondescript local bar to journal.

It wasn't that I still yearned for her. I just can't shake the feeling that God,

Dad, or the universe was trying to send a message, just like in Iceland. Why did fate intervene in Red Square? What was the ultimate motive? My only guess is that the encounter is meant to prove that we were both capable of the things that we had angrily screamed would never happen to each other. I left the comfort zone and bubble of Washington, DC. She turned away from her nomadic tendencies and dropped anchor. Maybe today was meant to be a reminder of how far we had come? A consummation of our growth as people?

Then again, maybe not. I mean, this has fucked me up. What the hell am I doing? Hasn't Katherine just proved that this all-or-nothing lens by which I have viewed my life the last two years, along with its idea of "freedom," is a bunch of bullshit? She married Mr. Perfect and is traveling the world *with* him. They're growing and experiencing *together*.

Why can't I have that? What's wrong with me? Why did that show itself? Katherine?! In Red Square? Millions of people from around the world here, and that was the draw I got? Katherine?! Come on, man. Everything is so goddamn confusing. I order a chilled vodka shot. The barkeep makes it tall without my asking. God, Russians pour it good.

The internal monologue doesn't stop. I scribble to the point of ripping the page with the point of the pen. Just like in Iceland, I'm ending my trip confused. So lost. What does it all mean?

I order another vodka shot. The bartender gives me two because she likes my Washington Capitals shirt with a Russian name on the back.

I feel my phone buzz and pull it out. It's Katherine. She hasn't texted me in years.

"Of all the gin joints in the world!"

I smile, let out a manic laugh, and recklessly toss the phone on the table. I get the *Casablanca* reference.

We always loved watching old movies.

I text her our photo back. I caption, "From Russia with love!"

No response.

TWENTY-FOUR

LA to Abilene

"Whoa, these are kind of tight."

I let out a nervous laugh.

The clothier looks puzzled: "You said thirty-six-inch waist, right?"

"Yeah, I mean, that's what I've worn for a while. I guess I kind of veer toward the stretchier fabric pants these days."

He grabs a tape measure from a shelf and walks over. I stand up on a box. "Don't suck in," he commands. In a circular motion he runs the tape around my waist. "You're more of a thirty-eight. At least, that's what you'll need to be comfortable."

It's mid-September and my summer travels have ended, but, like my waistline, I am not better. Maybe even more confused.

I'm at a department store in Los Angeles a few hours before the 70th Primetime Emmy Awards, ready to accompany Mom, whose twenty-year-old book, *Vulgar Favors*, was resurrected last year and became the basis of a hit TV series titled *The Assassination of Gianni Versace: American Crime Story* on FX. It's up for eighteen awards, more than any other show. Mom's book was the integral source of the production. The scripts drew from it, as did wardrobe and casting. It's a wonderful capstone for a project to which she gave nearly two years of her life in the late 1990s. We have a busy schedule of interviews, receptions, and promotional parties.

I own a tux left over from my NBC days on the banquet circuit. Thank God I tried that old thing on early this morning in the hotel room and discovered then that the pants couldn't button. It'd have been much worse to find that out a half hour before the red carpet.

The clothier brings me options. One pair of pants fits, but the price for the whole tux doesn't. I park my pride and open up about the situation. "Listen, I came out here with a tux. The pants don't button anymore. I think I can get by with the jacket, though."

He kindly nods along. "How about this: a pair of black dress pants? They won't have the satin stripe along the leg, but they're cheaper."

"Sounds good."

He comes back with a form-fitting pair, tight through the legs but loose in the waist.

"Don't worry about the stripe, man. Nobody will notice. It's LA and I'm sure half the crowd will be wearing sneakers and colorful velvet."

I walk outside into the customarily perfect sun of Beverly Hills. I think about the time I did a stint as a visiting NBC correspondent in nearby Burbank. From those few months I learned to like Southern California. I never progressed to *loving* LA because the cliché about a place predicated on style is true. Still, it was fun being away from DC, living on my own in a foreign place. This exposure to new things, California's eternal promise, may have gotten the travel bug going.

Maybe this LA swing will serve as my own capstone.

Mom is, of course, late to meet me in the lobby before the show. I study myself in the hotel hallway mirror. The cheap pair of five-dollar aviator sunglasses I bought off the street completes the outfit. My beard has grown so long that a friend recently joked, "You look like if the Unabomber joined the Taliban." But with the shades and slimming outfit, I tell myself I look presentable. A cool California cat even.

Louie Anderson of *Family Feud* fame hangs out in the lobby. He's been nominated for something. He graciously poses for any and all cellphone photos. One bellhop tells Anderson, "I grew up with you, man." For so many years, people approached and said that to me about Dad. "We spent so many Sunday mornings with your dad. He was family."

TV is weird like that, a family of Tim Russerts and Louie Andersons.

The elevator opens and Mom steps out. A colorful well-cut dress, her hair and makeup professionally done: she looks regal. I change my assessment of my outfit to *schlubby*. But there's no time to change. I walk ahead of her to the idling black car and open the door.

I will be Mom's handler tonight. Whatever she needs.

At the red carpet, a woman wearing a headset grabs Mom by the arm— "Maureen! Welcome!"—and leads her to the walkway. The woman makes no eye contact with me. I think back to the life I once led. I walked red carpets once. I even took Oscar-nominated actress Anna Kendrick to the ritzy White House correspondents' dinner when I was twenty-four. An up-and-coming actress and an up-and-coming broadcast journalist. Now she's A-list and, well, I'm a past life.

Another woman in a headset motions to stand behind the red-carpet tent. "Wait for her here." The first woman yells out: "Maureen Orth, writer, *The Assassination of Gianni Versace*, FX!" Shutters snap and Mom smiles. She answers questions and then meets me.

"That was cool, Mom!" I say with as much honest envy as condescension, because it's such a spectacle.

"I wanted you to walk with me."

"I have no business being up there."

"People like you. You look good tonight. Let them see you. You should've done it." Her comment, while well intentioned, frankly kind of pisses me off. Though it was not her intent, it feels to me like Mom wants to rekindle a career I left; her tone suggests I should've done more to stay relevant.

"People don't know me anymore. Which is fine. That's how I want it."

I don't know how convincing I sound.

We walk into the crowded concourse of the Microsoft Theater. Hundreds of well-dressed, important people mill about, many looking over their shoulder to see if they can spot a "someone." I don't know anybody. Soon Mom is whisked away. She'll sit with the cast and crew of the show. I sit in the back.

There's a concession stand selling twelve-dollar beers. I buy two and pound

221

them. Then I get two more and search for my seat. I find an unassuming older woman with a smile sitting in it.

"I'm sorry, I could be wrong, but I think that's my seat."

"No sorry needed," she says. "I'm a seat filler."

"Well, I guess I'm better than an empty seat, right?"

She just walks away.

Mom's show cleans up. It wins for director, lead actor, and outstanding limited series. For the final award Mom is onstage with the cast. She stands right behind the podium as the director speaks. I document the moment on my iPhone, like a parent at their kid's recital. My phone blows up with texts, many variations of "Your mom is onstage at the Emmys, dude!"

She deserves this. In the course of the evening I've found that most everyone around me is a seat filler, and one guy next to me sees me taking pictures and asks if I know anyone onstage. "The well-dressed lady, that's my mom."

"Cool! What do you do?"

I pretend not to hear.

Once Mom finishes with the post-show interviews, I give her a big hug. What a life. Peace Corps volunteer, documentary filmmaker, one of the first female writers at *Newsweek*, national magazine awards, *Vanity Fair* special correspondent, and now an Emmy winner for a hit TV show. As if to compensate, I tell myself that I also won an Emmy, in 2008, for being part of NBC's election night coverage. And now I lead a different life, a better life. Right?

"Great job, Mom," I say. "You could retire tonight and be a Hall of Famer!"

"Why? There's so much more to do! Let's get to the after-party."

We walk into a large, trendy event space. I spot LaKeith Stanfield of *Atlanta* fame, another show on FX. I shamelessly ask for a photo. He agrees, then ribs me: "You got the selfie, my man? Young, sweaty Santa Claus here."

The thing is, he's not wrong. The crowded room makes me sweat, and the beard doesn't help. I follow Mom around. Members of the cast ask for her photo. I dutifully offer to take it, and some people give me knowing glances. At a ritzy, posh Los Angeles party, a sweaty guy with a beard and a mismatched suit and a famous parent isn't exactly out of place. There are enough burnouts with trust funds to stock reality TV series for decades.

One eager lady in her fifties with black frizzy hair that matches her black glasses approaches. "I have to ask: Are you Luke Russert?"

I smile. Maybe I'm not totally washed up. "Yes, that's me."

"Oh my God, I loved your dad! You did such a great job too. I'm an MSNBC junkie. What are you doing now? I hardly recognized you. Your beard—and you're much bigger these days."

"You know, I'm just traveling."

I swill my drink and hold the icy coldness to my forehead. She seems puzzled, if not awkward that she stepped over a boundary. I try to comfort her with embellishment: "I got some projects I'm working on. There's stuff."

"Well, I'll look for you on TV."

"Yeah."

I'm even less convincing now.

The next day Mom and I fly to Tucson to visit one of her friends. Once on the ground I tell her I won't be flying home with her. Instead I craft a plan to drive to a hipster enclave: Marfa, Texas. Marfa is all over Instagram with its faux roadside Prada store and other quirky weird monuments. Might as well go see it. Why not? It's an eight-hour drive through the hills and flats of New Mexico and West Texas. It's another experience. I need an experience that is not LA. I need the anonymous travel in which I specialize now, where no one knows what I'm doing and I don't have to answer for what I've become.

Mom knows any effort to stop me is fruitless. "Please try to figure out some purpose; Marfa is supposed to be fascinating. What can you learn there? Maybe it'll inspire you." She's slightly agitated but doesn't want the high of last night's victories to crash down so soon. Warmly, with motherly concern, she says softly, "Drive safely, windshield cowboy."

ROAD TO MARFA

A few years ago in Maine, the open road felt like freedom. An hour into this trip in a rented SUV, a particular kind of loneliness hits. Soon after the sun rises, I see an email from Mary, the woman I've put through so much, who has tried to give me more chances during my travels. I've used her to lean on, but I've also weighed her down. Our relationship has disintegrated over the last few months, and, fearing the worst, I pull over to see what Mary wrote.

Her email says she cannot deal with what I've become. She cannot deal with the consistent uncertainty, the restlessness, the inability to commit. The poor diet. The lack of any clear direction. My endless staring into the abyss.

Am I really that bad? She's being a touch overdramatic, like Mom these days, but I understand why she's ending it over email. I never should have kept her waiting through this long search for myself. *False hope is so incredibly self-ish.* I sit on the side of the road and realize I'm not angry. I'm almost—I don't know—relieved?

I close the email without responding and hit the highway. I hit 75 miles per hour, then 85. There are no cops, no cars, and no reason to care. Soon 95 miles per hour becomes 100, and then 105. At this rate, I'm driving too fast to focus on anything but how the lines of the road narrow and how I must stay between them. I keep the pedal to the metal, pushing through to nowhere.

I stop only because I have to get gas. It's a nondescript roadside station, like the ones from 1950s movies, somewhere in the middle of the New Mexican desert.

"Welcome in, sir. How are you?"

The clerk is a heavyset Hispanic woman with thickly braided black hair. She sits on an upholstered rolling stool.

"A woman I loved very much kind of ended things permanently."

Saying this feels both true and feigned, melodramatic and somehow not dramatic enough.

The clerk nods.

"Well, we have a two-for-one special on slushies right now."

224

The fog I'm in doesn't lift. Everything rolls by like tumbleweed: New Mexico into Texas. How long have I been drifting? I think back to Sri Lanka, how I didn't really plan or research that trip. There for the likes, the content, the photos, the affirmation from people who live in my phone. Nepal too. The images I projected became more important than what I learned. I stopped trying to learn. Something weighed me down, something that hadn't been there before. When did the road lose its promise? It's easy to lose track of yourself when you give up looking for it. Katherine in Moscow was a reminder of just how lost I'd become. How alone I felt and continue to feel. Why? It's uncomfortable to think about. So I stop.

I hit El Paso and tacos. For no reason I decide to walk to the Mexican border, up to the gate. The streets and shops on the Mexico side look the same as the ones in El Paso. Maybe I should cross the border for a day? I think I have my passport. I keep it in my backpack. It would be a cool picture at the border for the gram, a good political statement about the meaningless wall. Score an easy win. I'm doing something meaningful, dammit!

Screw it. Too much effort.

Highway 118 runs through the Davis Mountains, the iconic foothills of West Texas. The altitude creeps up on me, north of five thousand feet. I was up even higher in Bolivia. I was so focused there. Whatever it took to see those salt flats. Hell, I fasted, no booze. Could I do that today? If I'm asking, does that mean I can't?

Near freight train tracks, I find the iconic Marfa Prada store. About thirty-five miles from the town, it's a permanent piece of "art," an unoccupied fake Prada in the middle of the desert. It mocks look-at-me pop-culture vapidity and is now legit pop-culture-elite-status vapidity. Celebrities flock here for fashion shoots. Influencers take selfies. Right now, two carloads of Los Angeles–looking bohemian cowboys get out of Cadillac Escalades to take pictures. They wear stupid scarves around their necks that scream *poseur*.

Am I any better than them?

What the fuck am I doing here?

I take a picture, though, and post it.

The likes come in. My mood improves, though deep down I know I just did the most basic deed of the professional Instagram influencer—the Marfa Prada shot. It's the Lynyrd Skynyrd "Free Bird" song request of Instagram shots. Oh, I'm painful.

I check into a low-budget motel in town. A guy in the parking lot brings crates of vinyl records into his room. "I don't do digital, man, and I travel with my music." Marfa in a nutshell: anachronistic and proud of it. The town features a batch of misfits, artists, adventurers, wannabe cowboys, and the rich folks sly enough to fit in but who still make a buck through a high-end restaurant or lodge. At the Lost Horse Saloon, there's an abandoned food truck with bullet holes near the front entrance. Lone Star beer is cheap, the guitar player in the band is decent. A local tattoo artist takes an interest in me, her hair a burnt orange. I'm now 100 percent untethered, so what the hell do I have to lose?

"Where you from?"

"DC."

"You escaping Donald Trump?"

I laugh. "I don't think he'd ever find himself here. Much less Ted Cruz."

"They're such assholes. I don't know how you DC people do it."

"Well, it's not exactly like I run into Ted Cruz walking his dog outside of Whole Foods."

"Whole Foods? What's that?"

"It doesn't matter."

I can't quite catch all of her story after she tells me her name, Daria, but she got to Marfa after working as a maid at a lodge near a national park. She left home from North Florida at eighteen and has been drifting since. I don't ask her age, but she seems a little younger than me. She invites me to a party. We go.

There's a donkey tied to a tree, chilling out; some carnival games like Skee-Ball happening in some gravel. Weird neon lights blink along a fence. I've never done acid, but this must be what a trip feels like. Around three in the morning, well served, I call it a night. Daria comes back with me, but I'm beyond a point where I can be of service to her needs.

"I have three roommates, so I'll crash here if you don't mind," she says.

I have enough sense to take my wallet and phone and hide them under the bed, rolled up in a shirt. I'm not the trusting kind anymore.

When I wake up, she's gone, the only remembrance some used towels. She took a shower and one of my T-shirts.

ABILENE

I leave Marfa. I skirted the outer rings of a different dimension and don't want to fall into a black hole. There's got to be something more meaningful out here to experience or at least give off the impression that I'm doing something worthwhile with my time.

On to Odessa, the home of Permian High School and *Friday Night Lights*. It's Friday, so maybe I can catch a game there. That'd be a kick-ass Instagram shot. I make it to the stadium in the afternoon. There's a game and the surrounding hotels are sold out, and there's a nasty rainstorm coming. The game could be delayed. I get a picture.

No sense in staying.

With the storm at my back, I head to Abilene.

Add it to the list of the world traveler, I guess. It's all so neatly compartmentalized in my brain. Sleeps in Bolivian salt huts, tents in sub-Saharan Africa, high-rises in megacities, and the fucking La Quinta Inn near the Abilene Mall. I stopped caring a long time ago. A bed and a toilet are enough. I text a kind friend, Noemi, who lived in Texas, and ask her if she knows Abilene. Turns out her old roommate went to college here. She sends the name of a place known for its signature Long Island iced teas—that drink of the devil, a mix of vodka, rum, tequila, gin, and triple sec. That'll be my night.

An Uber drops me off outside the Beehive Restaurant and Saloon in downtown Abilene, smack-dab between churches, banks, funeral homes, and a library. The boxy buildings of old Texas are preserved here. The bar is half-empty and underwhelming for a Friday night. A barkeep comes up to me: "Don't be sad. Everyone's at the Tracy Byrd concert now. They'll be here later."

The Long Island comes in a gargantuan cup. It hits hard but doesn't feel strong. Dad never drank liquor. Just beer. "You can keep control and count beer, buddy." Grandpa was the same way. They knew their limits. It's been ages since I've known mine. Every sip feels like a deal with the devil. The country music crowd comes in from the Byrd show. I get lost in some sports conversation with another drinker and order a second Long Island.

"Brother, best pay for these now," the bartender says. "I can't legally serve you another one."

Sure, whatever. "Hey, man, where are those bars with that stupid Texas dancing?"

"Stupid Texas dancing?"

The bartender is kind of pissed.

"The circle thing," I say.

"The two-step?"

"Yeah."

He sighs. "Check out a place called Guitars and Cadillacs. Here, have some water."

I sip water and put the destination into Uber. I arrive at a massive hangar behind a weird-ass strip mall. I compose myself for the bouncer and walk in tall and confident. There are rows of guitars on the wall, pool tables, loud Southern rock, and Texans in boots spinning like a laundry machine. I use the bar counter as a crutch. My elbow sinks into the lacquered wood, and it moans and creaks from my weight.

"Lone Star!" I say.

I down the cold beer. A woman asks me to dance. I can barely take one step, much less two. I laugh at my inability. She thinks I'm laughing at her. Shit. She kind of cries. Her friend tells me I should probably go home. In my fog I see she's right.

Another Uber. On the way back to the La Quinta, there's a Whataburger close to the hotel.

"Hey, man, leave me off here." The driver is happy to get rid of me. Time for the triple-meat burger with cheese. Extra-large fries. Onion rings. A milkshake and a large Diet Coke.

The walk to the hotel is deceptively far. Across the highway. Of course nobody walks on these roads. Cars go by hauling ass. I finally get a green light, but with people turning it feels like a game of Frogger. I drop the Diet Coke and it splatters on the pavement. I cackle. What was the point of that drink with this order, anyway?

In the room I gorge myself. First the burger, then every last fry and onion ring. I slurp up the milkshake and feel my stomach expanding.

I fall asleep with the TV on.

With the morning light comes immense pain. My brain feels like it's being assaulted by a jackhammer. My stomach feels like an anvil. My heart palpitates furiously. Anxiety creeps in. I'm going to die of a heart attack, just like Dad. I jump from the bed and brace myself on the wall, slowly walking to the bathroom. I feel like vomiting but can't. I take a sip of water and notice the face staring back in the mirror. Puffy, weathered, a grayness to the eyes, empty and full of sadness. I can't bear to look. I turn off the light.

It's a little after 6 a.m. and the sun is beginning to show itself. I creep to the window and see a guy my age, putting on his uniform while he walks toward his shift at a local diner. He looks tired, focused, and driven. He whistles cheerfully, ties up his apron, and slides through the door. I see my reflection again, now in the glass frame of some cheap-ass motel art. God, I look like shit. I don't even look like *me* anymore. This isn't what this journey was supposed to be about. This is a pathetic and shameful bastardization. This isn't self-growth, and it's far, far away from self-care.

What the hell is this?

PART 5

TWENTY-FIVE

Owning Up

The first thing I do when I get back to DC is see my cardiologist. I've been going to him biannually since Dad died, a son trying to avoid his father's fate. The doctor pores over my bloodwork. I notice him sizing up my physique too. He looks at me with something more than concern, something like admonishment.

"These numbers, the blood pressure, the cholesterol, they're a serious regression. They really wipe out the progress we've made over the last ten years."

I nod, embarrassed.

"What happened?" the doctor asks. "Are you . . . okay?"

How to answer that? Somehow on the way to finding myself these last few years, the travel became its own distraction, its own drug, its own exit lane from the path to understanding. The next trip was always going to be even more enlightening. I *had* to do it. There would be more answers, and that *aha!* moment was just around the bend. I somewhat acknowledged the distraction; I bought a journal in London, and the cover read: "You can't run away from your problems . . . *BUT I'm really fast!*"

Now my problems have caught me. Not only the bad diet and excessive drinking but the performing for a social media audience instead of focusing inward, all a result of not wanting to confront the possibility of disappointment. That I could, perhaps, remain unfulfilled. Forever untethered. A nomad without a cause. I kept myself from knowing me because I was afraid of really knowing me.

I still am.

"I'll clean it up, Doctor."

233

"You need to come back and see me soon."

Truth is, I don't have a clear sense of how I'll change. If the change you sought puts you in worse shape, what do you do?

As I leave, I mumble a faint "Have a good day" to the nurses I'm usually jocular and jovial with.

I walk the two miles back to my house, thinking.

How did I get here? I've broken away from my past: a job, a relationship that could have been a marriage, hell, even my hometown, for the better part of two years. I willed this, I wanted this. What was it? What is it that I needed? What do I have to show for it? These questions tear at me. Was this journey, all this travel, merely an escape—an escape from the self-doubt and sense of inadequacy I've felt?

No, the travel *had* to be more than that. For a long time, it was. It made me better. It opened my eyes to so much. But what am I to take from it now that I've seen the world? The more I think about it, the more anxious and upset I become.

I dig out some running shorts and a T-shirt, lace up my sneakers, and put my phone on the nightstand. No music for this run. Let this be the moment where I begin to "clean up," running in the silence of the Rock Creek Park woods to only the cacophony of my inner monologue, but running—and this time not running from anything.

My body isn't used to this. There's pain in my side, in my legs, and in my shoulders. As my mind circles in that familiar loop of self-hatred, I hear a whisper, an internal voice. It repeats itself and becomes a chant, one of Dad's old lines.

"You got this."

"You got this."

"You got this."

I rub the sweat off my left side, right near where I've had Dad's initials tattooed. He was horrified about that tattoo when I was eighteen, till I told him it was so he'd always be on my side. That made him cry.

I know he's on my side, but who else is right now?

I talk to myself: "Luke, *you* need to be on your side. Open yourself up to a world that's wider than your self-loathing, like the world opened itself up to you."

Miles later, I'm exhausted but at ease for the first time in months. No sweeter a sense of accomplishment than starting.

I cut back on booze, run more, eat less. I realize there is only so much you can do on your own. As an only child, I find comfort in the stillness of alone. But I can't live in the alone forever. I hate asking for help, being a bother. But I need to be picked up. I find a therapist to help me answer some of the questions I cannot answer on my own. What causes me the anxiety that leads to self-medicating? What am I searching for? Why did I feel so empty after living such a full, blessed, and privileged life?

I learn that it's best to embrace your anxieties and discomforts, because when you do, you learn to process them and live with them. They're part of you. Even if they're hidden, compartmentalized, or stored away behind a facade of an outwardly exuberant, energetic guy.

I realize I've been "white knuckling" my life. I'd say to myself, "Power through. Lots of people have it way worse than you—don't be weak." While that worked for some time, I didn't truly process the effect of losing Dad; my favorite uncle, Bill (husband to my godmother, my aunt Bea, who had died of cancer a few months before Dad); and Grandpa in a fifteen-month span from 2008 to 2009 that then morphed into my becoming a public figure. Being part of a legacy also meant I was living in loss. I come to realize that I'm also beset with not only inadequacy but also its sibling—fear of failure—along with a real fear of mortality. I've been good at deflecting, putting up shields. "Storing and ignoring" had been my mantra for years. Rarely has anyone been inside to see my vulnerabilities, including me.

A funny thing happens, I see, when I open the door just a crack to my therapist: I end up opening the door for myself.

Between weekly therapy appointments, I pray. I meditate. I begin to embrace the fear of looking deep within myself, and I'm able to look at that fear objectively until it begins to slowly melt away. And then I look even deeper into my depths, a real emotional autopsy. I read all the journals I've ever kept. Damn, they even start to make some sense! I was more honest on the page than I was in my mind.

A thought forms in my head: Would someone care about this? I shared pictures over Instagram with some occasionally deep captions, but that was social media. Could I write something about . . . all of it, from Dad's death to now? Could I explore the pain from that moment and be fearless enough to catalog my progression forward?

It was not my original intention to write a book, but I realize the journals are primary documents, real-time guides to who I've been as well as who I'm becoming. If I could inspire one person to better themselves or better understand themselves, to take a risk, change direction, or just realize it's okay not to have everything figured out, to keep missing their lost loved ones, to be vulnerable—then a project like a book might help me unlock my purpose.

The journey has been for my benefit, but I see how it can help others. I take a few days to jot down notes.

I find that I need to write. I need to get this out. I also realize I need to get out of DC. Washington is too full of distractions and the weight of my previous life. This journey, physically and mentally long, was inspired by changes in my environment. That was my catalyst to really think. The world within got clearer when the world outside changed.

So I head west.

TWENTY-SIX

By the Bay

It's grueling but it feels so good. *One, two, three, four.* Eventually, I make it up all 332 steps. This beautiful vertical cliff is known as the Lyon Street Steps. It's quiet here in the Pacific Heights neighborhood of San Francisco, next to the Presidio, the old military base now turned national park. The only noises are the panting of fellow runners or the wind cutting through the branches of the eucalyptus trees. It's a view not matched in any other American city. San Francisco's Marina District bleeds into the steel-blue waters of the Bay. The Golden Gate Bridge to the left of the domed Palace of Fine Arts sits not far from the shoreline. The gentle hills of Marin County wave back to you from across the water. There's an art installation of a painted heart halfway up the climb.

My heart is here now, the cliché of the Tony Bennett tune but just as true. The city's golden sun shines for me, it seems, at least when it's not covered by fog. I've been here about a month, and I try to do this run up these steps five times a week. If I don't run it, I walk it. Discipline, routine, order. These are my days.

I'm writing at the kitchen table of my late grandmother Mama-Mia, at her old apartment in the Cow Hollow neighborhood. She moved here in the mid-1970s from Piedmont, in the hills above Oakland. When Mama-Mia died in 2014, Mom and her sister, my aunt Christina, took over the building with a few units. Aunt Christina moved in full time upstairs. Mom kept Mama-Mia's as a pied-à-terre. Mama-Mia was the most creative member of the family: 100 percent Italian, born Helena Pierotti and nicknamed "Mama-Mia" because she was the "spiciest meatball." She painted, sculpted, and did collage here. The beautiful trees and flowers she planted are still blooming in the terraced back patio garden. Her artistic energy inspires. I try to channel it with candles when I write. Her portrait hangs on the wall.

When Mom calls, I tell her I'm writing every day and repeat how grateful I am that she's let me stay here to do it. She's relieved, because I've committed to a project in the Bay Area of her youth, no less. The city is far more tech-centric, far more Mark Zuckerberg than Jack Kerouac, but there remains a healthy iconoclastic culture that's a welcome change from stodgy DC.

I love it here. As the weeks turn into months and the months produce the tens of thousands of words I'm writing, I realize my routine and the Bay Area are replenishing my soul. I subscribe to the *San Francisco Chronicle*, follow the Giants and the Warriors, have a favorite coffee shop, meet new people, and reconnect with old friends. I'm a defender of the city too. I take umbrage when it's ridiculed in the national media for its issues. Yes, there are unhoused folks down on their luck who need to have better access to social services; yes, some streets could use a scrub; but overall there's no place like San Francisco. Here I can be myself with no pretense of a past life in the hallowed halls of powerful Washington. I'm free to be quirky and experimental. To lose myself in parks, beaches, and neighborhoods with character. I take up skateboarding for the first time since I was thirteen.

The writing is humbling. It's far easier to bloviate on television than to write something worthwhile. On TV I can hide behind performance theater. When you write, there is no cloak. I like the honesty of it. It reminds me of my travels. I have to give myself up to get there. Whether trusting a tuk-tuk driver on the highway in Cambodia, going back to that bench and crying in Hiroshima, or missing a girl like Maggie in New Zealand, writing out these experiences reminds me of the arc of the journey and boosts my morale. The miles, the planning, the cultural enrichment, the human connections, the time with Mom, the time alone. Being a foreign man in a foreign land for the better part of three years: no matter what, it was a hell of an undertaking.

And yet. And yet I can't ignore a whisper in my head. *Why didn't you go to the Holy Land?*

I saw enough houses of worship to last a lifetime but never went to the birthplace of my own. Every time I move, the whisper in the back of my mind keeps popping up. *Why not?* There are logistical answers, sure. The truth is, I was avoiding the Middle East. I was afraid of the solemnity of the Holy Land. I was not ready for what the Holy Land might tell me about my faith and myself.

I pray on it. The whisper becomes louder.

You must go to the Middle East.

I hesitate, though, wondering if the voice is the urge to escape, this time from writing.

One afternoon, after a day spent typing, I take one of my usual walks to clear the mind. Up the steep hills, the Bay off to the side. I always stop to watch it glisten and to make sure the Golden Gate Bridge is still there. I love that bridge. It centers me. I walk past a church school and come across one of those little free libraries—the large mailbox/birdhouses that have take-one-or-leave-one books inside. One book called *Life as Politics: How Ordinary People Change the Middle East* catches my eye. I flip through it and put it back. Interesting. Then I see the familiar blue binding of a book on the shelf below: *Big Russ and Me* by Tim Russert.

Oh, wow. I pull the book out. I know all the stories inside by heart. Incredibly, this is an author-signed copy. I laugh. I know Dad would have a chuckle. Somebody didn't want to keep a signed copy from a long-gone legend! I rub my finger over his familiar signature. Wow, he actually touched this copy. Part of him is on this page. His DNA. He always said we were bonded by the force of blood. What are the chances? Then the whisper perks up. I point to the heavens and yell, "I got it, man! I'm going."

TWENTY-SEVEN

The Holy Land

Behind me Amman disappears. The winding, desolate roads now take us through small towns, shuttered and asleep in the early morning dawn. The bridge crossing to Israel lies an hour away. I've started this trip as early as possible to accommodate the unforeseen. My driver, a young Jordanian, plays a nonstop medley of songs by Adele, his favorite artist. It's a calming sound ahead of something that could be anything but.

I've read horror stories of long delays at the border. I've read about shutdowns without notice due to security situations. I've read about Israel's understandably stringent border control officers, and I look again at my passport, heavy with stamps of countries that do not exactly have good relations with Israel.

Will I be let in?

I have to be. I feel like I've been called to Israel and the Holy Land.

Soon we come to an old rickety gate. Stray dogs run about, weaving between groups of soldiers and begging for food. My driver makes a U-turn and points to a dingy building past the gate to the left, some sort of processing center.

"There is you. Enjoy Palestine."

It's *Palestine* to him and all other Jordanians. Never *Israel*.

I get out and walk to the processing station. It has the trappings of one of those decrepit shelters you see in war movies: few windows, little natural light. Bright grocery store fluorescents seem to accentuate the dirty floors. Behind a glass panel stands a uniformed man who takes money for a state-sanctioned bus ticket across the bridge. He holds on to my passport until an acceptable

241

number of people have arrived at the station and then motions to us all to head to an idling bus outside.

A lanky kid in a black sweater with a military insignia walks the bus aisle, matching the passport pictures to the eyes staring back at him from the seats. Most on the bus are Europeans, the rest Palestinians. I'm the only American. The first checkpoint, on the Jordanian side, lasts ten minutes while the driver and a soldier compare documents. A few soldiers outside point the barrels of their guns down, their eyes on the windows, at the ready. Then the bus moves toward the bridge, through a desolate no-man's-land marked by watchtowers, outposts, and barbwire fencing. After a final checkpoint, the bus crosses the River Jordan and goes forth into Israel.

On the Israeli side I lock eyes through the bus window with a young Israeli woman, her long black hair unfurling past the shoulders of her white button-down. Her hands cling to her large military rifle. With it she motions for the bus to pull over into a specified lane. Another colleague of hers, no older than twenty-five and brandishing another rifle, boards our bus and looks over the group sternly. He checks a few passports and tells the driver to pull the bus in front of the processing center. Here there are tourist groups mixed with Palestinians from the West Bank who use the Jordanian border crossing as a way to visit other countries. Some people are stopped and questioned outside; most are told to go into the building. The amazing thing about all this—the decrepit buildings and barbwire and rifles and stern officials—is that I'm not afraid. I've been terrified at high altitude or nervous exploring a country on my own for the first time, but here and now, I tell myself that if fighting breaks out, if there's a terrorist attack—so be it.

I'm supposed to be here. I'm resigned to fate.

Once through customs, as my bus bops along a modern highway curving through the desert on the way to Jerusalem, I reflect not just on the last three years but the last few weeks. I traveled open and true on this medley, stretched the dollar and travel points I'd accumulated along the way as far as they could go.

In the United Arab Emirates I saw the Grand Mosque in Abu Dhabi, indoor skiing in Dubai. Ladies of the night walking the streets next to women in burkas.

Oman was serene and peaceful. I rented a car there and drove hundreds of miles along the coast and into the desert mountains. Gave an old man limping alongside a rural road a ride to his home and watched his wife and daughter sprint inside when I made eye contact with them, a taboo on my part.

In Doha, Qatar, I saw wealthy locals purchase $20,000 falcons for their falconry hobby and then retreat to shopping malls made of gold and marble, their lives made easy by an endless stream of cheap, controllable migrant labor.

I went to Eurasia too. In hipster Tbilisi, Georgia, I saw the birthplace of wine, the murderous tyrant Joseph Stalin's nearby hometown of Gori, and even joined in a protest against Russian aggression in the country. In Yerevan, Armenia, the world's first Christian country, I learned about the Armenian Genocide, an atrocity at the hands of Turkey the world has forgotten for too long. I finally got to see Istanbul. Safer now, I walked everywhere. Ate delicious kebobs and saw unmatched artistic culture and a blend of civilizations at the Hagia Sophia.

The pyramids just outside of Cairo were a world wonder. The city was a traffic-choked mess but beaming with pride and history. I went deep into the local souks, often the only white guy. Nobody in the world sells wares at a market as successfully and aggressively as Egyptians. I paid a visit to Our Lady of Zeitoun, a Coptic Catholic church where the Virgin Mary was said to appear as an apparition. They made me say the Our Father to get in, a security measure, along with armed troops to protect against Islamic extremists.

Then I got to Jordan. Floated in the Dead Sea. Saw the carved-out-of-rock-city of Petra, made famous by Indiana Jones. Slept in the Wadi Rum, the Valley of the Moon red-rock desert landscape that felt like Mars. There was no light pollution; I've never seen stars so bright. I snuck away from the camp just to feel the vast darkness, to literally run into the unknown—probably stupid, but necessary.

The climax of the trip, before Israel, was seeing my Buffalo Bills beat the Dallas Cowboys on Thanksgiving Day at a sports bar in Amman. For all the negative attention this sphere of the world has received, I never once felt unsafe. Inconvenienced, annoyed, or angry at undemocratic inequality? Sure. But always secure.

And already, amid my reveries, I'm in Jerusalem. Years of Sunday school, hours spent in pews, high school chapels, confessionals in college—I get goose bumps to know it all came from this low-slung city stretching to the horizon. I won't proclaim to be the best Catholic, far from it, but throughout this journey, whether visiting a mosque, synagogue, or temple—or even a local bar—I've never quite been able to shake my Catholicism. A good thing, because now that I'm in Jerusalem, I feel the need to embrace it. It guides, it protects, it cares.

HEBRON

As I walk the streets of Jerusalem, I feel something else, too: that no American visits Israel without some sort of implicit bias. Your understanding of the Israel-US relationship or how you've consumed news about the conflict between Israel and Palestine occupies a certain space in the American psyche. As a journalist I interviewed people who said Israel was a shining beacon of democratic ideals, *the* progressive country in the Middle East, among neighbors who execute gays and marginalize women. Others told me Israel was an evil force committing apartheid against the Palestinian people. It's evident being here that the actual truth is way more nuanced than either side's grandiose proclamations. The ex-journalist in me is curious to explore the conflict, but the Catholic in me whispers that I'm here to understand myself, first and foremost.

The next morning, I visit Hebron, the resting place of Abraham, of whom the world's three Abrahamic religions were born. It's an especially meaningful city for Jews and Muslims. Its religious significance for both faiths also serves as a microcosm of the conflict, of everything that's happened since 1948. It rests twenty miles south of Jerusalem.

I ride on a blast-proof bus to get there. Located in the West Bank, Hebron has over two hundred thousand people and is divided into Jewish and

Palestinian sections. There are roughly five hundred to one thousand Jewish residents, mostly settlers. They live in areas protected by roughly fifteen hundred Israeli soldiers. Palestinians with property in the Israeli-controlled area endure various checkpoints to access different streets and to travel to and from the Palestinian-controlled side. Innocent Israelis and Palestinians have been the victims of atrocious bloody violence in Hebron. In some sense, it stems from Hebron's religious significance. Attacks here are meant to make a statement.

Hebron is home to the Tomb of the Patriarchs, where founders of the Jewish nation are buried: Abraham, Sarah, Isaac, Rebecca, Jacob, and Leah. It's second only to Jerusalem as the holiest and most ancient site in Judaism. For Muslims, Hebron is a holy pilgrimage site. The Prophet Mohammed visited the city, and Islam, of course, carries its own connection to Abraham. So holy to Muslims is Hebron that a large mosque called the Ibrahimi is located near the Jewish Tomb of the Patriarchs. They are part of the same complex.

On my way to the tomb, I stop off for a quick slice of pizza near the visitors' center. I wait in line with Israeli soldiers, most fulfilling their nation's mandatory military service requirement. Their faces are so young and sprightly; most are eighteen or nineteen. They joke and laugh like teenagers anywhere, but military-grade rifles hang off their backs. One Black soldier catches me staring at him. "You never seen an Ethiopian Jew before?"

"No," I respond sheepishly.

"Now you have a souvenir!" He giggles and playfully nudges my elbow as I walk out the door toward the street, wearing a wide smile.

Past a few checkpoints, I make it inside the Tomb of the Patriarchs, where groups of Jews are deep in prayer. Men and women separate. Unlike the ostentatious displays that often mark significant sites in Christianity, the tomb is rather nondescript. Simple rooms for the faithful, folding chairs, and various writings in Hebrew on the walls. Each tomb is marked by a gate that leads down to a cave where the holy ancients are believed to be buried. Outside the room dedicated to Abraham, I notice a walkway toward a large reinforced wall. It keeps the Jewish area separate from the mosque next door, a tangible reminder of the division between the two Abrahamic religions. I join in the prayers.

Soon after, I cross through a checkpoint to the Palestinian side. The soldier asks if I'm Jewish.

"I am not. American Catholic."

I kick a soccer ball with some Palestinian kids who are using the blockade wall as a goal. I walk the souks, eat minced meat with rice, and am met with more smiles than scowls. I ask to see the Ibrahimi Mosque, attached to the tomb. I pass an Israeli checkpoint to enter. Inside, the faithful pray and, like on the Jewish side, they separate by gender. There is also a gate that marks the cave of Abraham. The mosque is well apportioned; my eye catches the intricately constructed minbar, green and red with accents of gold. I decide to pray again and have the same conversation with the patriarch that I had on the Jewish side of the wall. "Abe, if you're down there in that cave, are we not all trying to get to the same place? Give us the strength to overcome the divisions and learn the lessons from your unwavering fidelity to God. Because a blast wall between the synagogue and the mosque ain't it."

TWENTY-EIGHT

Salvation

I have to admit something: I expected the strife of the region to affect me more. But I don't feel that way. I understand the intensity of the religious passions. That solemnity I once feared, it engulfs you here. In fact, it helps make sense of the conflict. Tensions run high and beliefs are so fervent because you cannot escape feelings of faith. Wherever you walk has some thousandth-generation religious meaning.

The day after Hebron I move on to Jericho, where I feel locked in, like I'm in some sort of trance. At dawn, I travel just outside the city to the Mount of Temptation. Things feel slower here, even more methodical. I notice. I process. At this mountain, it's believed that Jesus fasted for forty days and forty nights just after his baptism, a way to prove his dedication to God and to strengthen himself for his future ministry. It is also where he was tempted by the devil three times. Jesus resisted temptation.

The Mount of Temptation is a tall, dry mountain in the Judean Desert. Seeing the physical mountain align with all the spiritual stories I was told over the years makes Jesus' temptation all the more real and believable. I think about what Jesus felt. In my mind I strip him of any spiritual superpowers, return him to a radical with ideas, rebelling against oppression. What better place to prepare than here? At this mountain there is nothing else to do except look inward.

It's hot, dry, and quiet. There are panoramic views of the Dead Sea and the Jordan Valley. A voice in my head tells me, *Notice things today.* I walk away from the tour group and find my own spot at the base of the mountain. I notice an inner calm spread from my core to my extremities.

After our desert tour, our bus moves on to Bethlehem, its clogged streets, and the Church of the Nativity, a Catholic and Orthodox church believed to be the site of Christ's birth. It's one of the oldest continuously used places of worship for Christians. Scores of pilgrims from all over the world here, many in tears, are overwhelmed by the significance of the place and its holiness.

A Palestinian Christian presents himself and whisks a small group of us downstairs to the grotto. Through a maze of crowded tunnels, we find a small, quiet room with colorful mosaics. The man leads the Our Father in Aramaic, the language of Jesus. It is here I feel my father. For the altar boy from South Buffalo, who never missed a week of Mass, this would have been so moving.

The line to see the literal star carved into the floor that marks the birth spot is long, disorganized, and realistically unfeasible. Instinctually I put my hand on the shoulders of the Palestinian Christian as the crowd grows chaotic. He guides me like my father did through crowded sports stadiums. He's an older man with gray in his beard, and most definitely a father himself. He has an idea, he says. He walks our small group to a quieter area, just behind the birthplace. It's reflective here. There's a small offering area for the Virgin Mary. We stand in silence. Some people bow their heads to pray.

I notice something. If you were to strip it down, a boy met his dad for the first time here. That beautiful bond lies at the root of so many modern connections between father and son. I think of my grandpa Timothy Joseph Russert. Another faithful Catholic, a man of few words who holds my dad asleep on the couch in family photos. I think of the home videos my parents took, my coming home from the hospital, Dad clutching me close to his chest. His whisper, caught on tape but one that I'm sure I remember as an infant: "Never has a papa loved a baby so much." I think of my grandpa Karl Orth, Mom's father and someone I never met. He attended Mass daily and would be so proud to know that his first grandson got here. I feel these ghosts.

They follow me.

The bus rolls back into Jerusalem at dusk. I turn off my phone and go for a walk. I want to stay locked in. I want to notice more. It's quieter now, the shopkeepers pulling down their metal gates. Tomorrow, I'll go to the Church of the Holy Sepulchre, shared by Catholic and Orthodox believers, the location of Christ's crucifixion and tomb and probably the holiest place in Christianity. But a voice inside tells me to go now.

I listen to it and start walking to the church.

A processional route traces Jesus' literal walk to his crucifixion. Christians call it the Way of Suffering. As a kid raised on the Stations of the Cross, walking them in reality is hard to believe. I start whispering to myself, "Jesus meets his mother; Simon carries the cross; Jesus falls for the third time . . ."

I arrive at the church thirty minutes prior to closing. There's hardly a crowd. Soft lights from countless offerings flicker against the shadows. I go to the Altar of the Crucifixion, the Rock of Calvary. It's heavy here. You're pushed down to your knees. I close my eyes and am transported: Christ on the cross, the Roman soldiers banging nails through his hands with a hammer, the blood dripping off his palms. I walk by the Stone of Anointing, where Jesus was anointed with oil after death. An older woman in a headscarf prays beside it in tears. The candlelight flickers in her moist pupils.

Go to the tomb.

There's a line to enter, and once inside, I'll have thirty seconds to pray before an Orthodox priest taps me on the shoulder to move along. Thirty seconds after thirty-four years. As I wait in line behind mournful pious people, many on the verge of tears like the lady I just saw, I gather my thoughts: What will I pray for? And for whom will I pray? The tomb is behind two doors, inside the aedicula, an ornate carved box, from the top of which candles hang.

I've seen where he was born. Now I'll see where Jesus died.

Beyond the first door is a waiting area. Large candles burn, steadied into sands held by a marble pot. Through the next door is the tomb of Christ. The priest motions for the woman in front of me. She gasps and tries to swallow her tears, then prays loudly in a language I can't identify. In his forties, with a short, dark beard, the Orthodox priest locks eyes with me. He motions with his hand. I kneel before the tomb of Christ, resting my forehead on the stone slab. To the left is an icon of the Virgin Mary. Above the slab is an intricate carving of the resurrected Jesus.

"Thank you, Christ, for my blessings, for the gifts bestowed on me, for the enormous privilege that has defined my life. Thank you for my two loving parents, who have done their best to bestow on me a moral code and strong sense of justice. I pray for peace and for all those sick, sad, tired, suffering, or alone, that they can find comfort and charity. I ask for two things, Lord. First, thank you for my safety, and may it continue on this journey and in life. Second, well, this is harder. Lord, I've seen the entire world, seen too many of God's marvels on this tiny earth. I've learned so much about myself and have had too many hours of self-reflection. Yet I still don't know what my purpose is here. Why was I given all of this? Why can't I figure out what I should be doing? What *could* I do? Dad was so good at guiding me. But I've been lost since he left. Just point where I need to be. Please, God."

Suddenly I feel a small tremble, like the stone is shaking. I sneak a look back at the priest to see if he notices. He is unmoved but makes no effort to come over. With a deep breath, I enter into a deep meditative space. I return to prayer and feel a pulsation through my forehead. I extend my palms atop the slab. My eyes remain closed; it feels like I'm spinning into another dimension.

I don't feel the physical space. The voice inside speaks: *He heard you. Go forward. Pray and you'll notice.*

"Pray for what, though? Pray more? Just pray? Pray for how long? What? Come on!"

The vibrations stop. The hand of the priest clenches my left shoulder. I come down. My eyes open. My moment has passed. I tear up and go forth into the mystery of faith.

I'm sweating at the neck and need to decompress. I walk in circles inside the church till the priests begin the process of closing for the night. I light a votive offering to the Virgin Mary as I leave and pray for clarity. My mind keeps coming back to the word *notice*. It's dark now in the narrow streets of Old Jerusalem. I know the Western Wall, also known as the Wailing Wall; the holiest site in Judaism is open twenty-four hours. I decide to walk there. On the way I see a Buffalo Bills yarmulke for sale from a street vendor still working. The Bills? Here?

That's *Dad*!

I pay for the yarmulke and find a small white plastic chair not far from the Western Wall Plaza. I pray as I was told. I breathe slow and take in the moment. I'm not sweating, not crying, not hysterical.

Again, I'm locked into faith.

I see the journey in my mind. Every experience seems to flash through. The woods of Maine, Patagonia, Easter Island, Vietnam, Rwanda, Nepal, Russia, West Texas, the California coast. All the different people who opened up their own slice of the world to me. If this journey over the last three years did anything, it forced a question I was too afraid to confront: *Who are you, Luke Orth Russert?* I think about a passage from Dad's book, in his letter to me: "Your opportunities are unlimited and with that comes a higher responsibility. As your namesake, St. Luke, tells us, 'To whom much is given, much is expected.'"[1] I even had *LK 12:48* tattooed on my inner arm after I read that. I pull up my sleeve and look at it. The faded green ink haunts me. It's haunted me for years. Makes me feel unworthy. That I've never done enough or been enough, that I'm not deserving of such a life. The inadequacy cuts deep.

Dad was so duty bound, that Irish-Catholic civil servant: up at dawn, in bed at dark, never missing a day. Grandpa too. He retired with all his sick days. Grandpa never questioned much because he worked so incredibly hard. Dad bottled up any self-doubt in his diligence, preparation, and focus. I never really thought about my own place in the world till he died. I lived to please him because I believed in him and loved him so much. The boy who wanted to make his dad proud. Who never wanted to leave his side. When he died, my rock was gone. I tried to do what I thought he'd want, to live up to that legacy, to continue his work. I tried to reconstruct a world of meaning after loss.

But I cannot bear the cross of a legend. That burden is too much.

I'm scared. This is tough to admit. It almost feels like I'm renouncing Dad and a life of duty, with its prescribed roles, for a different life—an open and free and unexplored one, and, because of that, an uncertain life. A vulnerable life.

"Aha!" I yell out. "Yes, Luke!" I begin to talk to myself. *Vulnerable. It's only because you put yourself in a vulnerable, uncertain position over these last three years, Luke, that you can really feel the life that can be your own. You opened yourself to learn, feel, and live with the seven billion other folks you share this earth with, away from the trappings of home, away from the world you knew. You took on that sense of uncertainty. You don't need the rock of Dad. You can forge your own rock. You can have what Dad never did: a sense of comfort within uncertainty.*

I sit inside that uncertainty in Christ's Tomb and now realize that this is the life for me: to find comfort within the discomfort of a life that is fully mine. Duty bound isn't for me: I did it for so long because I loved my dad. But as much as I'm like him, I'm perhaps even more like Mom, I realize. Spontaneous and creative, experimental. I love her for that, I love her influence on me. I love being her son.

And even more than being Mom's, I am mine. I'm my own person. I need not constantly look to others for guidance. I need to start noticing the voice within.

I begin to walk and to process. I begin to look for a sign, for proof that this is the right way to think. "Look for me there. You said that to me, Dad. Show yourself! Show me you approve!"

Then it hits hard. My eyes well up. It's like I'm still seeking permission from him. That young boy. "Is it okay, Dad?" I don't have to do this anymore. Of course he approves! He *wants* me to reach this truth, this self-reliance. More than that, he's been here all along, guiding me to it. In the rainbows in New Zealand and Iceland, in the signs of the Buddhist monastery in Cambodia, in the lessons from Senegal—he was asking me to lead my own life, free from his sense of duty.

I comprehend something that had been buried deep inside for over eleven years. I held on to a younger version of myself for so long, too long: "twenty-two-year-old Luke." The age I was when he died. In some ways it was an arrested development. Well into my thirties, I could not let go of that young man, young Luke. I thought that if I let go of twenty-two-year-old Luke, then perhaps I would let go of Dad too. But here, in Old Jerusalem, I can sense in the months and years ahead the man I'll be. One who holds on to the lessons learned on the journey, who keeps an open mind and an ingenuous heart. A man who meditates and takes in a diversity of global influences, some that Dad would have found strange, if not a little frightening. One who invests in causes outside himself, and outside media. One who sees the value and opportunity in storytelling to illuminate and inspire. A man who one day has a family of his own to nurture, provide for, and protect. And above all, one whom Dad smiles down on. There in Old Jerusalem I realize it: "Dad, I'll never lose you because you're here no matter what. I don't have to look for you. Your love is within me. As you wrote once, you just want me to live a good, decent, and meaningful life."

A life that I choose. A life I don't second-guess for choosing. A life that expands as my curiosities do. A life *I* can be proud of. That's enough and I'm enough.

I put on the Buffalo Bills yarmulke and walk to the Western Wall. I pass by rabbis, faithful Jews, and a few fellow Gentiles placing written notes into the wall. I take a piece of paper and scribble down a prayer. Second Timothy 4:7. Dad's favorite, read at his funeral: "I have fought the good fight; I have finished the race; I have kept the faith."[2]

I fold it, kiss it, and slip it into the crack.

Epilogue

Dear Dad,

You closed out your first book, *Big Russ and Me*, with a "Letter to Luke." I won't lie: it's been hard to read that letter since you passed. I can hear your voice, your inflection, your cadence. I can even see your mannerisms, the focused movement of your eyes, the creases forming on your forehead, the slow widening of your jowls that turns into a smile. I feel the slap of your hand on my back, then notice the slump of your shoulders as you step back and wait for me to speak. I'm happy my memories of you are so strong, all these years later.

In your letter you wrote, "But remember, while you are always, always loved, you are never, never entitled. As Grandpa likes to say, 'The world doesn't owe you a favor.' You do, however, owe this world something. To live a good and decent and meaningful life would be the ultimate affirmation of Grandpa's lessons and values."[1]

Thank you for the reminder that I'm never entitled. It's easy to forget in today's instant-gratification, "me first" society. No matter how famous you became, you never changed. You always did the work, and you always treated folks with respect. People noticed; I hear about it when your name comes up. It makes me so proud.

Grandpa was right: the world does not owe me a favor. And yes, I do owe it one. I want to tell the world's stories like I have in this book. Do my best to make the world a little smaller, a little more understood, a little more unified. I think that will be my "good, decent, and meaningful life."

Dad, I can recall only one occasion when you really cried. I was about ten. We were in New York City and you had just won an award from a charitable foundation for being "Father of the Year." You got up in the crowded banquet hall, began to read from your prepared remarks, and then absolutely lost it as you glanced down at Grandpa and me in the audience. Wiping away tears and blowing your nose, you spoke extemporaneously about how much you loved Grandpa and what he meant to you. How much you loved being a dad, how special it was for the three of us to be together. It was the most emotion you ever shared publicly and, to be honest, more than you ever did privately.

You wrote books about fathers and sons. Received countless letters about how your words helped people understand their own fathers better. I saw the happiness it brought you. I always admired how strong you were. You never got rattled. You were emotive and empathetic without being overly emotional. You understood people and made them feel welcome and secure. Though sometimes I wonder, what were your fears, anxieties, and inadequacies? What scarred you? What did you hold inside?

Dad, please know I did not write candidly in this book to elicit sympathy. You always said, "Nobody likes a martyr." You wrote a chapter about loss; I guess I wrote an entire book. But, Dad, by opening myself up, showing the scars, I feel so much better. I guess we're different in that way, but hopefully my words will help somebody else like yours did.

You liked to say Grandpa's phrase: "What a country!" Don't worry, I still believe in it. Even when times get tough, the power of the American promise forever uplifts.

I miss you and I love you. And Dad, the Bills are going to win a Super Bowl, and I promise I'll be there.

Love,

Luke

Afterword

When I was deep in the throes of writing the first draft of *Look for Me There*, full of self-doubt but also stubborn determination, before I ever dreamed of a publishing deal or becoming a bestselling author, a woman who is now my fiancée asked a simple question: "Why are you writing this?"

Tense and a bit touchy, I blurted out a passionate answer that came to be my guiding light during the writing process. "I don't care if this thing ends up in the bargain book box at a gas station and sells ten copies. If some kid who lost their dad finds it and it helps them feel a little less lost, well, that's the best reward I could ever have. That's what I'm trying to do."

A lot of people found this book, or it found them. More than I ever imagined. It was hard to make sense of it. As a first-time author, I just wanted to cut through and connect. But as letters, messages, and notes came hourly, daily, and then weekly—and I read every single one—I realized the book had done something more. It had provided readers an opportunity to take a deep look within themselves. It inspired them to process grief, loss, or regret, or just take a needed second to pause and reflect on the journey of life. *Look for Me There* let readers know they weren't alone in not having all the answers. We are bound together by our struggles and by seeking to understand the long-term effects of those thousands of moments, big and small, that make up our lives.

A common theme in the notes I received was the idea of purpose. "What's your purpose?" is such a simple question, yet at times it can feel impossible to answer. Grief can derail our sense of purpose. Whom do we carry on for after a loss? Many readers mentioned trying to live up to an ideal that their lost loved ones would want them to aspire to. But in that endeavor, many noticed in their

257

own lives what was a central theme in *Look for Me There*: if we're only living for others, forever chasing an elusive idea of what we think we *should* be doing, it's quite easy to lose a sense of self and end up unfulfilled. Deeper meaning ultimately comes from self-acceptance. It's okay to seek out what brings you joy. We are not perfect; we may never reach what we feel were the expectations of those who have passed on. But as one reader wrote me, "Notice the voice within. Remember the lessons from those we miss. Carry them, use them as fuel, but never forget to be proud of your own life."

It's not just those grieving who struggle with purpose. I read countless letters from seekers: people who appeared to the outside world to be productive and successful yet still felt stuck. They were unchallenged and desired to seek something new and find their true calling. I could relate. Seeking out a new path was a central tenet of my book.

For a time, traveling gave me a real sense of purpose. I was on a journey to enlightenment; things would show themselves, and at some point I'd have all the answers. But what I learned on my own journey (and it was amplified during the writing process) is that while I was searching for something—my own identity independent of my hometown, my family, and the life curated for me since birth—I was also running away from something. I was running away from the challenge of processing the grief of losing Dad. It was not until I sat in that grief and really understood it that I was able to look forward and figure out who I was and who I wanted to be.

But it's not always grief from which we're fleeing; challenges are omnipresent, and they present themselves in a myriad of ways. Can we handle rejection? Failure? The fear of the unknown? Are we up for real commitment? Can we endure risk? Avoid longing? Not fall under the weight of expectations and maintain faith? I learned from the outpouring of notes that I wasn't alone in working through these questions. One reader said, "There cannot be a worthy life without challenges. When we feel alone and unsure is when we must push forward to find ourselves. It's easy to wallow in self-pity; it's harder to find meaning. It takes work." I agree. It's only after embracing the challenge that one feels more fulfilled. But it's not easy. We must acknowledge the anxiety within and the discomfort of processing deep truths.

Where can we do that? One reader told me, "The more I seek, the more I realize profound moments come during self-reflection. If I've learned anything, it's that I need to forgive myself before I can move forward." Those words touched me to my core. I knew what she was getting at. Perhaps the ultimate challenge in life is self-forgiveness. Before you can forgive others, you need to forgive yourself. Forgive the missed chances and the personal failures, the parts of you that eat away in the back of your conscience, especially the dreaded whisper of *You have not done enough*. You can change for the better. You *are* enough. This forgiveness becomes a catalyst for positive change. It leads to being more open and present and thus finding a deeper purpose.

I received many letters about the sheer pain of loss. Some of these came from people proud of their lives, well accomplished and fulfilled, but who still feel that awful sting. Different from constant grief, the pain is more of a lingering void. It creeps up. One man wrote me, "I'm seventy-five now. I lost my dad young, when he was just fifty, and he told me to take care of Mom. I think about how I've lived twenty years longer than he did, yet he's been with me along the way—well, I'm tearing up writing this. I miss him still. I hope your journey inspired confidence to know he's with you." These types of letters reminded me of my grandfather. They came from folks of deep faith who didn't show much emotion, didn't question much, trusted God's plan—but were not spared from those "I miss you so much" moments.

These letters comforted me and spoke to the enduring weight of loss. It never fully leaves, even when you're at peace with it. Moments will come when memories resurface; you wish your loved one could see you, and you long for one more minute, one more chance to connect or say how you feel. But actually, why can't you? One elderly lady at a book signing, a bit teary-eyed, leaned over and whispered in my ear, "You know, you can talk to your dad every single day. Sorry if you think I'm crazy, but try it."

I responded, "Oh, I do! It's far from crazy!" I believe—and many readers, especially older ones, agree—you can speak to your lost loved ones. You're already carrying them with you. In those moments of longing, push toward a deep meditative state, close your eyes, and talk freely. Hold on to their energy and spirit. Often you know what they'll say; you can see their face, their smile, their habits. Don't feel strange if you do this; there are plenty of us who converse with people on the other side.

My original belief was that I was writing for an audience around my own age. What I did not expect was how the book affected older generations. Some of the most thoughtful, honest, revealing, and encouraging letters came from people in their seventies, eighties, and even nineties. Yes, there's a strong cadre of ninety-something-year-old *Look for Me There* fans!

I've thought long about why that is. Then I felt silly. People are people. You don't stop carrying a loss just because you get older.

I realized there was something beyond that too. So many bury that weight or ignore it, whether blissfully or painfully. Yet when given a chance to be vulnerable, perhaps to impart wisdom to a younger person, they share their experiences. Each time I read a letter from this kind of reader, I hoped their emotions were no longer bottled up, because they can sure help others. A ninety-six-year-old grandmother wrote, "The way you opened yourself was so transparent. That had to take real courage to be real and not fake it fine. I admire that so much in you. I told my grandson, who was valedictorian and had to write a speech for graduation, to share his struggles—for that is what people identify with. Real people don't break easily. At my age, you begin to see the difference of what is important and what is not." Whether they were young and starting out or were pushing one hundred years on this earth, readers reminded me vulnerability was one of the most important attributes one can have. It fosters connection and wards off loneliness and makes self-reflection and self-forgiveness more attainable. It seems that life gets easier the day you figure out how to be more vulnerable. For some it'll never come; it's too much of a challenge. But I can tell you—and my readers can verify—it's worth pursuing.

The day after *Look for Me There* came out, after a bevy of TV interviews, I awoke to the news that it was the top-selling book on Amazon. Of the millions of books in the world at that given time, it was number one. I started to shake in disbelief. Tears poured out of me. I knew Dad saw it; heck, he probably had a hand in it! Those were the happy tears. But there were more. All the grief, the doubt, the scars, the self-loathing, the forcing out of hard truths, the seven-year journey outside my comfort zone, the questions from many closest to me about my sanity, the lonely writing process that felt impossible—I knew now that it was what I was supposed to be doing. It was what I should have been doing. I saw it through. The dream wasn't dumb. The book was bigger than me. People cared about the message. It all had a purpose. The tears were of gratitude.

Look for Me There was a multiweek bestseller and received a lot of kind words and accolades. I'm so thankful for that. However, what I will hold dear and close for the rest of my life are the words of strangers. It was not always easy reading what was sent to me. Some notes—so raw, honest, and piercing—were not quickly forgotten. They could be all-consuming. But my faith reminded me this was my calling. I had created a forum for people to connect to something, to express themselves and share the parts of their past and present they often held within. Their vulnerability reminded me I'm not alone, that it's okay to be anxious or unsure about the winding path that is life. There's an entire community of us carrying that same cross.

Outside of marriage and, God willing, the blessing of children, I don't know if I'll ever do anything as meaningful in my life as writing *Look for Me There.* I hope to, and I'll try. But I'm aware this work is what could define me publicly, and I'm okay with that. In fact, I'm thankful for it. I grew from this book. It pushed me into being a better, more responsible, and more empathetic version of myself. Turning forty—the "halfway point" in life—is not far off, yet I feel at peace with the future. I do not fear the challenge.

I get asked in interviews if there's any knowledge I want to impart after writing the book and connecting with so many folks over the last year. I'll just say this: when we hold our lost loved ones in our hearts and picture them in our minds, remember they would want us to smile—not cry—at the memories.

Thank you to all the readers who made this author feel a little less lost. I'm eternally grateful.

LUKE RUSSERT
Early 2024
Washington, DC

Notes

Epigraph

1. Eddie Vedder, "Release." Words by Eddie Vedder. Music by Stone Gossard, Jeff Ament, Mike McCready, and Dave Krusen. Copyright © 1991 Innocent Bystander, Write Treatage Music, Scribing C-Ment Songs, Jumpin' Cat Music, and 3 Kick Heads. All rights for Innocent Bystander, Write Treatage Music, Scribing C-Ment Songs, and Jumpin' Cat Music administered by Universal Music Works. All rights for 3 Kick Heads administered by Universal Music Corp. All rights reserved. Used by permission. Reprinted by permission of Hal Leonard LLC.

Chapter 1: June 13, 2008

1. Tim Russert, *Big Russ and Me: Father and Son; Lessons of Life* (New York: Miramax, 2004), 318.
2. Russert, *Big Russ and Me*, 319.

Chapter 12: Vietnam

1. "Vietnamese Pay Tribute to John McCain," CBS News, August 27, 2018, https://www.cbsnews.com/news/john-mccain-vietnam-tributes-us-embassy-hanoi-memorial-pow-north-vietnamese/.

Chapter 13: Japan

1. White House, Office of the Press Secretary, "Remarks by President Obama and Prime Minister Abe of Japan at Hiroshima Peace Memorial," press release, May 27, 2016, https://obamawhitehouse.archives.gov/the-press-office/2016/05/27/remarks-President-obama-and-prime-minister-abe-japan-hiroshima-peace.
2. From the exhibit "Saigo no kotoba" ("Their Last Words"), Hiroshima Peace Memorial Museum, Hiroshima, Japan, 2016.

Chapter 15: Senegal

1. "The House of Slaves: Island of Gorée," UNESCO Multimedia Video & Sound Collections, video, accessed October 27, 2022, https://www.unesco.org/archives/multimedia/document-1333.

Chapter 21: Boxes

1. Richard Stengel, "Tim Russert: A Man This Good Is Hard to Find," *Rolling Stone*, February 14, 1985, https://www.rollingstone.com/culture/culture-news/tim-russert-a-man-this-good-is-hard-to-find-71566/.

Chapter 28: Salvation

1. Tim Russert, *Big Russ and Me: Father and Son; Lessons of Life* (New York: Miramax, 2004), 333.
2. 2 Timothy 4:7 NCB.

Epilogue

1. Tim Russert, *Big Russ and Me: Father and Son; Lessons of Life* (New York: Miramax, 2004), 333.

Acknowledgments

Writing is inherently lonely. The weight of the thoughts swimming in your mind can be overbearing—even if you're an introspective only child who enjoys solitude. I'm so thankful for those who helped me out along the way.

Without Paul Kix this book does not exist. We took a chance on each other at a crossroads in our perspective lives. Him more than me. I'm so thankful we did. Without hesitation and with no assurances, Paul reviewed "The Beast," hundreds of thousands of words of journaling and essays about travel that I wrote in San Francisco. From the outset, he believed in the project and helped make sense of the many complicated components of my journey. He asked thoughtful questions, identified themes, pushed me in the right directions all while never silencing my voice or forcing his hand. Most importantly, Paul held me accountable and brought a clarity and discipline to the writing and editing process with a sensible Iowan kindness that was constantly reassuring. For two years and counting we've spoken almost weekly, sometimes multiple phone calls a day. He never declined to help despite being a busy married father of three kids. Together we won, we lost, we lived. What started as a partnership became a sincere and caring friendship. I'm grateful.

As someone skeptical of agents, I was fortunate to find a great one in David Larabell. David was always honest, never overpromised, and gave crucial unfiltered advice throughout the project. He had my back.

The team at Harper Horizon was nothing short of spectacular. It's been an honor to play for them. Matt Baugher saw the potential in my writing and helped me fulfill it. I've never had such a decent and amiable manager. I'm beyond appreciative. During our time together Andrea Fleck-Nisbet was encouraging and warmhearted. Meaghan Porter and Janna Walkup were incredibly thorough in their edits; their professionalism and attention to detail made the book stronger. Belinda Bass made the cover shine.

Hilary McClellen was rigorous but always kind in her fact-checking, a true class act.

John A. Walsh was a valuable resource for the duration of the project. He was incredibly generous with his time and energy; his thoughts, opinions, and edits came from the heart, enhanced the finished product, and comforted a novice author. Much gratitude.

Wright Thompson, John King ,and Jake Sherman guided me to the right places. The only thing I respect more than their work is their friendship.

Thanks to the St. Albans mafia, some who I've known since kindergarten, for always loving me as Luke and never as Russert. And to my Boston College friends for the loyalty and laughs.

To all the kind souls during my time in media, from internships at ESPN and *Late Night with Conan O'Brien,* to the radio gig at SiriusXM and eight years in the NBC family: thank you for giving me the benefit of the doubt. Especially Erik Rydholm, Lauren Skowronski, Alex Moe, and Shawna Thomas.

To the underpaid and under-appreciated staffers I got to know on Capitol Hill, your patriotism and sense of duty keep our country afloat.

Thank you to my hometown of Washington, DC, and my beloved Buffalo, San Francisco, and Nantucket. All my neighbors have shaped me.

To those around the world who took care of me in sixty plus countries. Especially the talkative barkeeps. Thank you for your random acts of kindness. I believe in the global family.

For the viewer and the reader, I'm humbled. Sincerest thanks.

Thank you to RL and LB, my cardiologist and psychiatrist, for sound heart and mind.

To the pugs—Chamberlain, Charlie, and Shawkemo: you were and are pure joy.

Thank you to my extended family, especially my aunt Christina Orth, who gave me the space to succeed in San Francisco when I wasn't quite sure what I was doing but knew I needed to figure it out.

Dr. Laura Lomeli: you always believed even when it hurt. You showed me what it means to care. You inspire. Part of you lives in these pages.

Grandpa, Grandma, Mama-Mia, Grandpa Karl, Uncle Bill, Uncle Dan, and Corey: you're remembered fondly.

Mom, I did it. Thank you for the dedicated feedback, for never letting me settle, and for encouraging your son to get out beyond the world he knew. Your support has been paramount. I am in awe of everything you continue to do. I look forward to your memoir, as you are the most impressive story in the family! Much love.

Dad, I forever stand on your shoulders. I love you and miss you.

For the seeker, the wanderer, and the traveler—you'll always have a friend in me.

God bless.

Go Bills!

About the Author

Luke Russert is an Emmy Award–winning journalist and bestselling author who previously was an NBC News correspondent primarily covering Congress. His reporting was seen on *NBC Nightly News, Today, Dateline*, NBCNews.com, and MSNBC. He also spent time as an acclaimed radio host for SiriusXM Satellite Radio. A traveler, he has been to seventy countries and counting. He lives in Washington, DC, with his pug, Shawkemo.

To see more photos, get some travel trips, or to connect with Luke, go to www.lookformethere.com